"This book is an incredibly helpful addition to our knowledge of the practice of psychosexual and relationship therapy. Cate takes us on a journey through a comprehensive history of the profession, the complexity of DSM and the dangers this holds in pathologising clients, to the day to day problems that the client brings to our room. The assessment session is particularly helpful for those starting in the profession, as well as those looking to refresh their knowledge. A warm, empathetic and educational read which I recommend."

– **Jo Coker**, Psychologist, Accredited Psychosexual Therapist/
Supervisor and COSRT Professional Standards Manager

"Cate Campbell's new book firmly brings sex therapy practice into the 21st century. Students, sex therapists and experienced practitioners alike will find food for thought, as she encourages the therapist to assume a reflexive stance to their own practice. Cate uses her experience as a practitioner and lecturer to take an overall view of what the therapist needs as a secure base in order to develop their own, highly individual, practice. She addresses many important issues, which a sex therapist cannot afford to ignore, such as consent, trauma, culture, identity and gender, together with chemsex and FGM. Each chapter has a useful list of references, giving the therapist a starting point to undergo their own research. As a tutor and practitioner I would recommend this book not only to psychosexual therapists but to all practitioners in the counselling and psychotherapy field."

– **Michèle Logue**, Foundation for Counselling and Relationships
Studies, University Centre Doncaster

"I can't imagine what Masters and Johnson would have made of the very modern chemsex phenomenon, but I doubt they could have summarised it and put it into sexual therapy contexts as compassionately as Cate Campbell has, or with as much cultural competency. The modern convergence of technology with sexual subcultures, drug proliferation and pornography heralds a whole new era in sexual behaviour and therapy, that might leave many sex therapists feeling overwhelmed or out of touch. Cate explains that this needn't be the case, addressing the chemsex subject with a competent and much needed compassion."

– **David Stuart**, Social Worker and first to name
and identify the chemsex phenomenon

D1627045

Contemporary Sex Therapy

Contemporary Sex Therapy explores modern sexuality, its expression and problems, and some of the uniquely twenty-first century issues facing sex therapists and society as a whole. Seeking solutions to these and other common sexual and relationship problems, the book provides a practical, sensitive and modern approach, which tackles the complexities of contemporary relationships, identity, love and sex.

A comprehensive, stepped approach to psychosexual therapy is offered, demonstrating how to tackle blocks to sex and intimacy as well as providing an understanding of how and why they develop. Loss of desire, sexual pain and erectile and orgasm difficulties are seen within the context of modern life and relationship dynamics, so that comprehensive and realistic solutions are more readily enabled. The book looks at significant issues such as sexual consent, sexual and gender identity, sexual trauma and culture, as well as the more recent challenges of porn-related sexual dependency, chemsex, female genital cutting and technology. Throughout, the emphasis is on recognising and meeting the specific obstacles and needs of a wide diversity of relationships and experiences, providing a vast toolbox to appropriately address contemporary sexual issues.

Established sex therapists, as well as students, will benefit from the book's modern approach which focuses on each partner's experience, avoiding outcome and response anxiety entirely and appreciating the range of pressures experienced by modern couples. Relationship therapists and couples themselves will also be motivated by new ideas and explanations, which often challenge existing intuitive understanding to produce nuanced and effective solutions to improve sex and intimacy.

Cate Campbell is a relationship and psychosexual therapist and lecturer with the Foundation for Counselling & Relationship Studies, and provides training for a number of organisations including Relate and the College of Sexual & Relationship Therapists.

Contemporary Sex Therapy

Skills in Managing Sexual Problems

Cate Campbell

Routledge
Taylor & Francis Group

LONDON AND NEW YORK

First published 2020
by Routledge
2 Park Square, Milton Park, Abingdon, Oxon OX14 4RN

and by Routledge
52 Vanderbilt Avenue, New York, NY 10017

Routledge is an imprint of the Taylor & Francis Group, an informa business

© 2020 Cate Campbell

British Library Cataloguing-in-Publication Data
A catalogue record for this book is available from the British Library

Library of Congress Cataloging-in-Publication Data
A catalog record for this book has been requested

ISBN: 978-0-367-89896-0 (hbk)
ISBN: 978-0-367-89897-7 (pbk)
ISBN: 978-1-003-02188-9 (ebk)

Typeset in Times New Roman
by Apex CoVantage, LLC

Contents

Introduction

When relationship researchers Bill Masters and Virginia Johnson first devised their sex therapy programme they couldn't have imagined the ways society would change, bringing a revolution in attitudes to sex and relationships. They undoubtedly contributed to some of these changes, but would probably be amazed at the influence of the internet and delighted by the range of relationships, sexualities and gender identities sex therapists now encounter. This book is an attempt to build on the legacy of Masters and Johnson, explaining how to deliver contemporary psychosexual therapy (PST) which recognises the way our clients' experience of twenty-first century life affects intimacy and sex. In keeping with the original vision of Virginia Johnson, a core cognitive behavioural (CBT) structure is employed, here supported by psychodynamic understandings and systemic/social constructionist interventions which allow investigations of the history underlying clients' anxieties and identification of the relationship dynamics which perpetuate their problem(s). These are evaluated within the clients' cultural and contextual circumstances, contributing to a normalising approach which reduces shame and blame, facilitating the development of solutions.

The structure of PST treatment is explained, providing a clear process for students and a resource for qualified sex therapists, as well as information for relationship therapists interested in expanding their knowledge of counselling with a sexual focus. Masters and Johnson embraced the CBT tradition of setting homework exercises, in which couples relearned sexual response and acquired sexual skills, with feedback from their progress providing information for the next exercises to be set. The book will honour this with a clear progressive route through assessment and treatment, taking into account the range of modern relationships and issues which may be encountered. The aim is to provide confidence for practitioners in both the process and their ability to manage the process with a supportive rationale, regardless of the challenges they face.

Framing sex therapy as very much a stepped process places the emphasis on success, and the significance of each stage can be fully appreciated. Described throughout as experimentation, the value of building intimacy and enacting sexuality in this way is a core component of the book's approach. It differs from some PST versions of sexual task setting in that partners' attempts to arouse each other take a back seat to self-discovery at all stages, usually being spontaneously incorporated by couples once their confidence increases. Indeed, an outcome-driven approach is seen as detrimental to sexual success by causing anxiety and encouraging unrealistic expectations. As a PST supervisor and lecturer with the Relate Institute and Foundation for Counselling and Relationship Studies, I've been in the enviable position of seeing how a large number of practitioners manage and enact this process, benefitting hugely from their learning and experience as well as my own.

Chapter 1 summarises the development of PST from long before Masters and Johnson carried out their ground-breaking research into sexual response through to the present day. The proliferation of approaches and interest in sex from the twentieth century onwards has nonetheless failed to result in enjoyable sex for everyone. The rest of the book is devoted to explaining why this is and providing solutions.

In the USA, where codes for different illness are needed in order to make insurance claims, the American Psychiatric Association's *Diagnostic and Statistical Manual of Mental Disorders* (DSM) lists the 'sexual dysfunctions' commonly treated by sex therapists. While the rationale for the DSM is understandable, it has served to medicalise and pathologise sexual behaviours in ways that PST moves beyond. So, though sex therapists' work now encompasses the huge range of experiencing which affects sexual identity and behaviour, awareness of DSM sexual problems provides a starting point even for therapists with a broader remit. So the book's second chapter describes the dysfunctions identified by the DSM and the rationale for their inclusion.

The PST route followed here corresponds with a CBT approach of assessment, formulation, treatment and follow-up. Chapters 3 to 5 are devoted to the assessment and formulation process, detailing ways to begin engaging with clients, gathering information and using it to plan treatment. Practical guidance is given about ways to make PST work most effectively. For instance, Chapter 3 is devoted to conducting the initial assessment in PST, including how to engage with clients if the work has to be short-term or with an individual.

From this point onwards, the PST described in this book emphasises a stepped approach, with every step providing an opportunity for experimentation, learning and change. Consequently, no stage should be rushed, with the history taking stage described in Chapter 4 offering a sound therapeutic intervention which may even be sufficient without further work. Chapter 5 demonstrates how the information gathered is used to create a formulation of the individual or couple's issues, exploring why they have developed and what's happening to maintain them. This is discussed with them in a meeting where the decision to proceed into treatment is made and the first PST experiments are agreed.

It's emphasised, however, that assessment is ongoing throughout the PST process, with feedback from experiments providing more and more information. It's important to convey this experimental, information gathering approach at the outset, as it moves the emphasis from performance to discovery. Both clients and student psychosexual therapists often think of the PST process as a series of obstacles to overcome or stages to work through as quickly as possible. In fact, adopting this approach is counterproductive. As most of our clients are affected by performance anxiety, any sense of working through a process 'successfully' to reach the next stage is liable to create more anxiety. Instead, framing the entire process as experimental allows clients and therapist to work collaboratively on learning rather than achieving. The experiments aren't about accomplishing a particular outcome, but concentrate on providing information and experience. Goals are seen as movable stepping stones towards a discoverable outcome rather than a set of aims to accomplish, though satisfaction with outcome may considerably exceed clients' expectations. This is made clear in Chapter 6, which explains the PST treatment process, showing how progress is determined and responded to in ways which maintain clients' engagement and positivity. The importance of therapeutic positioning is emphasised, with a non-judgemental, interested and not-knowing stance modelling the approach clients are encouraged to adopt. The PST process itself is presented as a treatment model which can be followed with adaptations until such time as it becomes embedded for the practitioner. The expectation is that therapists will develop practice based on what works in their experience, using this model as a basic and functional starting point.

Chapters 7 to 9 look at DSM dysfunctions in more detail, offering interventions to add to the treatment skeleton outlined in Chapter 6. Chapter 7, for instance, deals with the issues surrounding desire and arousal, including relevant social and gender issues and the relationship dynamics which can maintain problems. Causes of desire and arousal problems are explored and treatment programmes are offered. Loss of desire is addressed, including the way responsive desire can develop in relationships, allowing misconstrual of a partner's motivation and willingness to be sexual. Gender differences, collusive desire dynamics and erectile difficulties (ED) are also examined. Use of medical investigations and interventions for ED (including PDE-5 inhibitors, such as Viagra) are looked at alongside a psychosocial approach which takes into account the way a man's or couple's beliefs affect their progress and 'performance' and what motivates desire.

Problems with orgasm are discussed in Chapter 8, acknowledging that these can be matters of perception and may be unnecessarily pathologised. Many people have unrealistic expectations of orgasm or response anxiety which affects their ability to climax. The pressure now associated with women's 'right' to sexual pleasure has, ironically, led to increased pressure for straight couples, with men often so focused on causing their partner's orgasm that they miss out on much of their own pleasure as well as the development of intimacy and building of arousal. Women, meanwhile, feel increasingly required to satisfy their partner's need to give them pleasure, which can cause pleasure-preventing anxiety.

Chapter 9 explores the development and management of genital and pelvic pain, plus some disorders of sensation, such as persistent genital arousal. The emotive subject of female genital cutting then has its own chapter, describing what it is and what help is available for affected women who wish to improve their sexual response. Other 'medical' issues affecting sexual response are considered in Chapter 11. Almost any physical or mental health 'problem' can have a huge impact on sexual functioning, often related to the ways we think about the issue. This allows much scope for change. As well as offering some practical solutions, this chapter explains ways to work with unhelpful thinking or, at least, look for positive approaches to difficulties.

Chapter 12 delves more deeply into the management of blocks with advice on what to expect and how to manage the unexpected, as the ability to anticipate and manage blocks can make or break sex therapy. Shame and fear are often at the root of blocks so this is explained, showing therapists how to understand and work with underlying trauma and anxiety. The influence of personal beliefs and social discourses is revisited to thicken appreciation of the many influences inhibiting the expression of sexuality.

Consent is discussed in Chapter 13 as an essential component of PST which can be overlooked by therapists anxious to make a difference. Many of us are social-ised to believe we should comply with the wishes of others, however inconvenient or unpleasant that may be. The management of sexual consent is consequently awash with misunderstanding, as couples often unwittingly struggle with consent issues on a daily basis. Clarity around sexual consent is never more important than when someone has experienced sexual abuse, the focus of Chapter 14, with information about the potential effects of sexual trauma, how it can be assessed and managed, and the suitability of PST when it's untreated.

Trauma and attachment issues underlie sexual dependency just as much as they do any substance or process addiction. The spectacularly easy access to online pornography has dramatically increased the number of people developing sexual problems which make it difficult to have partnered sex. In addition, many young people are growing up with a distorted view of sex and intimacy due to pornog-raphy viewing, to the extent that some begin their partnered sex lives believing that fear and pain are a normal part of sex. However, the notion of sex addiction remains controversial, with many sex and relationship therapists unaware of how to assess and manage sexual dependency. Frequently, sexual acting out escalates as dependency grows and it becomes harder to feel normal without an increas-ingly elusive dopamine hit. Where this isn't recognised, sex therapy won't be effective, so Chapter 15 gives information about what sexual dependency is and isn't, how to assess and treat it, when to refer and how to help partners.

A relatively recent phenomenon, chemsex is often regarded as if it were simply a drug addiction issue, due to the way sex and drugs are combined to provide emo-tional regulation in some groups of gay men. Chapter 16 explores this, arguing that self-soothing abilities, trauma and attachment issues should be the focus of therapy, as concentrating exclusively on drug use does nothing to heal the under-lying pain which leads to chemsex nor to acknowledge the role chemsex may have in healing.

Many of us have a mono story about the vast range of sexual and gender pres-entations we may encounter. For instance, asexual partners can sometimes find it

difficult to be understood when they seek PST, and people with specialist preferences may present less commonly and also be less understood. Chapter 17 consequently aims to thicken the stories around different or alternative sexualities,
and particularly to expedite openness for clients. Therapists also need an ability
to facilitate conversations about relationship choices, such as polyamory, so it's
important to recognise and be open to the variety of sexualities that may present.
We need to be equally responsive to our changing culture, context and the range of
differences in beliefs and attitudes our clients bring. Chapter 18 highlights some
hidden contexts, as well as more obvious effects on sexual expression and PST,
advocating openness and creativity in our practice. A snapshot of contemporary
psychosexual practice in Chapter 19 is followed by an appendix containing case
examples which can be used to practise creating formulations and treatment plans.

While the approach taken in this book focuses primarily on creatively supporting our clients towards optimal intimacy and sexual expression, it nonetheless recognises the help offered by medical methods. The importance of clinical
awareness is stressed, both to treat clients appropriately and spot potential medical problems. It sees the psychosexual therapist as a creative conductor, able to
explore, assess and direct treatment responsively, knowledgably and flexibly.
Nonetheless, we all have to start somewhere with some sort of structure. The core
cognitive behavioural approach anticipates the end of therapy from the beginning,
regarding the entire process – from assessment to ending – as providing treatment.
This means some clients will choose to step off at an early point while others
will continue through many stages, benefiting from each step. The interventions
offered in each phase make it possible to exercise therapeutic discretion in choice
and pace.

Many new PST students are anxious about the CBT process which they assume
to be didactic, placing them as experts. However, this is where skills are utilised to
determine when it's appropriate to give information and advice and when clients
will benefit from more collaboration. It's often clients themselves who assume
there are right and wrong ways of approaching PST. They're often surprised and
fascinated to discover our approach is much less linear than they imagine and,
often, counterintuitive. It's to be hoped that readers being introduced to PST
through this book will be as surprised and enchanted with the approach as our
clients. For those already practising, welcome! Whether you're approaching this
book as a refresher or looking for new ideas, dip in, bringing your own imagination and originality to reinvigorate your enthusiasm and ingenuity in this most
rewarding of therapies.

Chapter 1

History and philosophy of psychosexual therapy

There is evidence that ancient civilizations around the world used forms of sex therapy which were not just concerned with sexual problems, but also with sexual enhancement and pleasure seeking (Niak, 2017). However, from around the fifth to the fifteenth century, Western sexual behaviour became dictated by religious ideals which exercised social control. It was insisted that sex was for reproduction only, and that sex solely for pleasure was both aberrant and bad for health. Health increasingly took over as the rationale for sexual proscription from the sixteenth century, as medicine became more professionalised (Atwood & Klucinec, 2007). Women's health, in particular, was bound to their sexuality and reproductive potential rather than their sexual pleasure. Just being a woman has historically been seen as a cause of neurosis. The root of the word 'hysteria', for instance, comes from the Greek *hystera*, meaning 'womb'. From the days of the ancient Greeks to the present, female hormones and the womb itself have been thought to affect women's mental health. At one time it was even thought the womb could move around the body, afflicting organs and mood on its way (Adair, 1996).

As industrialisation took hold in the West, sex became as subject to market forces as everything else (Foucault, 1990), albeit sometimes obliquely. From the mid-nineteenth to early twentieth century, for instance, French physicians promoted the idea that women's routine was too sedentary and that they needed exercise to prevent physical, mental and sexual health problems. Recognising the importance of women's role in servicing the family, and thereby keeping the workforce afloat, they were encouraged to be as active as possible, taking on more strenuous household tasks, such as chopping logs (Quin & Bohuon, 2012). For girls and young unmarried women, sports were imported from England with the intention of preparing them for healthy childbearing and rearing. That they readily took to activities such as cycling and riding then created the problem that they were mobile and often, therefore, out of sight. Ultimately, swimming, cycling and horse riding – all of which somewhat challenged modest dress – were medically banned during menstruation. No other justification for control was available as the exercise did, indeed, promote fitness and enhance mood.

In the nineteenth century UK women were expected to service men's sexual appetites, but not to experience the same desires and pleasures as men. Towards the turn of the century a medically trained social reformer named Henry Havelock Ellis began championing women's rights, including sexual rights (Ellis, 2012), claiming that women *could* enjoy sex given sufficient appropriate stimulation. So outrageous were his ideas that his writing could only be seen by doctors until 1935 (Goodwach, 2005a). Many years ahead of his time, he normalised practices such as oral sex and masturbation, as well as homosexuality, and researched transgender issues, influencing many future practitioners, including Freud.

Gender

Ellis truly was transgressive as, for example, he questioned a binary approach to gender. Gender difference had become much more important in the eighteenth century, once again as medicine and science sought empirical evidence to explain the world. Certainly, 'proof' was offered to bolster power differentials, and 'expert' opinions were respected even in the absence of evidence. The gender dichotomy developed alongside racism; for instance, the hugely influential German psychiatrist Richard von Krafft-Ebing (1886) claimed women from – what he defined as – more primitive races than Europeans showed less gender difference. Before and since, the search to define a gender binary has failed, despite exploration of promising anatomical, genetic, hormonal, gonadal and neurological possibilities (Sanz, 2017). Indeed, the more a definitive explanation of gender has been sought, the more elusive it has become. While one in 2000 of us has been classified as anatomically – that is, genitally – 'intersex', there are also multiple versions of human biology which make it no simple matter to assign gender in other ways, while genital and gonadal anatomy is often so ambiguous that assigned gender has merely been a matter of parental choice (Associated Press, 2005).

Knowing and enacting gender has been of varying importance in different cultures and at different times. Nevertheless, even ancient societies emphasised social/sexual characteristics as indicative of good enough masculinity/femininity (Berry, 2013). Erectile failure in ancient Rome and Greece, for instance, was not just enthusiastically treated with the currently popular concoction, but prophylaxis was employed to avoid this misfortune. This becomes more understandable in relation to the idea that, at the time, and for centuries afterwards, physical adversity was associated with metaphysical or spiritual malady, including as punishment for some sort of unsociable thought, deed or aspect of temperament. Once science began to replace mysticism as the dominant authority on sex, from the eighteenth century, sexual behaviours other than straight intercourse were vilified. Krafft-Ebing made a living from pathologising sexual behaviours and creating fear about sexual response and mere thought, never mind behaviour. Perhaps this explains why adequate masculine gender performance has so much significance even now; we have become habituated to the idea that any lack, however minimal or blameless, is a cause for shame.

The twentieth century

The theories of Sigmund Freud in the early twentieth century ushered in a different approach to sexual problems, which he viewed as the root of most internal conflict. Human instincts, including drives related to procreation and pleasure, were thwarted by social convention, Freud asserted (1905/2016), and this conflict was at the root of much psychological distress. This related to issues such as resolution of the Oedipus complex, the incest taboo and penis envy, which became the focus of treatment for most psychological complaints, while sexual issues themselves weren't directly addressed.

It wasn't until the mid-twentieth century that interest began shifting to physical sexual problems. However, research and 'treatment' focused entirely on pathology rather than enhancement, with the emphasis on deviation rather than normality, but without any clear idea of what 'normal' was (Atwood & Klucinec, 2007). This meant practitioners were looking for extremes of behaviour or arbitrarily applying norms. Researchers like Alfred Kinsey and Masters and Johnson sought to determine people's actual sexual behaviour rather than pursuing fairytales about what they ought to be doing or what was deemed 'right'. The research by Kinsey and colleagues (1948) involved thousands of people and demonstrated the wide variety of sexual behaviour being enjoyed, often covertly. This was highly important at a moralistic time when aversion therapy was being employed to treat 'perversions' like masturbation and, particularly, homosexuality, which the American Psychiatric Association still considered treatable until the 1990s.

The physiology of erotic pleasure finally became the focus of scientific research when physician William Masters and his assistant, Virginia Johnson, brought sex into the laboratory, painstakingly measuring the effects of their subjects' arousal. Though Masters began his work investigating sex workers, of the approximately 700 subjects that were studied, few were not white, middle-class and well-educated. Yet the context of the research cohort was, at the time, entirely irrelevant.

Masters and Johnson's (1966) research set out to determine what happens to the body during sex, establishing stages of sexual response from arousal, through a plateau phase and orgasm to resolution, when the body returns to its homeostatic state. Though they promoted male and female sexual response as analogous and linear, they revolutionised the thinking of the time, asserting the role of the clitoris and debunking Freud's idea that 'vaginal' orgasms reflected ego maturity. Having also identified the common sexual problems people experienced, Johnson realised that the behavioural interventions of practitioners like the South African psychiatrist Joseph Wolpe (1958) could potentially be used to treat what Masters and Johnson now termed 'sexual dysfunctions'. Using relaxation and a hierarchical progression through a series of challenges to an individual, Johnson hoped patients would be able to overcome sexual anxiety through the gradual desensitisation which Wolpe was using successfully.

At about the same time, scepticism was growing about the efficacy of psychoanalysis, which was seen to take too long to achieve results and to have poorer outcomes than other interventions. This interest in other approaches was heavily influenced by the now contentious work of psychologist Hans Eysenck (1952) who reviewed the effectiveness of therapeutic modalities, finding Freudian psychotherapy fared worst. Since Eysenck was, at the time, using behavioural therapy at the Maudsley Hospital, he wasn't unbiased. Nonetheless, behavioural interventions gained in popularity and Masters and Johnson's (1970) treatment advice offered a cognitive behavioural (CBT) approach, introducing systematic desensitisation through 'sensate focus'. They also sometimes used – mainly female – sexual 'surrogates', who stood in for partners under their direction. However, this controversial approach never gained general momentum and remains within the domain of specialist sex workers, primarily helping disabled clients.

Helen Kaplan-Singer (1974) elaborated Masters and Johnson's CBT approach, including psychodynamic attention to the antecedents of couples' sexual problems, which she saw as a symptom. She later (1979) discussed a triphasic sexual response cycle, involving desire, arousal and resolution, which inevitably contributed to the idea of low or absent desire as abnormal. US psychiatrist Harold Lief was also interested in desire disorders, suggesting that low testosterone may be responsible for loss or lack of sexual interest. He also acknowledged the role of psychological, relationship and contextual issues, however, setting up and encouraging sexual awareness and education as part of medical training.

Sexology

Sexology as a discipline was developing around the world in the second half of the twentieth century, not always fully embracing the Masters and Johnson approach. In Eastern Europe, where sex therapy tended to be a state-funded, multidisciplinary offering, for instance, women were sometimes taught how to have 'vaginal' orgasms, the rationale being that this was what they wanted (Wislocka, 1978). The concept of empowered women with access to the workplace, contraception, childcare and sexual satisfaction sounds ideal. However, priests were often members of the multidisciplinary sexology team, and women were encouraged to pursue sexual satisfaction in tandem with domestic responsibility, with the ideal of stable marriage and family at the heart of the project (Košciańska, 2014). Thus, while Western sexual emancipation was overtly linked to the economy and the commodification of sex and the body, in the Eastern Bloc the economy still benefited as stable families contributed to the workforce, reducing the need for state aid.

The 1970s

Not everyone interested in learning about sex had an economic motive. *The Hite Report* (Hite, 1976) into female sexuality exploded popular understanding around women's sexual response and interests. US graduate student Shere Hite had collated more than 3,000 questionnaires from women which made public the – then – shocking 'secret' that women often faked their climax to comply with Freud's myth that penetrative sex was responsible for 'mature' female orgasms. So much male hostility had greeted the idea that female orgasms were all 'clitoral' in origin, and that a minority of women experienced orgasm through penetration alone, that when Masters and Johnson presented this to the medical community they were forced to play down their findings. Hite's work made it possible for women to share their experiences and realise there was nothing wrong with them if penetrative sex didn't always, or ever, result in orgasm. Practically overnight, women began seeing themselves as entitled to sexual pleasure, as female sexual needs became increasingly normalised and encouraged. More effective and available contraception, and liberalising of attitudes towards sex in the 1960s and 70s, led to more sex positive discourses, so that many couples were becoming less inclined to automatically tolerate sexual difficulties.

In the UK, the Institute of Psychosexual Medicine was established in 1974, initially just for the medical profession but now for all practitioners who routinely examine their patients, such as nurses and physiotherapists. The emphasis of treatment is on the patient's reaction to a physical genital examination which offers information about their comfort with their bodies, ability to relax and to manage an unusual situation. Practitioners don't take a history but hope to create a safe environment in which the patient feels able to speak about their problems freely. Attention is paid to the relationship between practitioner and client, including the transference. This provides a helpful additional layer to the practitioner's clinical skills – an adjunct to their medical offering rather than replacing it.

The term 'psychosexual' was adopted by UK sex therapists in general. The British Association of Sexual & Relationship Therapy was formed at around the same time, as a specialist organisation for sex therapy practitioners, applying professional standards and accrediting individuals and training. These days known as the College of Sexual and Relationship Therapists (COSRT), its members are not primarily medically trained but come from a wide range of disciplines, including counselling and psychotherapy, sexual health, psychiatry, nursing and midwifery, and medicine.

US psychologist Jack Annon's (1976) PLISSIT Model, discussed further in Chapter 3, provided a structure for the exploration of sexual concerns. Davis and Taylor (2006) proposed an EX-PLISSIT Model which emphasised the consent stage of the process, which they felt was often skipped. Stepped approaches like this fit well with modern PST, where therapeutic need can be gradually assessed while therapeutic intent is present from the beginning.

Medical approaches

The 1980s saw an even greater shift towards medical solutions for sexual problems, with vasodilator injections, vacuum pumps, hormones and surgery now being offered to treat erectile difficulties. Among other medical interventions, antidepressants were used to combat early ejaculation, while vaginal stretching and relaxation exercises, physiotherapy and surgery were applied to combat vaginismus. On the face of it, both psychoanalytical and biopsychosocial approaches to sexual problems couldn't compete with potentially less time consuming and cheaper medical fixes, especially once drugs like Viagra became available in the late 1990s and early 2000s to treat erectile problems (Berry, 2013). There's no doubt that they were warmly welcomed by their users, and their market grew as individuals and couples became increasingly intolerant of *any* erectile glitches. Ironically, because treating the symptom ignores not just the cause but also the interpersonal and psychological consequences of the symptom, a satisfactory resolution is not always achieved (McCarthy & McDonald, 2009; Althof, 2006), with many users giving up the medication despite achieving erection.

After Masters and Johnson, there had been an expectation that sex therapy would become plain sailing, with 'targeted interventions for clearly defined sexual problems with easily assessed outcomes' (Meana *et al*, 2014: 541). However, far from simplifying the sex therapy process, experience only added to its complexity. The focus on function alone didn't take into account satisfaction, which may be very different, as the Viagra experience demonstrated. Achieving pain-free erection, arousal, penetration and orgasm sounds ideal, but not if it's perceived as an empty, unloving or hurried experience. It also won't work if it conflicts with a person's image. While expectation and appreciation can be managed with therapy, a prescription won't help someone who feels he ought to have an erection easily without medical intervention, for instance, and that not to do so reduces his masculinity and self-image.

Another massive issue has been distinguishing between arousal and desire, particularly once it was discovered that arousal often precedes desire in women (Basson, 2007). This was only a small part of increasing evidence that men and women not only don't respond physically in the same way, but often have very different sexual objectives, such as women hoping to feel wanted and close and being less focused on orgasm. Men want this too, but the prizes of erection and orgasm are often seen by men as providing both what their partners want from them and also personal reassurance around their identity and performance (Campbell, 2015). Thus, Masters and Johnson's sexual response cycle can only really be applied to men, and not all men, not all the time.

Moreover, where sexual problems have a clinical root, the psychological and inter-personal consequences of the problem may continue beyond medical treatment, which is where skilled psychosexual therapy is so valuable. Even where clinical interventions do offer solutions, some of the 'problems' complicate this. Genital pain and dyspareunia are primarily pain disorders which affect sexual functioning, but often seem to be pathologised or treated as imaginary because of their association with sex (Meana *et al*, 2014). While psychological interventions, such as mindfulness, CBT, and Eye Movement Desensitization and Reprocessing (EMDR), may help alleviate genital pain, they're potentially no more or less helpful than with pain in other parts of the body. This has led many to wonder whether we should end categorisation of some sexual issues as 'dysfunctions' and instead be willing to consider absolutely anything that compromises sexual expression or enjoyment as the problem (Meana *et al*, 2014).

Late twentieth century

The second half of the twentieth century saw an eruption of sexually related issues, from the appearance of HIV infection to awareness that action must be taken to recognise and assist the many vulnerable adults and children who were being exploited, abused and subjected to cultural practices such as genital cutting. Medical advances have meant there are more people living with disability which creates challenges to their sexual expression, and issues of sexual identity are increasingly being creatively addressed. An additional massive contributor to the development of sexual and relationship issues has been the availability of internet pornography. Though porn films began replacing magazines in the 1970s, as more people owned home video players, it wasn't until the late 1990s that pornography started really becoming an issue (Goodwach, 2005b). Within a decade it had been recognised as contributing to compulsive sexual behaviour, sexual dysfunction and relationship breakdown.

Feminism

While Western attitudes were becoming increasingly more liberal as we entered the twenty-first century, rather than being interested in what most people enjoyed or found difficult about sex, there remained the belief that penis-in-vagina (PiV) sex was normal and satisfying – if, that is, satisfaction was desired and understood. Sociologist Michel Foucault (1990) argued that discourses and mores around gender, reproduction and sexual behaviour change over time, reflecting potentially subjugating influence over the way people treat their own and others' bodies and experience. His views influenced more wide-ranging and interpretive attitudes to sex, gender and sexuality, with more curiosity about the ways attitudes and beliefs influence these on a micro and macro level.

Feminist philosophers like Judith Butler (1990) highlighted the dangers of believing in 'natural' behaviours, beliefs and traits, as any difference from what had been deemed 'natural' was seen as a deviation from the normal and thereby could become pathologised. Decades earlier, French academic Simone de Beauvoir (1949) had challenged the notion of natural gender tendencies, which she said were socially constructed, referring to women as 'the second sex' given that their conduct was compared with that of men. That it had been unacceptable for Masters and Johnson to promote too many ideas of women's sexual difference, and that the male sexual response cycle was thus applied to both men and women, supports de Beauvoir's point. Yet, despite attention being drawn to the inequity of these distinctions, they persist to this day.

The need for a systemic and social constructionist response to sex was highly evident, yet family and systemic therapists who used these approaches traditionally seemed to avoid talking about sex (Markovic, 2007). This has changed considerably since 2000, as a systemic approach pays attention to the way couple dynamics affect the development and maintenance of sexual difficulties as well as being interested in social and contextual influences. Much has now been written about 'systemic sex therapy', emphasising and showcasing an integrative approach (Weeks *et al*, 2016; Hertlein *et al*, 2015). Given the diversity of attention needed within sex therapy, there are clear benefits to integrating more than one method. A number of models of integration within psychosexual therapy have been proposed, mainly uniting cognitive behavioural and systemic approaches, but also suggesting some novel methods (Markovic, 2013). There is some difficulty, however, in determining the most efficacious ways of working. Both lack of research and the need to optimise the approach for individual client(s) conflict with the current trend for outcome evidence, which is as useful for inspiring confidence in clients as it is in encouraging treatment commissioners.

Markovic (2013), for instance, points out the utility of research and empirical data in providing reassuring normalising information for anxious clients. For many people, a DSM diagnosis offers hope as it makes clear that their issues are not unique and that treatment is possible. However, the medicalization of relationship distress can also be pathologising, particularly in relation to the patterns of disturbance which evolve as a way of reducing, if not fixing, the sexual problem. Markovic highlights the benefits of a postmodern approach to sex therapy which seeks the optimal result for the individual client or couple rather than seeking a 'best', most effective or utilitarian approach to common problems. What makes each sexual problem, *and* its resolution, utterly unique is each couple's response and the therapist's ability to hone their skills, utilising emerging research in the most helpful way. While there may be some common dynamics, which it's incredibly helpful to recognise as a therapist, our challenge is to appreciate what each individual feels and needs, and how partners are relating to each other and the therapy. Through experience, we each develop tried and trusted ways of working, deciding which intervention to offer, the timing of this and, crucially, the ability to anticipate and manage difficulties in response to treatment and triggering events.

This is not the way sex therapy was framed even a decade or two ago. With the emphasis on deficit, couples were expected to want sex to please one another as part of a normal relationship. Consequently, partners who were clear that they didn't want sex – whether they saw this as temporary or permanent – were heartily encouraged to do it anyway. Though this can work in the context of a loving and sensitive relationship, it often felt abusive. For therapists using task setting and Sensate Focus, traditionally there was also an expectation that couples would progress to naked touch as soon as they agreed to treatment. However, obligation isn't sexy and unwanted behaviour just generates anxiety. It's no wonder Masters and Johnson saw its obliteration as the key to sexual success.

PST

Simply restoring function may actually create sexual problems, since so many couples avoid sex or develop low desire as a way of escaping the anxiety associated with sex. When clients believe that sex is 'natural', any difficulty is evidence of abnormality, either in the relationship or in one or both partners. The responsibility to please then hangs heavy when it comes to enjoying our own experience. The need to perform and respond is not just explicit but reiterated in the media and social discourses we all contribute to. So effective contemporary sex therapy can't just be about restoring/improving function or removing pain. It has to address beliefs, anxiety and context while recognising interpersonal reactions and personal response. It has to be able to spot common difficulties and be open to the unexpected. Therapists need to be as open to help and suggestion as we would wish our clients to be, and willing to share treatment with other professionals who have appropriate expertise.

There is currently no one-size-fits-all approach to sex therapy. Whereas, 20 years ago it may have been appropriate to require a DSM sexual dysfunction in order to provide 'sex therapy', clients are now approaching sex therapists with a far wider range of issues (Niak, 2017), including drug-related sexual concerns, compulsive sexual behaviour, identity issues, trauma and abuse, and sexual health matters, not to mention simple lack of knowledge or relationship misunderstanding and conflict. This requires the therapist to have more knowledge and a wider range of skills than ever before. It's clearly impossible for every therapist to personally completely meet the needs of every client they see. It's therefore incumbent upon modern sex therapists to know where and how to access more information as necessary and to be able to refer clients to other services when appropriate. Never has there been more need for co-operation between disciplines and practitioners, and for healthy respect and interest in each other's approaches. Specialist practitioners, working in sexual health, addiction, contraception, obstetrics, gynaecology, urology, oncology, mental health, learning difficulties, disability, mindfulness and yoga, physiotherapy, allergy and pain clinics are among the many relevant sources of support for individuals and couples with sexual problems. The contemporary psychosexual therapist needs to be able to work independently and to conduct or map the additional or alternative resources which may be helpful.

Though we wish to, as much as possible, avoid labelling and pathologising our clients, it's helpful to be familiar with DSM diagnostics, if only because we sometimes have to work with others who use it faithfully. Dysfunctions *will* therefore be referred to throughout the book, and the following chapter takes a look at the clinical picture provided by DSM-5.

References

Adair, M.J. (1996) Plato's view of the 'wandering uterus'. *The Classical Journal*, 91;2, 153–163.

Althof, S.E. (2006) Sexual therapy in the age of pharmacotherapy. *Annual Review of Sex Research*, 17, 116–131.

Annon, J.S. (1976) *The Behavioural Treatment of Sexual Problems*, New York: Harper & Row.

Associated Press (2005) Doctors rethink assigning gender to intersex babies. *St Louis Post-Dispatch*, February 20, A10.

Atwood, J.D. & Klucinec, E. (2007) Current state of sexuality theory and therapy. *Journal of Couple and Relationship Therapy*, 6;1–2, 57–70.

Basson, R. (2007) Sexual desire/arousal disorders in women. In: Leiblum, S.R. [ed] *Principles and Practice of Sex Therapy*, fourth edition, New York: Guilford Press, 25–53.

Berry, M.D. (2013) Historical revolutions in sex therapy: A critical examination of men's sexual dysfunctions and their treatment. *Journal of Sex & Marital Therapy*, 39, 21–39.

Butler, J. (1990) *Gender Trouble: Feminism and the Subversion of Identity*, New York: Routledge.

Campbell, C. (2015) *The Relate Guide to Sex and Intimacy*, London: Vermilion.

Davis, S. & Taylor, B. (2006) From PLISSIT to Ex-PLISSIT. In: Davis, S. [ed] *Rehabilitation: The Use of Theories and Models in Practice*, Edinburgh: Churchill Livingstone, 101–129.

De Beauvoir, S. (1949) *The Second Sex*, Paris: Éditions Gallimard.

Ellis, H.H. (2012) *Studies in the Psychology of Sex*, Kindle version: Amazon Media.

Eysenck, H.J. (1952) The effects of psychotherapy: An evaluation. *Journal of Consulting Psychology*, 16, 319–324.

Foucault, M. (1990) *The History of Sexuality*, New York: Vintage Books.

Freud, S. (2016) *Three Essays on The Theory of Sexuality: The 1905 Edition*, New York: Verso.

Goodwach, R. (2005a) Sex therapy: Historical evolution, current practice. Part 1. *Australian & New Zealand Journal of Family Therapy*, 26;3, 155–164.

Goodwach, R. (2005b) Sex therapy: Historical evolution, current practice. Part 2. *Australian & New Zealand Journal of Family Therapy*, 26;4, 178–183.

Hertlein, K.M., Weeks, G.R. & Gambescia, N. (2015) *Systemic Sex Therapy*, New York: Routledge.

Hite, S. (1976) *The Hite Report: A Nationwide Study on Female Sexuality*, London: Collier Macmillan.

Kaplan-Singer, H. (1974) *The New Sex Therapy*, New York: Brunner Mazel.

Kaplan-Singer, H. (1979) *Disorders of Desire*, New York: Brunner Mazel.

Kinsey, A.C., Pomeroy, W.B. & Martin, C.E. (1948) *Sexual Behavior in The Human Female*, Philadelphia: Saunders.

Košciańska, A. (2014) Beyond Viagra: Sex therapy in Poland. *Czech Sociological Review*, 50;6, 919–938.

Krafft-Ebing, R.V. (1886/2018) *Psychopathia Sexualis*, London: Forgotten Books.

Markovic, D. (2007) Working with sexual issues in systemic therapy. *Australian & New Zealand Journal of Family Therapy*, 24;4, 200–209.

Markovic, D. (2013) Multidimensional psychosexual therapy: A model of integration between sexology and systemic therapy. *Sexual & Relationship Therapy*, 28;4, 311–323.

Masters, W.H. & Johnson, V.E. (1966) *Human Sexual Response*, Boston: Little Brown & Co.

Masters, W.H. & Johnson, V.E. (1970) *Human Sexual Inadequacy*, Boston: Little Brown & Co.

McCarthy, B.W. & McDonald, D.O. (2009) Sex therapy failures: A crucial, yet ignored, issue. *Journal of Sex & Marital Therapy*, 35, 320–329.

Meana, M., Hall, K.S.K. & Binik, Y.M. (2014) Sex therapy in transition: Are we there yet? In: Binik, Y.M. & Hall, K.S.K. [eds] *Principles and Practice of Sex Therapy*, fifth edition, New York: Guilford Press, 541–557.

Niak, D. (2017) Sex therapy as a technique for psychiatric patients. *Indian Journal of Health and Wellbeing*, 8;5, 368–375.

Quin, G. & Bohuon, A. (2012) Muscles, nerves, and sex: The contradictions of the medical approach to female bodies in movement in France, 1847–1914. *Gender & History*, 24;1, 172–186.

Sanz, V. (2017) No way out of the binary: A critical history of the scientific production of sex. *Signs: Journal of Women in Culture and Society*, 43;1, 1–27.

Weeks, G.R., Gambescia, N. & Hertlein, K.M. (2016) *A Clinician's Guide to Systemic Sex Therapy*, second edition, New York: Routledge.

Wislocka, M. (1978) *The Art of Love*, Warsaw: Iskry.

Wolpe, J. (1958) *Psychotherapy by Reciprocal Inhibition*, Stanford, CA: Stanford University Press.

Chapter 2

Sexual problems and the DSM

The American Psychiatric Association's *Diagnostic and Statistical Manual of Mental Disorders* (DSM) has been used since 1952 to categorise mental health conditions. In theory, the manual offers clinicians the opportunity to find the best diagnostic fit for a client's experience and, thus, to provide the most effective treatment. As there are new versions every 15–20 years, though, with interim versions more frequently, a person's treatment and even the categorisation of their 'disorder' can change, sometimes dramatically. It isn't so much that state-of-the-art research replaces outmoded interventions, but that social conventions and pragmatism affect attitudes to behaviours so they are either categorised as illness or not. For instance, homosexuality was seen as a mental illness in early editions while the latest edition has failed to classify sexual addiction, despite lobbying to do so. As the DSM is used for US insurance purposes, cynics might argue that the prevalence of problematic internet porn-related behaviours could present a severe challenge to US medical insurers were it to be included.

The World Health Organization's International Classification of Diseases (ICD), covers all health conditions, not just mental health, and is more often used by UK psychiatrists for diagnostic criteria, while UK sex therapists tend to use the DSM. Both the DSM and the ICD still base classification of sexual disorders on the original Masters and Johnson descriptions, though the ICD's remit is slightly broader. Traditionally, some UK sex therapists only worked with DSM dysfunctions, but their work now is more likely to be influenced by their workplace. People with sexual problems also present in other clinics, such as those for skin conditions, pelvic pain, urology, gynaecology and psychiatry. It has, thus, been argued that the diversity of the work implies there is no such thing as sex therapy as a discipline (Wincze & Weisberg, 2015). However, it can also be argued that the difference between more general treatment which addresses sexual issues and sex therapy is the range of skills practitioners possess. So, though a practitioner may be trained and equipped to work with sexual issues, the contemporary *psychosexual therapist* has a range of skills *and* is also able to treat all the DSM dysfunctions. The inclusion of DSM sexual disorders here does not, therefore, suggest they're the exclusive work of 'sex therapists'. The broad categories of condition and the treatments developed for these do provide neat options for sex therapy, though it's always the clients' feedback rather than the treatment plan which should determine the route of interventions and most appropriate practitioner(s).

In deciding on treatment routes, it's important not to rule out clients who don't present with an obvious DSM sexual dysfunction, as these are heteronormative and inevitably limiting. Many couples, for instance, attend with general dissatisfaction about their sex life which wouldn't qualify them for PST using DSM criteria. This does not, however, mean they wouldn't benefit hugely from a PST programme. Often, too, DSM 'dysfunctions', which have been unrecognised by the clients, emerge during history taking or even later. Such clients would never receive treatment if they were turned away on the basis of presenting with no qualifying dysfunction at initial assessment. In other words, the contemporary sex therapist is aware of, and can treat, DSM dysfunctions but is not governed by them, utilising a flexible and creative approach.

DSM categories

The disorders recognised in DSM-5 are categorised as:

- **Disorders of desire**, which are sexual interest/arousal disorder and male hypoactive desire disorder.
- **Erectile Disorder**: This is also known as 'erectile dysfunction' (ED). Clients may prefer 'erectile difficulty'.
- **Orgasmic Disorders**: Premature (early) ejaculation; delayed ejaculation and female orgasmic disorder (anorgasmia).
- **Sensation Disorders**: Genito-pelvic pain/penetration disorder – previously referred to as dyspareunia and vaginismus. Persistent genital arousal disorder (PGAD) is currently a non-DSM condition, but is presenting more often.
- **Substance/medication-induced sexual disorder**: Conditions come into this category when they occur around the time of beginning, increasing dose or stopping medication known to cause the problem. It's important to get details of all drugs being taken, as this category refers to recreational drugs (substances) as well as prescribed and over-the-counter medication.
- **Other Specified Sexual Disorders**: These are conditions which don't meet full criteria but which cause distress and for which a specifier can be identified; for example, sexual aversion disorder, which now appears in the category of phobias.
- **Unspecified Sexual Disorders**: These are problems which don't meet the DSM categories, and the reason is clearly given, perhaps because there is insufficient information.

Specifiers are employed in the DSM to refer to the types or characteristics of a problem. For instance, sexual problems may:

- **Be lifelong versus acquired**: If they're lifelong, the condition will have been around since a person's first sexual activity; acquired disorders will not have been experienced previously.

- **Be generalised versus situational**: When they're generalised, problems crop up in every sexual situation, whereas situational problems only happen in certain particular contexts, such as with a long-term partner and not casual partners, or they may have started following a particular event.
- **Cause mild, moderate or severe distress**.

Paraphilic disorders also occupy a DSM category, but a paraphilia of itself is not considered to necessarily have mental health implications. DSM-5 (APA 2013) defines paraphilias as 'intense, persistent' sexual interest which doesn't involve genitals or foreplay and isn't with physiologically 'normal' human adults. These include behaviours such as fetishes and sadomasochism. For a practice to be considered a dysfunction, there must be persistent distress or impairment. It's therefore quite common to meet paraphilias in the course of sex therapy. Most are incidental to the work and not problematic if they don't interfere with desired partnered sex or cause other relationship issues. Occasionally, clients present with considerable distress or the behaviour underlies a sexual or relationship issue, so it's important to be prepared and aware of personal prejudices. Very occasionally, clients mention interest in an illegal practice, such as viewing child pornography, exhibitionism or non-consensual sex. It's therefore sensible to be aware of your agency's response in such cases or to discuss this possibility with your supervisor and colleagues.

Female sexual interest/arousal disorder

Sexual interest/arousal disorder has been a controversial inclusion as it rolls together desire and arousal, which were separate in previous editions, based on research suggesting women don't distinguish between arousal and desire.

There are a number of factors which contribute to a diagnosis of sexual interest/arousal disorder. It's necessary to have three for a diagnosis.

- Having no or little interest in sexual activity
- Little or no sexual or erotic thoughts or fantasies
- Little or no initiation of sexual activity
- Not responding to a partner's sexual initiation
- Little or no sexual excitement or pleasure in at least 75 percent of sexual activities
- Little or no interest or arousal despite potential cues
- Little or no genital or non-genital experiencing in at least 75 percent of sexual encounters

Male hypoactive desire disorder

This is diagnosed when there has been at least a six-month history of persistent or recurrent reduction or absence of sexual or erotic fantasies or thoughts and desire for sexual activity, which is causing distress.

Erectile disorder

ED is diagnosed when someone has, for at least six months, experienced significant difficulty in obtaining an erection during sex or a clear decrease in the rigidity of their erection.

Premature (early) ejaculation

Early ejaculation involves a minimum of six months with ejaculation occurring before the individual wishes to ejaculate and within about a minute of 75 percent of partnered *vaginal* penetration attempts. They must be distressed by this and it mustn't be caused by any clinical condition or treatment. However, distress and dissatisfaction about length of penetration before ejaculation are not alone considered dysfunctional.

Many more men present with early ejaculation than actually meet the criteria, frequently having unrealistic expectations about how long they should be able to 'last'. Few are aware that humans are unusual compared with most animals, which ejaculate upon penetration, and that three-quarters of men ejaculate within two minutes of starting intercourse (Kinsey *et al*, 1948). Criteria, thus, specify length of time to ejaculation following penetration as severe when occurring within 15 seconds, moderate in 15–30 seconds and mild within 30–60 seconds.

Delayed ejaculation

Though it's considered the most infrequently reported sexual dysfunction (APA, 2013), people are presenting with delayed ejaculation more often. This is possibly because having a sexual problem has become more normalised or because increasing use of pornography has led to reduced desire for partnered sex (Park *et al*, 2016).

A diagnosis is made when, despite adequate desire, arousal and stimulation, there's at least a six-month ongoing history of ejaculatory problems with a partner. Specifiers include: whether the problem has always existed or been acquired; whether it happens in both solo and partnered sex (generalised), or only with a partner or in specific situations (situational). The severity of the delay is another specifier. A clinical cause may be evident – for instance, some antidepressants may have a role – but there are often multiple, complex contributory factors.

Unlike early ejaculation, it may not cause distress, at least initially, as 'lasting' can be seen as a sign of control or masculine prowess. However, lengthy thrusting can cause physical injury, not to mention exhaustion, and partners may feel undesirable.

Genito-Pelvic Pain/Penetration Disorder (GPPPD)

GPPPD replaces dyspareunia (pain during intercourse) and vaginismus (involuntary tightening of the pelvic muscles that prevents penetration), as the two conditions were found to frequently co-exist. The diagnosis requires one or more of the following:

- Not being able to have vaginal intercourse/penetration
- Genital or pelvic pain when penetration is attempted
- There is fear or anxiety about the prospect of sexual pain
- Pelvic floor muscles are tensed when vaginal penetration is attempted
- Distress or damage is evident.

Specifiers include how long the problem has existed and how bad it is. GPPPD may be seen in a variety of settings, as there are often conjoint medical and psychological issues, not least distress and weariness caused by the length of time it can take to get a diagnosis and/or treatment. Currently, GPPPD relates to pain in women but, as more men are being diagnosed with chronic pelvic pain conditions, definitions may be expanded in future.

Female orgasmic disorder

Diagnosis requires at least a six-month history of problems with orgasm at least 75 percent of the time, for no apparent reason. Inability to orgasm regularly – or at all through intercourse – is not considered dysfunctional and response pressure may be the actual cause of distress.

Critique of the DSM

There has been much criticism of the DSM, not least that it ignores the complexity of most sexual problems. Tiefer (2010) points out that most couples don't feel equipped to manage their own sexual problems and may feel the only help available to them is medical. Tiefer (2002, 2010) has been a particularly stern critic of what she sees as the medicalisation of sexuality, driven by the pharmaceutical industry (Conrad, 2007). Indeed, the widespread availability of drugs like Viagra to treat ED may have boosted public belief in the possibility of a quick fix for sexual problems (Meana *et al*, 2014), promoting the idea they can be easily treated by clinicians with no relevant biopsychosocial experience or training (Kleinplatz, 2015). Moreover, the evidence base for social and contextual issues is harder to come by than pharmaceutical research, simply due to lack of funding.

While needed for statistics, research and funding, a manualised response doesn't necessarily achieve results. Clients respond more quickly when the practitioner is able to provide a unique approach (Bobele, 2018). However, although brief notes on aspects to take into consideration when making a diagnosis are included in the DSM, the concept of categorising sexual problems and restoring sexual function largely ignores the underlying causes of 'symptoms' and other contributory relationship and contextual factors. What's most concerning, however, may be that problematizing sexual behaviours and experiences creates a market for treatment and promotes feelings of inadequacy.

Qualified and experienced psychosexual therapists are in an excellent position to normalise many sexual problems and explore solutions. This is not the same as trivialising sexual issues or expecting endurance, which recent media interest in sexual performance purports to overcome. However, media attention has increasingly created impossible sexual goals which generate aspirations to acquire sexual interest, skills, response and knowledge – which then results in dissatisfaction and anxiety (Frith, 2015). Effective contemporary psychosexual therapists consequently need to be aware of the potential for disempowering clients by inadvertently following a medical and/or populist agenda. Most importantly, they must be able to recognise and address the multiplicity of issues experienced by people with sexual problems, not just their dysfunction. Chapter 3 considers how to assess for PST.

References

American Psychiatric Association (2013) *Diagnostic and Statistical Manual of Mental Disorders*, fifth edition, Arlington Virginia: APA.

Bobele, M. (2018) Unique problems, unique resolutions: The case of the bad orgasm. In: *Quickies: The Handbook of Brief Sex Therapy*, third edition, New York: W.W. Norton & Co.

Conrad, P. (2007) *The Medicalization of Society: On the Transformation of Human Conditions into Treatable Disorders*, Baltimore: Johns Hopkins Press.

Frith, H. (2015) *Orgasmic Bodies*, Basingstoke: Palgrave Macmillan.

Kinsey, A.C., Pomeroy, W.B. & Marton, C.E. (1948) *Sexual Behavior in the Human Male*, Philadelphia: Saunders.

Kleinplatz, P. (2015) The current profession of sex therapy. In: Hertlein, K., Weeks, G.R. & Gambescia, N. [eds] *Systemic Sex Therapy*, second edition, New York: Routledge, 17–31.

Meana, M., Hall, K.S.K. & Binik, Y.M. (2014) Conclusion. Sex therapy in transition: Are we there yet? In: Binik, Y.M. & Hall, K.S.K. [eds] *Principles and Practice of Sex Therapy*, fifth edition, New York: Guilford Press, 541–557.

Park, B.Y., Wilson, G., Berger, J., Christman, M., Reina, B., Bishop, F., Klam, W.P. & Doan, A.P. (2016) *Behavioral Sciences*, 6;3, 1–26. www.ncbi.nlm.nih.gov/pmc/articles/PMC6000996/. Accessed May 26, 2018.

Tiefer, L. (2002) Beyond the medical model of women's sexual problems: A campaign to resist the promotion of "female sexual dysfunction". *Sexual and Relationship Therapy*, 17;2, 127–135.

Tiefer, L. (2010) Still resisting after all these years: An update on sexuo-medicalization and on the new view campaign to challenge the medicalization of women's sexuality. *Sexual and Relationship Therapy*, 25;2, 198–196.

Wincze, J.P. & Weisberg, R.B. (2015) *Sexual Dysfunction: A Guide for Assessment and Treatment*, third edition, New York: Guilford Press.

Chapter 3

Initial assessment

Though assessment is considered a distinct phase in PST, consisting of an initial meeting, history taking and formulation, assessment continues throughout PST treatment. Not only is information continually being added to, but it should be regularly revisited. As new information is gathered, it adds to and contextualises existing information, offering even more insight and providing an invaluable resource. Consequently, no information which seems puzzling or inconsistent should be dismissed, because it will probably make sense at some point. There is more than just information gathering to consider at the initial assessment, however. This is usually the therapist's first contact with the individual or couple, who may have been considering sex therapy for a long time and be extremely anxious and unsure of what to expect. A positive first session should offer hope and reassurance for the client(s) and provide the therapist with a reasonable idea of what treatment will be needed; hypotheses will be further explored during the PST history taking stage. It's also often possible to normalise clients' issues; for example, loss of desire is common when couples are experiencing work stress, financial problems, tiredness, since having a baby, and so on.

The initial assessment elicits the reason for attending and offers a preliminary impression of the clients' suitability for PST. Sex therapy may not be suitable for all clients, or the factors contributing to the sexual problem may make PST difficult. Contraindications might include insufficient time, severe mental health issues, coercion, drug or alcohol dependency, severe relationship difficulties and, sometimes, pregnancy. Though couples often want to fix their sexual problems before the arrival of their baby, it should be explained that pregnancy changes the body's sexual response, and being pregnant inevitably also changes the way a person feels about their body and sexuality. It's also possible that some of the physical and psychological changes affecting sexuality which occur during pregnancy may not persist afterwards. For instance, it may be easier or more difficult to climax. Having said this, PST in pregnancy usually still provides considerable learning about closeness and intimacy, which stands couples in good stead when the baby comes and sex may not be their top priority.

Introduction to PST

Many clients attend an initial assessment with mixed feelings about what they're embarking on. Sometimes a crisis has triggered the consultation, some clients have been referred from another therapist or health care practitioner or a couple may have been waiting for the appropriate moment to attend. In many cases, couples wait as long as possible before seeking help because it's reassuring to feel that the possibility of therapy is there if their situation becomes bad enough. Once embarked on the process, they may feel this is their last chance to find a solution.

Permission giving

Permission to discuss sex needs to be clear. For those working in a medical, rather than therapeutic context, it may be more difficult to initiate or respond to a conversation about sexual concerns. Jack Annon (1976) conceived the PLISSIT Model which stands for Permission, Limited Information, Specific Suggestions and Intensive Therapy. While the model was devised for use in general health care settings, rather than PST, its principles can be useful to us all.

Permission – In healthcare, asking patients' consent to discuss sexual matters may be framed also as offering advice: 'I wonder if you'd like to talk about the way your condition is affecting your sexual expression?' Clients seeking PST or relationship therapy, however, are more surprised if sex isn't mentioned, and may conclude as a result that there are matters that can't be brought up. In relationship therapy, mentioning sex at an early stage gives clients permission to do so too. Even though in sex therapy you'll obviously discuss sex, it's still helpful to acknowledge that it can be difficult to take the step of coming for PST, not least having to discuss very personal matters with a stranger. It can also be helpful to ask clients at the end of the session how they found it and whether you could have done anything to make it more comfortable.

In sex therapy, it's important to seek consent if you're doing anything other than *talking* with the clients, such as showing them pictures of genitals. It's also extremely helpful to know how clients identify sexually. For instance, bisexuality isn't obvious when couples present and it's easy to make the assumption that they're gay or straight. Far from being intrusive, asking about sexuality is normalising and non-judgemental.

Limited Information – In healthcare, this is the kind of general information which is found in handouts or is relevant to a large number of patients. In sex therapy, this may be the initial psychoeducation offered during assessment conversations or as information to take away. In both cases, bibliotherapy or films may sometimes be suggested.

Specific Suggestions – This stage addresses individual concerns and often requires a more thorough knowledge of the issues being raised. Some doctors, nurses and physiotherapists develop extremely in-depth knowledge of sexual matters in relation to their area of health expertise and are able to address sexual concerns directly themselves. More often, their skill may be in knowing to whom they can refer their clients or pointing them in the direction of appropriate sources of help. Relationship therapists also develop knowledge and skills to enable them to discuss their clients' sexual relationship helpfully. It's to be hoped they know enough about sex therapy to explain what it entails to their clients and to refer them as appropriate. Specific suggestions are made throughout the PST process, though more often, and in more depth, from the formulation onwards.

Intensive Therapy – This would generally be outside the remit of health providers and relationship therapists, though there are times when they would offer specific solutions to particular problems, perhaps collaborating with, or accepting referrals from, a sex therapist. For instance, physiotherapists may work on strengthening pelvic floor muscles and skin specialists may treat vulval skin conditions or sensitivity. The PST process should be considered intensive therapy, as its providers are specialists with considerable knowledge, skill and experience.

Nurse educators Bridget Taylor and Sally Davis (2007) emphasised the importance of permission giving, which they felt was being skipped by many health professionals. They consequently developed the Extended PLISSIT Model (Ex-PLISSIT), which sees permission giving as important at all stages of the PLISSIT process. For instance, rather than assuming permission, giving out a leaflet and believing the job is done, they suggest asking patients if they'd like further information or have questions before giving information. They then urge practitioners to check at a later date whether the information has been useful and whether any further help is needed. They also encourage practitioners not to wait until after the first three stages before referral to 'intensive therapy', as this might be required at the outset.

In PST the stages may overlap or you may need to move back and forth between them, with less intensive therapy needed as PST progresses and partners take over responsibility for the process, for instance.

Curiosity

You need to be interested in the clients' presentation, the content of their story and how they relate to you and to each other if they attend as a couple. Therapists need 'a warm, active state of mind' (Cecchin, 1987), using systemic curiosity to both thicken their stories and avoid favouring one point of view over another. It's, therefore, important to ask questions and not just take the stories being brought at face value. For instance, someone with erectile problems may tell you, 'It happens all the time'. Does this mean erections can't be relied on or that the client never gets an erection anymore? Does something trigger loss of erection? Does the client ever have an erection on waking in the morning? Can he masturbate without losing his erection? What is his partner's reaction?

Not all therapists realise how important the initial assessment session can be. It's the beginning of the therapeutic relationship and an opportunity to set the scene for the work you'll be doing together. This may be the only session some clients attend, either because they were put off or because the session has sufficiently addressed their needs. It helps to structure the session so that it's calmly paced and you're able to fit in all the necessary elements. As well as collecting information about identity and contact, it's useful to learn what clients see as the problem, what they've already tried to remedy it and what they hope the outcome of therapy will be. It's not uncommon for each partner to have a different idea of what the problem is and to have different goals. For instance, the problem Rob identified was early ejaculation and the outcome he wanted was more control over when he ejaculated. This was news to his partner Stella, who thought the issue was lack of sex. She saw herself as partially responsible for this as she rarely initiated sex, having felt rebuffed a couple of times. Her goal was more intimacy of any description.

The therapist saw their issue as avoidance of sex and intimacy due to Rob's fear of failure and Stella's fear of rejection. To Rob's astonishment, Stella hadn't even realised that Rob felt he ejaculated too soon. She agreed intercourse was brief but found this quite flattering, as it indicated to her that Rob was highly aroused. She thoroughly enjoyed the rest of their sexual encounters and usually climaxed herself. Rob's reluctance to be intimate had affected her sexual confidence, however, which returned once she recognised the dynamic the couple had been engaged in.

Information gathering

Sometimes it can be helpful to send out a form to gather some basic information before the session. Knowing that the therapist is aware of the problem can also be helpful to clients who are embarrassed to speak about it and who don't have a referral letter. Some people don't like writing down what's wrong, though, so 'description of the problem' could be optional. Where therapy is time-limited, it's essential to give clients a questionnaire in advance of the first session so it can be used to clarify information rather than collect it. E-mail or online questionnaires need to be encrypted.

It's helpful to have your own questionnaire as an *aide memoire* during the session. Some therapists like to split the questionnaire into two columns, one for each partner, so they can record their answers and immediately see what differs. Different therapists and agencies will have their own preferences about what's important to know at this stage, but it's helpful to include:

- Age and occupation
- Length and type of relationship
- Each partner's definition of the problem, how it affects them and why they're coming for help now
- How long the issue has been troubling them, what they've tried to fix it, whether anything has changed and each partner's view of what has caused the problem
- Any exceptions to the problem; for instance, times when painful sex is comfortable or someone with early ejaculation takes longer when they masturbate

- The way the partners identify sexually – for instance, one or both partners may identify as bisexual
- Details of health and current medication may be helpful; many drugs can affect sex, as can many medical and mental health conditions
- Similarly, it's helpful to know about alcohol, recreational drug use and smoking
- Counselling history.

Information giving

A brief overview of the process should be given at a relevant point (see Box 3.1 and details on page 53). When discussing the history taking process, it's explained to couples that, unlike most counselling sessions, what they say will not just be kept between the therapist and each partner, as the information is used to create a formulation of their issues and may be referred to throughout treatment. However, this should not deter them from disclosing information which will be helpful to the process. They just need to point out anything they really don't want to be shared.

Though PST treatment depends on feedback, and is individual to each couple, the work always begins with a sex ban. This may seem counterintuitive, but it gives couples space to learn about their physical responses and reduces performance pressure. Discuss the sex ban before starting history taking. If couples aren't having sex together already, an explicit ban on partnered sex may allow them to enjoy touch without the fear that it will become sexual and fail or that rejection will follow. If, however, the couple are still being sexual together, albeit with some difficulties, continuing partnered sex during the history taking process may be helpful. Couples often notice changes occurring as a result of the thoughts and conversations provoked by history taking, for instance.

It's also helpful to warn couples about the commitment involved in PST. Regular therapy sessions, individual and couple exercises take time, plus couples need to be aware of potential financial costs. PST isn't necessarily a quick fix. It's impossible to predict how long a couple or individual will take to feel there's been sufficient improvement, so they could be in therapy for anything from a single session to many months.

Box 3.1   PST Process

- Initial Assessment
- History Taking
- Formulation
- Treatment
- Follow-up

Assessment with individuals

The initial assessment is ideally conducted face-to-face with both partners. This ensures they're both given the same information and the therapist is able to observe the way they interact. A high level of conflict is often unrecognised or minimised by one partner attending alone. However, this may be a contraindication to treatment, as PST is unlikely to succeed if the couple are seriously at loggerheads. Nevertheless, it's common for one partner to present alone, usually assuming the problem is theirs, and not expecting the other to attend. If this is the case, you can discuss whether the other partner will come if invited, and whether they'll want to have a joint or individual session before beginning the history taking process.

Though some clients remain adamant that the problem is theirs alone, sometimes it's actually the unseen partner who's insisting the problem is nothing to do with them. It may be that the absent partner is frightened of being blamed or feels too ashamed to face the idea they've contributed to the issues. Understandably, some are just anxious about the process. Often, try as you might, they cannot be persuaded to attend, even if attendance is framed as being to support the other partner. Interestingly, as the history taking develops, it's common to clearly see how the absent partner's attitude and behaviour affects the problem and the relationship, even when the identified sexual problem existed long before the relationship began. Moreover, it's extremely common for both partners, and the relationship, to develop issues even if the problem starts with only one partner. For instance, where something like pain or erectile problems leads to sex feeling shameful or disappointing, partners often lose desire and avoid sex. This can lead to the development of further problems if, say, one partner feels the other doesn't want sex and loses his erection, can't climax due to anxiety or hurries sex.

The therapist needs to ensure individual clients have a realistic expectation of what can be achieved, to understand why they've chosen to come at this point in time, to find out what they've already tried to help and whether anything obvious has contributed to what they're experiencing. They should visit their GP to rule out organic reasons for their problem(s).

Ending the session

Sufficient time needs to be left at the end of the initial assessment for the clients to ask questions, as well as to explain what will happen next. Some won't need further sessions; some will be eager to get started with history taking and others will want a chance to think about their options. Sometimes couples decide further sessions are unnecessary, as their communication and confidence has already improved to a point where they feel able to find their own solutions. This is especially common with poorly informed or inexperienced couples, when the therapist is able to normalise what's been happening, offering information or reassurance that help is possible. Knowing that therapy is there if it becomes necessary leaves the door open for them to come back. Such couples tend to do well if they return, being highly motivated and believing both in their ability to make changes and the therapist's potential to help.

Some couples want to think over their decision, often because they hadn't appreciated the commitment involved. It can feel disheartening to new therapists when clients don't continue beyond the first stage of the process, but they need to remind themselves that PST is a stepped approach. The first session can be highly therapeutic, even if clients don't have the time to give to further therapy.

It's beneficial to end by summarising what you've heard in the session and what *appears* to be the focus of the work. Take care not to suggest one partner is responsible for the problem or that taking care of a single issue will fix everything. Even when an obvious problem and its cause strike you immediately, it's likely other issues and contributing factors will emerge during history taking.

At the end of the initial assessment, clients often comment that it's been much less embarrassing and stressful than they expected, with many saying they're very much looking forward to the next stage of the PST process, history taking.

References

Annon, J.S. (1976) *Behavioral Treatment of Sexual Problems: Brief Therapy*, Oxford: Harper & Row.

Cecchin, G. (1987) Hypothesizing, circularity and neutrality revisited: An invitation to curiosity. *Family Process*, 26;4, 405–413.

Taylor, B. & Davis, S. (2007) The extended PLISSIT model for addressing the sexual wellbeing of individuals with an acquired disability or chronic illness. *Sexuality & Disability*, 25, 135–139.

Chapter 4

History taking

History taking is an essential component of the CBT process, and is necessary to develop an effective formulation of the issues, especially how the past is operating in the present and what's maintaining problems. When used effectively, it's also an opportunity to build the therapeutic relationship and offer psychoeducation. It's the first time some clients have really considered themselves and their relationship in detail, so they often process what they say in a different way when they share their experiences. Hearing themselves speak, the way the questions are asked and the therapist's responses can change their perception (cognitive restructuring). The process can also stimulate discussion between partners.

Practitioners who see PST as just a series of exercises to be worked through may rush the assessment phase. Indeed, there are even couple agencies who recommend that it's completed in a single session. However, it's impossible to create the formulation without sufficient information. Without a formulation, treatment is reduced to a series of exercises which may or may not be appropriate. Then, when blocks to progress occur, neither therapist nor clients will have much insight into why therapy isn't progressing. As a result, the therapist is frustrated, the clients feel uncontained and there's an overall sense of failure. However, when adequate time has been spent on assessment, the therapeutic relationship is stronger and clients are more likely to be trusting and honest. Most importantly, it establishes a necessary sense of collaboration which encourages therapist and clients to tackle blocks with faith that they can be understood and overcome.

Sometimes clients want to rush through the assessment process and get to the treatment phase as quickly as possible. Usually, they want to rush that, too, and get results without really engaging. However, they've probably delayed seeking help and had the problem for a while, so it's unrealistic to think it can be fixed in a flash. Couples are also often at different stages in the change process, so it isn't helpful to be influenced by one partner's need to move on. Often, too, clients in a rush have had unpleasant experiences in the past – which may include physical or sexual abuse – which they've tried to get over with quickly. It doesn't help to collude with the possibly unconscious idea that sex therapy is an ordeal to be endured.

While it can be tempting to offer clients exercises during the history taking process, this isn't normally a good idea, as you won't yet have had the chance to fully ascertain their suitability for treatment. Nor will you have the full story available to assess whether particular care is needed with tasks which could be triggering. Given that many clients don't reveal abuse of any kind until late in the history, if at all, it has to be assumed that all clients are vulnerable and that the setting of exercises and experiments needs to be cautious and appropriate. The same goes for setting tasks for a couple when only one partner is attending therapy. You can't know what's going on for the other partner, so it's unethical to set tasks involving them. When one partner has attended initially and then dropped out, it's a terrible idea to set tasks involving them. Whatever reason they gave for leaving the process, they may have found it too triggering. They may then, consciously or unconsciously, sabotage attempts at experiments because they're uncomfortable or they don't want to be sexual, making the situation considerably more painful.

We also need to be careful, when exploring people's lives and identities, not to collude with internalised self-hatred or to impose our own views of how someone should be. UK counselling and psychotherapy agencies have all signed up to a memorandum of understanding on conversion therapy (Stonewall, 2019) which agrees that no practitioner or organisation will attempt to change a person's gender or sexual identity, even if this is what the client requests. For example, it wouldn't be considered ethical to encourage someone to have, say, a straight sexual relationship if this was being done to try to fix their genuine desire for another kind of relationship. This is one of the reasons why assessment is so important and no tasks should be set before a really thorough history taking has been carried out.

Confidentiality

Some therapists worry about how they'll manage knowing secrets, but respecting confidentiality is part of the work. If something you're told makes it difficult to work with a couple, you need to be honest about this with the partner who made the disclosure and consider options together. A trauma history requires particular sensitivity about how and whether the other partner should be told.

Clients need to be aware you'll be taking notes, usually using a generic booklet containing questions about them, their family and the relationship. Additional questions may be added about any dysfunctions that emerge. Notes should be destroyed once treatment is complete.

Whether or not they're relaxed about therapeutic talking, many clients feel uncomfortable or apprehensive about the personal nature of assessment at the outset, so do acknowledge this. Also be aware of your own comfort with the material. Therapists need to take a non-judgemental position, making no assumptions, especially in relation to sexual orientation or practices. Avoid shaming language and binary explanations, and attempt to use gender neutral terms. Interestingly, some clients are more comfortable with questions about sex than about intimacy or emotions.

Needless to say, history taking should be conducted in a safe environment where there is privacy, quiet and comfort. This may not be the case if the consultation is conducted using digital messaging. Clients often like to use something like Skype for their history taking in particular, as it can seem easier to arrange for each partner. However, do ensure that partner and children are not around during the appointment and that there won't be interruptions. Some clients choose to conduct the appointment from their office or bedroom, both of which may have stressful and distracting connotations, so advice may be needed about this.

At the beginning of the first history taking session, it's always worth briefly explaining the process again, going over appropriate boundaries and establishing the limits of confidentiality. Make clear to clients that they can skip questions, come back to questions or add information they think would be helpful to you.

The questions

The following is a general guide to the areas to be covered and questions it would be useful to include in your history taking booklet. You can make the booklet up by printing two copies of each page of questions so that the same sets of questions are on opposite pages, one for each partner. Always ask the full set of questions to both partners. Partners often answer the same question differently, so don't assume you know what's going on just because one partner has commented.

The topics below will generate a number of questions, and it's up to you whether you just stick to these or supplement them, especially initially. Once you're actually using them, there's no doubt you'll discover that some reveal more fruitful information than others and that they'll prompt ideas about further questions. It's therefore likely that you will be honing the booklet over time.

Information about the client

What's it like being you?

If you haven't gained much sense of the client previously, it can be helpful to open with a general question, such as this one, which allows the client to choose what to disclose and can give helpful ideas about what they find oppressive or affirming. Some respond to this very general question with descriptions of sexual behaviour, but many will have already spent time on this in the initial assessment. Partners joining the process may benefit from an initial question about what's been happening and what they want from the process, though this often comes out in the general introduction and explanations before starting. A generic question right at the beginning suggests that PST does not see sex in isolation but will have a more systemic approach.

You may want to clarify information gleaned at the initial assessment or gather basic information if the client is a partner who wasn't present. What's the client's job, for instance, and do they like it? Is this what they always wanted to do or do they have other ambitions? Will work affect their ability to attend therapy? Someone who works away for weeks at a time, for instance, may find it difficult to maintain momentum. Similarly, some hobbies are time consuming. There is some evidence that extreme sports are associated with a trauma history, so this would be useful to know about.

Details about the client's birth

This may seem an odd subject, but it can be enormously revealing. Some clients know nothing at all, suggesting a family which doesn't share this kind of information, perhaps feeling it's too personal or inappropriate. Some have heard detailed happy stories about the delight their parents had in their conception and arrival, while others have heard horror stories about their delivery, in which their mother has been torn, haemorrhaged or 'nearly died'. Sometimes these stories have a direct impact on the individual's ability to be sexual, inducing fear of damaging their partner or of being hurt themselves. As early attachment injuries have the potential to affect sex and intimacy later in life, check whether there was any separation at birth – for instance, a premature baby may spend considerable time away from its mother in the Special Care Baby Unit – or whether their mother had postnatal depression.

Feelings about their body and appearance

Body image conversations can reveal information about anorexia and bulimia, use of steroids, genital cutting, self-harm and abuse, so always ask clients how they feel about their appearance and body and whether they've ever had surgery, an accident or illness. Ask, too, whether their feelings have changed over time. Many people report disliking or being alarmed by the changes in their body at puberty, discuss image issues related to weight gain or loss, post-pregnancy body or body features they have strong feelings about one way or the other. It's surprising how many people experience distaste about their breasts and genitals, often believing them to be abnormal. These days, some people will have had genital enhancement surgery, so this may be something to ask about. Discussing tattoos, Botox, piercings, exercise, body building and attitudes to makeup and body care in general can reveal a great deal about someone's comfort with their body, whether they use enhancements to glory in it or disguise it. It's always helpful to ask specifically how they feel about their breasts and genitals, as self-consciousness can get in the way of sex. Women with heritage from places which practice genital cutting need to be asked about this (see Chapter 10). Men should be asked about circumcision.

It's helpful to explore attitude to gender at this point if it didn't emerge in the initial assessment. Is the client comfortable with their gender? This can bring out stories around the childhood realisation that someone was stuck with their gender, insightful reflections on gender, gender celebration or anything from full-on gender dysphoria to mild irritation that siblings were treated differently. Parental discourses on gender often emerge here too.

It's also useful to enquire about parents' attitude towards nudity, their own and their children's bodies, and whether the client was aware of their parents being sexual. Some parents can be too open in their sexual behaviour and flaunting of their bodies, while others hide their sexual selves and make their embarrassment obvious. Clients often have stories about walking in on parents having sex, which they often regret. However, many find everyday parental affection and touch both charming and reassuring.

Sexual anxiety

Ask clients whether they've ever had any performance or response anxiety, as this is often at the heart of sexual problems. Be as specific as possible, trying to find out whether the anxiety has only been with the current partner or occurs when relationships become closer and there is more to lose. Clients may have ideas about what has contributed to their anxiety, revealing some unhelpful beliefs and discourses around sexual performance.

Health

Illness can have a profound effect on an individual's relationship with their body, and childhood illnesses sometimes affect a person's ability to trust their body and feel it belongs to them. This may be exacerbated if there has been any examination or involvement of genitals, such as urinary catheterisation or circumcision. Some people who've had long periods in hospital as children feel deep shame about being different or abandoned if their parents couldn't be with them.

It's understandable that early exposure to pain and separation could affect body confidence. Many people have only sketchy memories about illness or surgery and don't make a connection with their current sexual problems. However, early and traumatic memories are embodied and can present as distress or sexual aversion without any cognitive awareness that a memory has been triggered. Family of origin attitudes to illness can also affect the way a child feels about their body. For instance, if distress about illness and injury is dismissed in childhood, the person may not feel entitled to complain about sexual discomfort and avoid sex as a result.

You need to know about any sexually transmitted infections as these can seriously impact self-image. The client also has to manage risk in the relationship if an infection is long-term, such as herpes or HIV. Women who've never been near a sexual health clinic are often shocked when a smear test reveals they have an HPV infection. This sometimes requires further investigation or even treatment to prevent or treat cervical cancer.

Current illness or disability may be the reason for attending PST. Clients may need help to manage sex more comfortably, deal with body image issues arising from their treatment or have sexual issues related to side-effects of their medication. The way clients refer to their health offers many clues about their ability to manage difficulty and their expectations about the help they can and should expect.

Far more conditions are now known to be stress-related, and many are understandably exacerbated by stress. You'll consequently want to know what makes existing illness worse and whether the client has ever developed stress-related behaviours, such as nail biting, hair pulling, bed wetting or sleep walking. How do they know they're stressed? What happens when they're stressed now and how do they manage that? Do they and their partner have different approaches to stress management? Does this ever cause clashes? Anxiety about 'getting it right' in everyday life may be accompanied by anxiety about getting sex right. Some clients believe they should just carry on, however bad they feel.

Some with known mental health issues feel their partner should be more understanding of them, while others blame themselves exclusively for any problems in their relationship. Still more ignore or deny being affected by stress, depression or anxiety but will admit, if you ask the questions, to recently being more irritable or experiencing a low mood. Those who've ever had any intrusive thoughts, or felt compelled to perform repetitive behaviours, will benefit from discussion of how this is managed.

Check how much clients are drinking and smoking and whether they've ever used recreational or party drugs, which can interfere with sexual function. Also ask whether they feel they're eating well, whether this has changed and how they're sleeping. Dietary neglect, comfort eating and early waking are all associated with depression.

Sexual development

It's interesting to discover how clients reacted to sexual development – whether they had been prepared for the onset of puberty and what sex education they received. Commonly, people learned about sex and reproduction from school, family, friends and practice. More recently, gender beliefs about what sex entails have been influenced by viewing pornography, for both boys and girls. Some clients have absolutely no mental image of loving sex and many erroneous ideas about what partners enjoy sexually. Ironically, this has meant clients have begun presenting with a considerably increased need for education. As well as asking how they acquired their original sex education, and what that entailed, it's helpful to know whether they've actively sought particular information more recently and where they found help.

Ask when menstruation/wet dreams started, whether this came as a surprise and how it was dealt with. Usually, clients describe preparation for menstruation as part of their sex education, though they haven't all had a good experience. Older clients, in particular, may have been terrified by their first period and tell stories of how they coped for months without telling anyone. Preparation for wet dreams is less common, partly because parents don't know when to have the conversation. Though around eight is the average age of pre-puberty hormone changes in boys, some begin much younger or older, and many boys are never aware of wet dreams at all. Many have erections throughout puberty, with or without arousal. Often clients tell anecdotes about trying to conceal their erections once puberty arrived.

A conversation about becoming aware of sexual feelings can be helpful. Explain to your client that many children notice feelings they can't explain but may enjoy, and don't realise until sometime later that these were associated with sexual arousal. Asking when they first noticed such feelings can be hugely enlightening for clients who'd assumed they were different in some way. They often describe experiences such as orgasming when climbing ropes during PE at school or rubbing their bodies on surfaces because 'it felt nice'. Awareness of *sex* may occur much later. Many children are aware of reproduction – sometimes due to observing animals – and sometimes of sex for pleasure, without making the link to their own experience.

Sexual experience

Ask at what age they started masturbating rather than whether they masturbated, as this normalises the behaviour. Some boys are shocked by their first climax if they weren't expecting to ejaculate, and some people say they found the intensity of their first orgasm overwhelming and even off-putting. Discuss current masturbation, including frequency and what prompts the client to masturbate. Is masturbation used to relieve stress or boredom? Has their experience of masturbation changed at all? For instance, has it become more difficult to climax or get an erection? Is masturbation accompanied by fantasy, erotica or porn? How much porn are they using? If more than about five hours a week, has partnered sex become less satisfying as porn use has increased? Ask about use of sex workers and cybersex, which may also interfere with the experience of sex with a regular partner. Check whether porn use ever involves children or young people under the age of 18. Is the person using chatrooms? What sort of people is the client talking to? Is this always a lone activity or sometimes/always shared by the couple?

Asking about the age of first non-penetrative sexual experience with someone else often elicits memories about early relationships and finding opportunities for sex. Often, the first penetrative sexual experience was with the same partner. Discuss the effect becoming sexual had on the client and how they think it may have affected their attitude to sex subsequently. This may be a good time to ask how the client identifies sexually and whether this has changed. Ask whether, as far as they know, they were ever touched inappropriately *after* discussing the first experience. Sometimes the inappropriate touch came first but is discounted by the client. If the client is aware of sexual abuse, ask what therapy they've had. Clients often say they've worked through the abuse and are over it, but many mean they've actively repressed memories, not that they've had therapy to help. Ask, too, whether any of their sexual experiences have been non-consensual, as they may not think of this as 'inappropriate touch'. Now may be a good time to ask whether they've ever felt guilty about sex or whether their faith or culture impacts their attitude towards sex.

Has the client ever experienced sexual pain? Common reasons for pain include tension, inadequate lubrication, a tight foreskin or infection. Even if the client says they have no sexual problems, ask about issues with arousal, erections and whether they orgasm when they want to. Is there anything else about their sexual history they think you should know?

Reproduction and fertility

Even when couples have already told you about the children they have together, it's important to ask about any previous relationships which produced children or pregnancies, any miscarriages or terminations, whether there has been any fertility treatment and how they managed that. Ask all clients whether they have plans for (further) children or feel their family is complete. It's not that uncommon for clients to have regrets or to be planning fostering, adoption or surrogacy.

Ask about current contraception. Even if a straight couple aren't having sex now, they may be soon, so this needs consideration. See if they've had any problems with contraception in the past. If the client has more than one partner, do ask about safer sex practices. If they have children, how did seeing/going through the delivery affect them? Ask about the effects of the menopause, where relevant, and whether the client has had hormone replacement therapy.

This section could usefully end with a more general chat about the client. Their reaction to being asked to describe themselves in five words is often more revealing than the answer. Some just say they can't do it. Prompt with questions about what they do and don't like about themselves, how they think other (perhaps, specific) people would describe them. If all else fails, ask how they would like to be and how this differs from the way they are. Particularly notice whether they find it easier to describe their faults than their good points or whether their descriptions are grandiose and unrealistic, as this may manifest in therapy. Do they generally find it easy to talk about how they're feeling? Do they avoid conflict or prefer anger to the expression of other feelings, such as vulnerability or emotional pain?

If it hasn't already emerged, ask whether they've ever felt bullied or subject to oppression of any form. If they were bullied at school, ask how this was handled and by whom or whether they dealt with it alone. If so, why was this?

Always end the session by asking how the client found it and whether there's anything they want to return to.

Information about the family

This section potentially takes less time than the previous one, in that it contains fewer topics. Often, though, clients' answers are more detailed. Clients who are uncomfortable talking about their families often have poor recall and actively don't want to dwell on their childhood.

Description of the family

What sort of family does the client come from (for example, traditional nuclear, single parent, blended, same sex)? Ask about siblings, their ages and how they got on. Did anyone else live at home, such as grandparents or lodgers, or were there other influential people in the child's life, such as an aunt, teacher, nanny or childminder? How did parents get on? Were any family members absent for long periods and what was this like? How was divorce managed? Were there step parents and siblings?

Ask about the relationship with parents. Did the client confide in them? Did they discuss sex openly? What sort of ideas were communicated by the family about sex? If family members had a motto about sex, what would it be? Were there any family skeletons? If so, were there unknown stories or events which were known by everyone but not discussed? Indeed, what was the family attitude to openness and emotion? Was unpleasantness talked about or avoided? Were children encouraged to be brave in adversity or fussed over too much? How were tears coped with? What made the family feel close? Was this, for instance, a family that used banter? This can be problematic with a partner who finds banter bullying. Were there any obviously traumatic events (accidents, bereavements, separations, for instance), and how were these managed?

It can be helpful to ask clients to describe each parent in five words and to tell a story to illustrate one or two of the words. The way the story is told can be illuminating. Some clients are triggered to great distress when recalling anything at all about childhood, while some revel in entertaining anecdotes and some tell stories which are incongruous. For instance, a client who said his mother was 'great fun' illustrated this with stories of how she locked him in the cellar for hours when she was angry. Asked how this could be considered fun, he said his mother described this as 'a prank'. Such disowned trauma may interfere with intimacy, or more distressing memories may emerge as PST progresses.

Ask how family members behaved when they were cross with one another. Did the clients see parents arguing and making up? Some parents try to completely hide their disagreements from children, who then only witness the very worst rows that can't be hidden. They may consequently believe *any* differences are a major problem. Living with constant parental arguing can normalise unhealthy relationship conflict.

Rules

Not all children are clear about what's expected of them, so punishments appear out of the blue, sometimes creating hypervigilance and fearfulness. As adults, they can then develop strict rules for themselves which they find difficult to adapt when partners are different. Find out what happened to clients when they were in trouble. Stories of severe physical punishment can be considered traumatic, but apparently more minor sanctions can have long-term consequences. Carers' withdrawal/not speaking can have a devastating effect, creating chronic trauma in children, as can lack of attunement. The client's view of this is often to protect the carer, claiming they were difficult children: 'I was a brat'. Don't just accept this. Dig deeper, and find out who said this and why. Was the carer under stress?

Schooldays

Did the client and siblings all attend the same school? This question can bring out stories of rivalry, disappointment and expectation. It can be helpful to discover how the children were described; for example, 'the clever one', 'the joker', 'the good girl'. These early labels can have a powerful effect on the way people see themselves throughout their lives.

Were there any sexual experiences associated with school? Boys who have attended boarding school sometimes develop early or delayed ejaculation associated with fear of being discovered masturbating. This can also affect those who shared bedrooms. While some children adore boarding and thrive, others feel abandoned and experience extremes of bullying which can affect their ability for intimacy in adulthood.

Ask whether the client feels they met parental expectations and how they know this, as this can affect feelings of self-worth around all aspects of life, including sex.

Checking the client's well-being at the end of this session is important, as it may have triggered some disturbance or, at least, food for thought. Check how they will spend the rest of the day and how they will take care of themselves.

The relationship

This section could be considered the nitty gritty part of history taking, and the only part some practitioners bother with. Though it might seem helpful to plunge straight into this, it's better to warm up the clients with the previous sections so they may be more relaxed and open by the time they reach this point, as well as providing more useful information.

Relationship history

Check how they see the relationship. Sometimes one partner will say the couple are deeply enraptured soul mates while the other says their relationship is just casual. You may want to address the discrepancy at some point; meanwhile, you'll be looking out for reasons to explain this difference. Questions such as 'how did you meet?', 'how did your first sexual experience together happen?' and 'how long were you together before marrying/moving in?' often bring out differences in memory or perceptions. Questions about what attracted each partner and how moving in together changed the relationship are more personal. Have there been any separations or blips in the relationship, and how were these managed? How did having children change the relationship?

Relationship quality

Ask how they would describe the relationship currently and what's missing. Have either had affairs or sex outside the relationship? If so, how was the other partner's affair discovered? Does the partner know about their own extra-relationship sex?

Previous relationships

How is this relationship different to previous long-term relationships? Are any previous partners still around, and what effect does this have? If there are children from other relationships, where do they live and how do they affect the relationship? Did the sexual problem being experienced occur in previous relationships?

The current sexual problem

Ask the client to describe the sexual issues that brought them to counselling. Which partner's idea was it to come? What made them come now? How long have they been managing the problem and when did it start? What else was happening around that time? What have they tried so far to fix things? Does anything else help? Or make matters worse? Ask the client why they think they have the problem and what's keeping it going. What effect does it have on the relationship? Which partner is more distressed about it? How do they show this? How do they each behave when the problem happens? This question, in particular, may give clues about the way the problem is being maintained. What difference do they hope PST will make? You may want to ask additional questions about the problems being experienced when a particular dysfunction is suspected.

Sex in the relationship

This section helps explain what is going on sexually between the couple and how they feel about it. It's helpful to begin by asking what qualities each partner has that have enabled them to cope for this long. Framing the question this way is enabling and provides an opportunity to celebrate resilience. Partners often give considerable thought to the answers in this section, and can be quite chatty. Helpful questions include:

- How would you define intimacy? Would your partner say the same?
- Do you find your partner physically attractive?
- How important is sex to you? Would your partner say the same?
- Do you think you and your partner have roughly the same level of desire?
- Do you feel your sexual needs are met? If not, what is missing?
- Which of you enjoys sex the most?
- What is it that you each enjoy the most?

- On a scale of 1 to 10, how much would you say you enjoyed the last time you made love? When was that?
- Was that fairly typical of your recent lovemaking? If not, what was different?
- How often do you normally make love?
- How often would you like to make love?
- Do you guide your partner(s) or show them what you enjoy during lovemaking?
- If not, what do you think stops you?
- Do you both enjoy giving and receiving oral sex? Have there ever been any problems?
- Is there any anal stimulation or penetration? If so, who likes it more? Have there ever been any problems?
- Where and when do you usually make love?
- Who is most likely to initiate sexual behaviour?
- Do you think you ever misread one another's sexual advances?
- Does sex usually end in intercourse/penetration?
- If so, how long do you normally spend on foreplay?
- Is there anywhere either of you doesn't like to be touched?
- Is there anything that puts you off?

Hygiene issues are among the most common reasons for rebuffing a sexual advance, so it can be liberating for the client to be specifically asked whether this is relevant. An unclean partner is an understandable turnoff, but *feeling* unclean can be even more aversive. Partners may be very aware of coffee breath, feeling sweaty or that they haven't washed since their last poo.

Ask about any practices that haven't already been mentioned, such as kink, role play and use of sex toys/dressing up. Is there anything that gets in the way of sex? Or makes it better? They rarely do? Sometimes partners stop enjoying an activity. For instance, they may feel differently after starting a family. Whether there is an obvious landmark or not, it's important to maintain an open, curious dialogue, regularly checking how both partners are feeling and experiencing the relationship and sexual behaviours.

Relationship quality

Very damaged relationships, or couples who can't countenance difference or adversity, may not survive the PST process. This risk may not be evident at first presentation or if you've only met partners individually. You also need to be alert for any signs of domestic abuse or coercive control. It's not uncommon for a partner to present for PST without really wanting to be sexual with this partner. Some are unaware their relationship is abusive. Sometimes one partner has threatened the other that the relationship will end if they don't have sex – this is a contraindication to PST. While lack of sex can threaten a relationship, making threats or coercing is a different matter. Some partners expect the therapist will help persuade the other to engage in practices they don't like. Helpful questions to assess coercion include:

- What do you think your partner likes about you? And doesn't like?
- Describe your partner in five words? Tell me a story to illustrate this.
- How do you make time for yourselves?
- What would you say about the way you communicate?
- Can you talk about sex?
- How do you manage conflict in the relationship?
- Does this ever get out of hand?
- Do you ever feel obliged to make love?

All the above answers may need follow-up if you have a monosyllabic client, but most elaborate on the answers themselves. Any suggestion of coercive, controlling or violent behaviour needs to be explored, with safety being the most important factor, overriding the PST process. Supervisory support is essential, as is documentation of what you've been told – not speculation.

Asking clients whether they think people have any rules and responsibilities towards each other when they make love usually brings out ideas about consent, independence and avoidance of coercion. However, some clients believe they have a *duty* to please their partner sexually, expressing some oppressive ideas which they may expect the therapist to endorse. All discourses around sexual duties are important to note, as the pressure they create may be a major cause of the sexual issues being experienced. A very few clients say their partner ought to be more sexually obliging. There's a difference between regret that sex is infrequent or unsatisfactory and a sense of entitlement to sex.

Ending

Finish the process by asking again how it has been for the client, whether there's anything they don't want the partner to know or anything they want to go back to. Briefly explain what will happen next – the formulation meeting followed by starting treatment if you all agree this is appropriate – with a brief reminder of matters like the sex ban, time commitment and fees. This is a good point to ask whether anything is worrying the client. Don't end without asking again whether there's anything else they think you should know.

Individual and time-limited clients

Even though not all the questions may be relevant to individual clients, they still benefit enormously from history taking. In many ways, it can be even more therapeutic in itself than it is for couples.

Suicidality is much less common in PST, but can still occur, especially with individual clients who are highly self-blaming. Suicidal thoughts always need to be explored and a safety plan made. Once mentioned, this takes priority over the PST process. Has the person thought about what they would do? What would make them enact this? What will they do to avoid carrying it out? Who can they turn to? In common with other forms of counselling, it's important to offer a confidentiality contract, clearly stating that this may be breached if there is considered to be a risk to someone.

You won't have the luxury of a full history taking interview if you only have a limited number of sessions. In this case, you may resort to a partial history taking or it can be completed as a questionnaire to be returned before you next see the client(s). If this is done online or e-mailed, the questions and answers must be encrypted. Clients often enjoy completing the questionnaires, frequently saying it encouraged communication with their partner. There should be enough information to create a formulation, but it's still helpful to have a brief clarifying session or conversation with each partner beforehand, perhaps by phone. This also offers the opportunity to allay any anxieties about the process and explain what the next steps involve. Now the therapist has the job of creating the formulation.

Reference

Stonewall (2019) *Memorandum of Understanding on Conversion Therapy in the UK*. Version 2, Revision A, July 3, London: Stonewall.

Chapter 5

Formulation

With the information gathered in the history taking process, the PST formulation is an opportunity to discuss how partners each regard what's been happening to their relationship and to share your assessment of why these issues should affect them. Most importantly, you'll have examined the thoughts, behaviours and relationship patterns which are maintaining the problem. You should also, by now, have some ideas about the best way to start making changes and a skeleton treatment plan (see Appendix). Though all this may seem daunting, when you compare each partner's history taking responses, ideas seem to leap from the page. As you become more experienced, this should help you to anticipate potential blocks to progress and issues with the therapeutic relationship. For instance, a very perfectionist client will be more likely to focus on getting the exercises 'right', may have difficulty in treating them as experimental and may expect the therapist to judge their effort.

The process of compiling the formulation is the same if you're working with individuals. If your work is time-limited, and the clients have filled in the history taking answers themselves, you may want to see what's missing before any clarification calls or meetings so you'll have a better idea of what it's helpful to focus on.

Having given thought to the formulation, it's helpful to type up some bullet points as an *aide memoire* for delivery. Though you'll be referring to it during the post-history taking meeting, the formulation should not be considered a definitive document. It's possible it will need to be changed as you discuss points with the clients. They may disagree or add important information that is useful to include. The feedback from experiments conducted during treatment may also contribute to a different view. Consequently, the formulation and history taking need to be considered live documents which assist the therapist in guiding clients through the PST process. As such, they're the therapist's to amend and refer to, and would not normally be given to clients. Though some CBT therapists do give copies of formulations to their clients, sometimes in the form of letters or diagrams, it can be counterproductive in PST where couples can view it as evidence of their failure, blame one another or see it as an unchangeable truth rather than a prompt for the therapist. It's also not a good idea to create the formulation on the spot with the clients. Though this may seem empowering to them, it's easy to leave out crucial points. Even more importantly, it denies clients the opportunity to appreciate the care you've taken to study their history taking answers, which may help to strengthen the therapeutic relationship. Most clients are incredibly interested to hear what you've come up with, and the ensuing collaborative conversation offers a sense of immediacy and momentum.

Formulation

If you're working with a couple, it's important they both attend, as the formulation is about them both and you can't get started on the treatment, if that's appropriate, without both of them present. First of all, ask them how they found the history taking sessions. They'll often tell you the sessions have already made a difference to the relationship and that their communication and understanding has improved. Some say sex has already improved too.

It's also helpful to remind them at the beginning that the reason for the history taking is to work out why they should be affected in the way they have been, what they want to change and what's the best way to do that – the formulation is your assessment of this. Explain that what you've come up with is inevitably hypothetical and that you actively welcome comments and interruptions. If you don't feel PST would be beneficial, now is the time to say so, as you can refer to the reasons for this as the formulation is delivered. The main reason not to do the work is when one or both clients are not in a position to engage with it. This could be because they're too busy, too mentally or physically ill, preoccupied with caring for someone, struggling with an addiction, affected by unresolved trauma, unable to afford treatment or don't actually want PST. Unless there is extreme conflict, abuse or coercion, relationship problems are not a contraindication provided the therapist has had relationship therapy training. Often, PST can accelerate recovery. After all, if the couple are motivated to seek PST, they're motivated to improve the relationship.

If you or the clients are still undecided about whether to proceed to treatment, the formulation discussion should help all participants agree to a decision. Some clients don't want to continue because the process isn't what they'd expected, but far more often it's because they've already experienced so much improvement. They'll still be interested in your formulation, which may prompt further ideas which they want to explore or clarify.

Therapist notes

There's no need to feed back all the information you've collected – the skill is in teasing out what will be relevant and helpful to the client(s) and not overwhelming, insulting or boring. An example of how history taking details can be transformed into a formulation is given in the book's Appendix (page 197). As you'll see, the formulation notes to yourself can be easily charted under these headings:

- The problem
- Precipitating factors – PST
- Precipitating factors – Problem
- Predisposing factors
- Current triggers
- Discourses and beliefs
- Maintaining factors
- Positives
- Goals

Point out to clients when the content of sections overlap. For instance, triggers and beliefs are often maintaining factors, and realising this puts change back within the clients' control.

Don't be tempted to write yourself a script, as this doesn't lend itself to a collaborative conversation. You won't maintain eye contact either if your head's down reading. Just make sure you've written enough to be an adequate prompt, but not so much that the formulation sounds like a lecture. Make sure the typeface is big enough and legible enough to glance at rather than have to scrutinise, that you have your reading glasses if you need them and that there's adequate light in the room to read by.

The problem

This describes the sexual problem as it appears to each of the clients, and is what the therapy will be addressing. However, it may be that the couple's view of the problem is simply that they aren't having sexual intercourse. *Your* view may be that they're putting too much pressure on themselves to do so and that *this* is the main problem to be addressed. You'll most likely be mentioning this as a maintaining factor later on. At this stage, however, it's helpful to just describe what the clients say *they're* worried about. If you're lucky, they'll see the issues as multifaceted, but they're probably initially going to be focusing on what they see as their problem.

Precipitating factors – PST

This is whatever made the client(s) decide to seek psychosexual therapy. Common precipitating factors to attend PST include wishing to have a baby, children leaving home, an affair, illness/surgery or, for individuals, a new relationship.

Precipitating factors – problem

The precipitating factors in this section refer to whatever may have started the problem. Common precipitating factors for the problem include wishing to have a baby, children leaving home, an affair, a 'failed' sexual experience, infertility treatment, getting married/cohabiting, having a baby, stress, fatigue, young children, retirement, work problems, unemployment, illness/surgery, menopause, relationship issues and organic causes triggering a psychological response.

Predisposing factors

While the precipitating factors are what clients think contributed to their problem, there are likely to be a whole lot more elements which influenced its development. These are also sometimes referred to as 'vulnerability factors' and generally involve events, ways of thinking, context, and culture that make this couple or individual more likely to have their problem. Some may have always existed and others may be acquired. Common predisposing factors in PST include illness, repeated 'failed' sexual experiences, family comments (for instance, about body, development or masturbation), poor communication skills, abuse, neglect or trauma, lack of sex education and family of origin coyness about sex.

Current triggers

Anything which contributes to, or makes the client(s) aware of, the identified problem can be considered a trigger. Clients may already recognise some of these, but others may be unconscious. Triggers may not relate directly to the problem but may have caused the problem, perhaps just by making a partner feel uncomfortable. For instance, the smell of alcohol on their partner's breath may make someone feel extremely ill at ease. They may or may not be aware that this is because their uncle always had alcohol on his breath when he abused them. Such triggering life events or even just unhelpful beliefs may appear or become more evident once treatment commences.

Common triggers that clients may recognise include any physical contact, consciously avoiding sex, references to sex in conversation on television and so on, special occasions and holidays, awkward/'failed' sex or attempts at initiation, and reminiscent situations. Avoiding triggers provides protection, so it's easy to see how avoiding touch, developing different bedtimes or not even watching television together can exacerbate an existing problem. These are done as ways of avoiding or reducing the problem but can create new issues, such as a complete lack of intimacy or communication. Couples frequently stop going for nights out together because of the danger that sex will be expected or the problem may be talked about. If they do go out, they may spend the whole time feeling jittery.

Discourses and beliefs

Our lives are organised by discourses and beliefs which reflect behaviour and standards as well as ideas about ourselves. These are also often protective, providing a structure for how to be. Often, if we're even aware of them, they can feel helpful, positive and safe, but they can also be erroneous and oppressive. Many can be gender specific; some are shaming and/or marginalising. They may be what we've been deliberately brought up to believe in or they may have developed as a response to our environment or family behaviour. Other people may influence us to think we're especially clumsy or clever, for instance, or that we need to be perfect.

Such ideas may have been influenced, reinforced or acquired from clients' context or surroundings, such as from friends, community, culture, religion, education or via the media. What is observed may also be influencing. For instance, a girl who sees female relatives teased for acquiring sexual characteristics as they grow up may respond by hiding or disliking her breasts, disowning or repressing sexual feelings, or be devastated when she starts menstruating. Whether or not it was intended that she feel negatively towards her body and sexuality, she may receive the message that adult female bodies and sexuality are dirty, shameful or wrong. She may feel that she shouldn't grow up, and adopt childish or childlike ways to make herself more acceptable. Or she may not be affected at all.

The psychosexual therapist looks for anything which may be helpful or unhelpful, so the information can be used to benefit therapy. CBT emphasises the importance of noticing negative automatic thoughts (NATs) or global ideas which are unhelpful or limiting to the client. People are usually unaware they have negative thoughts, or they may assume that whatever they think must be true. Noticing negative thoughts offers the opportunity to explore them. A thought such as, 'I'm no good at sex' says nothing about what this means. It could mean, for example, that the person doesn't enjoy sex, that they think they have poor sexual technique or that they don't experience arousal or orgasm. Often, this kind of statement is something the person has either been told or the belief has resulted from a single event.

Knowing about negative thoughts means the therapist can watch out for them and challenge them. It allows therapists to demonstrate how unhelpful thoughts and ideas can interfere and to either encourage alternative thoughts or experiment to see if they're really true. It also helps to anticipate problems with treatment. For instance, if someone believes they're rubbish at sex, they may believe they'll be rubbish at any experiments you set, and so avoid them or find they provoke high anxiety.

Common (but far from exclusive) unhelpful global ideas which are especially relevant to PST include:

- Men are responsible for women's pleasure
- Partners should always try to do what the other one wants
- Men can't cope for long without sex

- Masturbation is a type of infidelity
- Men are always ready for sex
- Sex always goes off the boil when you get married
- Women don't like sex as much as men
- It's important to be a good lover
- If you can't please your partner sexually, they'll look elsewhere
- Partners should know how to please each other
- Gay men always prefer either insertive or receptive sex
- If you don't enjoy anal sex, you aren't properly gay
- Penetrative sex is the only real sex
- Lesbians aren't interested in penetration
- Having regular sex will stop your partner from being unfaithful
- If your partner has sex with you, it means they love you
- It's wrong to have sex if all isn't perfect with the relationship
- All men use pornography.

Clients are often very certain their ideas are 'true' and shared by everyone. Religious or cultural beliefs may need to be respected, but it's also helpful to explore the effect of clients' global ideas on the relationship and each partner's self-image, thinking and behaviour. For instance, there are many powerful discourses about pleasing your partner sexually, but there's a difference between wanting to please for its own sake and wanting to please due to the consequences of not doing so. Some people, for example, genuinely believe partners should demonstrate their love by engaging in sexual practices they don't like. This idea should be discouraged. To make someone have any kind of sex they don't want, or to coerce, is not loving at all.

Maintaining factors

Maintaining factors are what PST will address. While precipitating and predisposing factors help the therapist to anticipate blocks and interest the client, they're in the past. Maintaining factors are whatever is keeping the problem going. This may include behaviours which are aimed at reducing the problem, such as avoiding sex. Let's say, for instance, one partner who expects to be rejected has avoided initiating sex because refusal is so hurtful. This may make the other partner feel unattractive and unwanted, and so they also avoid any form of intimacy. If they don't talk about this, they'll each continue assuming the other partner has gone off them.

Patterns like this often begin with misunderstanding, such as one partner not wanting sex in the morning until after they've cleaned their teeth or being too tired for sex in the months after having a baby. These precipitating factors are often long forgotten. Even if there are issues, such as early ejaculation or loss of desire, these are not usually what's preventing sex and intimacy – collusive avoidance of sex is doing that. Consequently, identifying the maintenance cycle and bringing it into the open is a crucial first step in creating change. Often, there are multiple maintaining factors, such as poor communication, lack of a language for sexuality, body issues, unhelpful beliefs and fear of failure.

Positives

Positives are elements of the clients' lives, beliefs and relationship which bode well for the work and them. We're particularly interested in exceptions, 'unique outcomes' (Goffman, 1961) or 'sparkling moments' (White, 1995) – times when the problem doesn't happen or has been overcome. Examples of positives in PST would be the strength of the couple's relationship, their problem-solving skills in other areas, their commitment to the PST process and/or each other, their physical attraction and the way things have changed so far, such as better understanding or processing during history taking and improved communication. It's important to include positives to offset what may seem like a catalogue of problems and to offer hope.

Goals

The formulation will have produced ways to recognise and negotiate what clients need going forward. Some will fulfil their objectives during the first step of PST or shortly after beginning treatment. As presentation of the formulation is intended to be as collaborative as possible, clients may have expanded on it and clearly discussed what they're now looking for. This may not be what they said they wanted at the outset, as views tend to change during assessment. Some partners keep repeating what they think the other wants, so they end up pursuing what neither wants just because they're trying so hard to please each other. Sometimes, having experienced a problem for years, they're in a tearing hurry to fix it, preferably with little or no effort. It's up to the therapist to manage expectations and dissuade clients from unrealistic goals. For instance, someone who says they want penetrative sex with their partner five times a week isn't going to achieve that if one or other of them works away a lot. There will be other goals which are more rapidly achievable and realistic.

Goal setting still needs to involve the clients, however. You could start by looking at their ultimate goal and working backwards. If their aim is pain-free, relaxed penetrative sex two or three times a week, but they both have little desire and haven't made love for several years, they're probably aiming a bit high. This goal is perfectly possible, but there'll be a number of steps on the way. If they could identify what would help to make sex relaxed, for instance, that could be what they aim for to start with. They may say they need to be more comfortable with one another or not afraid to talk about sex or state their needs. These communication issues need to be addressed long before they consider the bigger one. Generally, once the small goals start being achieved, the big ones almost solve themselves.

As far as possible, goals should be SMART – Specific, Measurable, Achievable, Realistic and Time-limited. There are likely to be individual *and* joint goals for couples, so there's a lot to consider. Though, to some extent, PST goals will be subjective, it's helpful to make them more SMART by asking the couple what would need to happen for *them* to feel the goal had been achieved. It's also useful to ask them to score how far it has already been achieved, as a baseline, and perhaps to identify what might help get them up to the next level (for example, from a 'two' to a 'two and a half' or 'three') and how long they think this might take. This collaborative way of working helps to give the couple agency and ownership. Some therapists like to create a ladder of goals, to be regularly reassessed and amended, since goals may change as treatment progresses.

If a couple don't want to continue into therapy, or you think it's inappropriate, you can finish the session by discussing when or whether PST may be possible in future and what they can do to help in the meantime. If they want to go ahead, you can set the first experiments.

First experiments

A CBT approach to PST requires that clients are given homework experiments and that their subsequent feedback informs the next experiments set. Similarly, the clients' reaction to the formulation may inform what you feel would be realistic. It's important to frame homework exercises as experimental, since PST clients are usually already affected by performance anxiety. It's helpful to explain that the experiments offer a win:win outcome. If they go well, the clients will be pleased and, if not, you'll have much more information on which to base the next steps. It's also important to emphasise that the PST process isn't a series of exercises to just work through in order to reach an outcome. It's a process of change which is utterly dependent on clients' needs. Though you may have ideas for treatment, these will change depending on how the work goes. It's not, therefore, helpful to tell clients specifically what you've planned. This is likely to change, and they may then feel they've done something wrong or else be hurrying to reach the next stage. It can also increase anxiety, not to mention spoil the surprise.

Discuss with clients how they feel about starting treatment. The more nervous they are, or the longer it's been since they were sexual, the more cautious you should be. It can be too much to ask a couple to be naked together straightaway if they haven't done this for some time or if all recent experiences have been negative. Setting a simple Pre-Sensate task (see page 54) and some self-focus (see page 58) is probably enough for the first time. If a couple has recently been actively sexual together and has continued being sexual during the assessment phase, they may be comfortable starting straight into Sensate Focus (see page 64). However, even they may welcome a change of gear and some preparatory work before starting exercises which include touch. This is also the time to impose a sex ban, and to go over practical points such as appointment frequency, the commitment necessary and payment.

You may be relieved to have survived your first formulation session, but the formulation itself is not a document to deliver and then put away. It should be seen as a living, dynamic entity which is referred to, appended and amended throughout the work. Another important document, even if it ends up being highly edited as the work progresses, is the treatment plan, the subject of Chapter 6.

References

Goffman, E. (1961) *Asylums: Essays in the Social Situation of Mental Patients and Other Inmates*, New York: Doubleday.

White, M. (1995) *Re-authoring Lives: Interviews and Essays*, Adelaide: Dulwich Centre Publications.

The PST treatment process

As we've discovered in previous chapters, the PST process follows a stepped programme using a core CBT model. This means a great deal of hard work and progress has probably occurred before the treatment phase begins. Some clients will even feel their situation has improved sufficiently not to proceed further. Discussion with the clients and the therapist's judgement during the formulation determines the pace and content of treatment, but it's helpful for beginning psychosexual therapists to have an idea of the trajectory of the work at the outset. This chapter consequently offers an overview of the PST process. While interventions related to particular sexual issues are covered in their specific chapters, this segment contributes general interventions which could be offered to the majority of couples. The self-focus interventions can obviously be used with individuals. Further interventions for individual clients are discussed in the sections dealing with specific problems.

The PST process

Initial assessment – this is the first contact with the client(s), giving the therapist insight into their 'problem', history, context, attitudes, solutions they've tried, level of distress and their hoped for outcome, as well as explaining what therapy can offer, giving information about the process and answering the clients' questions.

History taking – individual sessions with each partner of a couple provide the therapist with detailed, helpful information, as well as providing an opportunity to explore beliefs, offer psychoeducation and build a therapeutic alliance.

Formulation – the therapist's assessment of the client or couple's issues based on the information received in the history taking is discussed before goals are agreed and the first experiments are set.

Treatment – consists of individual and joint physical and cognitive exercises/experiments, psychoeducation, discussion and feedback. Treatment involves nine phases of Sensate Focus, each of which may last for many sessions. Phases should always be followed in sequence. Sometimes the work moves back to a previous phase but, as they build on each other, from Sensate

Focus I onwards, phases should never be skipped. Phases include: Pre-Sensate Experiments, Sensate Focus I, Sensate Focus I with additions, Sensate Focus Interim Phase, Sensate Focus II, Sensate Focus Plus, Sensate Focus Mutual Phase, Containment Phase and, finally, the Creative Phase. Many clients are satisfied with their progress long before this.

Follow-up – clients are often offered an appointment three months after the final session, so they can celebrate their progress and any remaining problems can be addressed.

Pre-sensate experiments

Many sex therapy approaches dive directly into sensual and sexual touch, even when couples have had no physical intimacy for many years. However, clients approach PST in different stages of readiness, and therapists need to assess the most appropriate response. When clients are very anxious or haven't been sexual for some time, have a history of any form of abuse or trauma, or have very little sexual experience, Sensate Focus experiments, in which a couple explore each other's naked body, may initially feel too challenging. For couples like this, Pre-Sensate Exercises provide a more gradual introduction to intimacy, communication and touch. These exercises can be used alongside Sensate Focus to address any deficits in these areas as well. They're also helpful if there are blocks which stall the process, until they're assessed and/or overcome, and when there are other reasons for the process to tread water. For instance, this can happen due to an unexpected event such as when bereavement, work stress or illness make it impossible to focus sufficiently on the programme to move forward. Usually, the couple doesn't want to lose the momentum of the process or their developing intimacy, so Pre-Sensate Exercises help maintain their progress. Individual self-focus exercises, described later, are also given throughout the process, as these help develop body awareness and sensuality as well as treating some problems.

Clinical psychologist and relationship therapist David Schnarch (1991) works with couples on tolerating and strengthening intimacy. His work provides considerable inspiration for us all, as the management of intimacy is often at the heart of sexual and relationship issues. Two of the Pre-Sensate Exercises offered here – Gazing and Hugging – are based on Schnarch's exercises.

Gazing

- Lie on your sides, facing each other but without touching, with your heads on your own separate pillows.
- Gaze directly into your partner's eyes.
- Try to maintain the gaze for at least five minutes, noticing your reactions (giggles, discomfort, wish to break the gaze, feelings of connection).
- Vary the exercise once mastered by placing a hand on each other's hip, clasping hands or touching the face and head.

Hugging

- Take off your shoes.
- Stand firmly on your own two feet.
- Hug.
- Calm yourself by focusing on yourself.
- Concentrate on what is happening to your body.
- When you become good at this, you can focus on the relationship.
- If you topple, re-balance, re-hug and continue.
- Do this for 10–15 minutes daily.

Both these exercises can be a useful way to begin Sensate Focus experiments. Notice how easy clients find them and how well they manage any associated discomfort. Many couples feel extremely close and make the exercises part of their intimate repertoire long after therapy has ended. Others find them completely intolerable and avoid them. It helps to reassure clients it's normal to initially feel awkward and self-conscious, but that this subsides after a few attempts. When one or both partners wish to persevere with an experiment they find particularly difficult, they may need considerable help with strategies to manage their anxiety, such as mindfulness, relaxation and guided imagery. It's helpful if they're able to tune into what's happening in their bodies and recognise any thoughts that accompany their discomfort. Such skills can be helpful if they feel uncomfortable as PST progresses into more intimate touch.

Hands on hearts

Once the gazing exercise has been mastered, it can be extended and adapted with further kinds of touching, such as kissing the face, then returning to the gaze. Staying on their separate pillows for the gazing, couples can each place a hand gently on each other's body. This can be helpful when gazing is found unbearably exposing. Though developing the ability to tolerate the gaze independently is part of the purpose of the exercise, this is too much for some people initially. Wendy Maltz (2012: 277) suggests that when there is a background of sexual abuse, couples can try placing a hand on the other's heart and imagining sending and receiving love, respect and appreciation. Once the gazing exercise has been mastered, this can be a lovely addition for all couples. Some find this level of closeness difficult, while others find it bonding right away.

Tracing

Virginia Johnson reported that, when she was tired or stressed as a child, her mother used to trace her face or hands with a finger, gently drawing or writing words on them – what Johnson called 'nonsensical nothings' (Maier, 2013), which she found soothing. This non-sexual way of comforting gave Johnson her ideas for Sensate Focus. It may be found easier than gazing by some clients and is a great way to begin or end exercises at all stages of treatment.

Creating a habit   ~~touchpoints~~

Finding the time to schedule experiments can be an exercise in itself. It's important to discuss this and to agree that, if an experiment has to be missed, a new time for it will be set immediately. It's not uncommon for couples to turn up having only just done an experiment but with stories about several near misses. These can be revealing in themselves and make clear issues within the relationship – such as one partner's avoidance and the other's reaction – or any collusion to avoid the exercises.

While they're making the effort to find time for their experiments, couples can also be encouraged to think about what they can do to create everyday intimacy if this is missing. For instance, they could create a nighttime routine where they always say a proper goodnight, hug and kiss even if they have different bedtimes. Or they could make sure they always greet and leave each other with a kiss and hug, something children find reassuring to witness, too. A cup of tea together when they come in from work, or some space, regular times to talk or go out, even collaboration on household tasks can create a sense of cooperation and safety.

Therapists come across or devise their own variety of additional exercises of all sorts (see Campbell, 2015, 2018) as well as using those they find most helpful. They are just as valuable as Sensate Focus experiments, particularly as they can be used to help with blocks later in the sensate phases, as well as promoting skills which make Sensate Focus possible.

Talking points

Typically, behavioural patterns between clients which are never actually discussed, but are a source of dissatisfaction, resentment or pain, can lead to avoidance of sex. Resentment over something like their partner's spending or contribution to housework can get in the way of loving and sexual feelings (also see Chapter 18). Some couples need help to have productive conversations which aren't just blame-laden. Setting conversation as a homework experiment can be helpful if it's then fully explored in-session. Find out how comfortable the conversation was and whether both partners felt their viewpoint was heard and validated. Couples who feel conversation is 'pointless' or 'daft' need help to understand that, without talking, they're basing their entire relationship on assumptions. Clients can be given guided discussion topics or they can just explore a single theme, such as:

- Consent
- Confidence
- Sexual rules
- Responsibilities

- Safer sex
- Hurt feelings
- Managing rejection
- Sexual myths
- Expressing sexuality
- Sexual losses
- What constitutes infidelity
- What constitutes sexual behaviour
- Body image
- Embarrassment
- Fantasies or wishes
- Appreciation

Sex ban

When to impose a sex ban is a matter of judgement. It can be helpful to start this from the formulation onwards, applying it to all forms of sex including masturbation. This emphasises the focus on sensuality rather than sexuality, as well as creating more sexual tension between the couple. Exceptions would be where masturbatory self-focus exercises are needed or when the Pre-Sensate Phase is expected to be protracted. In this case, masturbation can continue. Even if the Pre-Sensate Phase is lengthy, the sex ban should still be in place by the time Sensate Focus begins, apart from any prescribed masturbatory exercises.

Some couples are surprised or annoyed by the sex ban, so it's important they're made aware from the beginning that it's a vital part of the process. They may say they don't need it because they're not having sex anyway, but a ban is very different. It creates boundaries around the experiments, with no fear of more sexual behaviour being required, and allows the couple to enjoy touching for its own sake rather than worrying it will lead to intercourse. Response and performance pressure are, thus, also removed. This allows the couple space to relearn their sensual and sexual response.

When setting the ban or reminding clients of its importance, it's worth mentioning that couples sometimes break the ban, especially when Sensate Focus is bringing them closer. Potential loss if the relationship were to end, therefore, increases. Similarly, the risk of failure may seem greater, so a resurgence of performance anxiety may lead to outcome sex in order to avoid the experiments. Fear of failure if therapy ends is another reason for breaking the ban. Point out, too, that it's frequently the less likely partner who initiates boundary violation. Having this conversation initially seems to reduce the incidence of ban breaking and also makes it easier to discuss if it does happen.

There *are* times when the therapist is delighted that a couple have moved on the process independently, but in the early stages it can be unhelpful as it keeps them trapped in their existing habits, with no room to relearn their responses and ways of communicating sexually. Nonetheless, it isn't helpful to adopt a judgemental approach, which just drives the non-compliance underground. A useful therapeutic stance would be curiosity about what happened to make the couple abandon the process and how that happened. There is usually considerable learning from the experience. Collaborative hypothesising about the underlying causes for what happened helps the couple to take control. This should include planning how to manage temptation next time. However, don't move the couple on to the next stage of treatment yet, as their process has been interrupted. Indeed, they may need to go back a step.

Self-focus

It's not just individual clients who benefit from individual experiments – most clients benefit from some individual work alongside the joint experiments. Self-focus experiments may be especially helpful at the beginning of therapy, but can also be usefully employed later on to deal with specific issues as they arise.

Readiness for therapy

The following questionnaire can be given to clients during the history taking process, but is often more useful as they embark on therapy. It can be offered as homework at the formulation or after the first session, especially if this has produced some blocks. Given during the history taking phase, it can help in assessing readiness for Sensate Focus or whether to start with Pre-Sensate Exercises. Generally, the questionnaires are completed separately and not shared with the partner until the PST session, when they can foster illuminating discussion. However, they can also be set as a Pre-Sensate Exercise to help ascertain when to move the clients on to Sensate Focus.

- On a scale of 1–10, how ready do you feel for emotional intimacy?
- What would get in the way?
- On a scale of 1–10, how ready do you feel for physical intimacy?
- What would get in the way?
- On a scale of 1–10, how ready do you feel for naked touch?
- What would get in the way?
- Currently, how do you express emotional intimacy?
- What gets in the way?
- Currently, how do you express sensuality?
- What gets in the way?
- Currently, how do you express sexuality?
- What gets in the way?
- Which of you do you think is more anxious about these experiments?
- Why is that?
- What could happen to make you both more comfortable?
- What are you most interested to discover?

- What are you most excited about?
- What worries you the most?
- What questions do you have?

It can be helpful to keep copies of the completed questionnaires in your files to revisit as part of the ongoing assessment process and to help clients monitor their own progress.

Kegel exercises

Since the 1950s, when gynaecologist Arnold Kegel noticed that exercising the pubococcygeus muscles prevented and treated urinary incontinence, their sexual benefits have also been increasingly recognised. The sling-like pubococcygeus pelvic floor muscles, which extend from the base of the spine to the pubic bone, holding pelvic structures and organs in place, can become lax due to age or damage, such as childbirth. Many women are already familiar with the exercises, which are encouraged during pregnancy and the post-partum period to strengthen the pelvic floor and reduce risk of injury. In fact, they're of benefit to both men and women throughout life, not only to prevent incontinence but also to improve genital control and the intensity of orgasm, possibly due to the increased blood flow to the area achieved by exercising. The basic exercise is as follows:

1 First, you need to find the muscles you're going to exercise. You can do this by stopping passing urine in mid-flow or imagining you are trying not to fart – this uses the same muscles. Don't make a habit of stopping mid-flow, and don't do this if you have any difficulty emptying your bladder or are pregnant.
2 Sit or lie comfortably and contract these muscles for a count of 10.
3 Release slowly to a count of five.
4 Repeat 10 times.
5 Then contract and release the muscles as quickly as you can 10 times.
6 Now contract and hold for as long as you can.
7 Repeat these exercises at least twice a day, remembering not to clench your buttocks or tense your thigh or stomach muscles – all the activity should be in the pelvic floor.

Advise clients to build up the number of exercises they do and the length of time they squeeze the muscles. Women can feel the muscles tightening and releasing by putting a finger inside the vagina. If they have an erection, men can also see the effect of the exercises as their penis moves.

Once they're used to the exercises, clients can do them anywhere – on the bus or train, at traffic lights, while cleaning their teeth or doing the washing up. Combining them with another activity like this can help remind clients to do them. They aren't essential, however. They're an option which makes clients much more aware of their genital area and may offer the bonus of perkier erections as men age, continence and more intense orgasms. Kegels can also sometimes initiate orgasm if the person is close to climax. This is an advantage if they have difficulty with orgasm, but can be a nuisance in clients with early ejaculation. They shouldn't be offered to clients with vaginismus and vulvodynia who benefit from reverse Kegels exercises to relax the pelvic floor (see page 109).

Relaxation

The ability to relax and avoid distraction is essential to PST. There are many excellent relaxation exercises available, mostly focusing on breathing. It's also helpful to use mindful awareness of different feelings states to recognise a relaxed state and its physical difference from a stressed state (Ogden & Fisher, 2015). For instance, if someone realises they hunch up, tense muscles and breathe quickly when stressed, then slowing breathing, standing tall and shaking out those uptight muscles may produce a calmer state with no need for specific exercises.

Guided imagery

This can be extremely helpful to assist clients when they become preoccupied with ideas about what their partner is experiencing in the experiments or when they're generally worried. They aren't for use during experiments, when clients need to be present in the experience, but can help calm them beforehand and manage anxiety generally.

Some guided imagery experiments describe a tranquil place, such as a tropical beach, which clients are encouraged to visualise, perhaps concentrating on slowing their breathing at the same time. Some practitioners go on to add other relaxation effects, such as feeling the stress leave each part of the body as it's warmed by the sun or lapped by gentle waves.

For those who find it difficult to concentrate on such descriptions, imagining their own calm place – which has real relevance to their life – may be more helpful. Ask the client to close their eyes and describe a place where they can be calmly and comfortably alone, giving details about the sounds, smells, sights and sensations they're experiencing. Surprisingly few clients choose a tropical paradise, though many do opt for some sort of holiday venue. Some feel at peace in the anonymity of a busy area, such as the top of the Eiffel Tower in Paris or the Shibuya Crossing in Tokyo. Others like to imagine doing a favourite activity, such as painting or feeding ducks. This is fine so long as there aren't distractions; the place they're imagining needs to provide personal calm and well-being. Some people even choose an everyday familiar place, such as their kitchen or bedroom.

To begin with, it may be helpful for you to describe the place to them whilst they imagine themselves there. It may assist them to describe the emotions and bodily sensations they have as they experience their imaginary refuge and begin to feel soothed (Shapiro, 2018). Try to avoid referring to the place as 'safe', as this can be triggering – many people have been abused in a place that should have been safe.

The exercise should be repeated daily, if possible, and whenever the client seems triggered during a session. It needs to be clear that the intention is not to avoid emotion, which is perfectly acceptable, but to be able to manage difficult feelings when necessary. Explain this is a skill which has to be learned, and that many people never acquire, avoiding emotion rather than managing it.

Fantasy

Some clients feel guilty about fantasy, having developed ideas that it's wrong or unfaithful. Sometimes partners express this view, too. Indeed, researchers have found some benefit from requiring partners to imagine themselves in sexual fantasy to avoid jealousy (Newbury *et al*, 2012). However, sexual fantasy is often necessary for people to see themselves as sexual beings. Imagining being creative in their love making with their partner is inhibiting for clients who prefer an unlikely scenario. Some benefit from imagining other people having sex, rather than identifying themselves as the star actor.

Those who feel sex is wrong, or whose fantasies involve any form of force, may not find it arousing to imagine this as something they'd do with their partner. Forced or coerced sex is a common subject of sexual fantasy (Kowalik, 2018), which shouldn't be pathologised (Stockwell & Moran, 2014). It may make sex permissible for some people to imagine themselves engaging in it unwillingly. Others feel their desirability is increased when their fantasy partner can't control themselves.

For fantasy to be liberating, it has to be accepted as unreal and that anything is possible. It's an opportunity to imagine the wildest, most unlikely scenarios without inhibition. Once this is understood, clients are free to let rip alone or with their partner. Significantly, the incidence of sexual fantasy has been demonstrated as higher in women in cultures where female sexual modesty is expected (Kasemy *et al*, 2016).

Fantasy can be 'set' as an exercise to accompany masturbation or just as an experiment to see what's possible. When clients feel too anxious or guilty about fantasising to relax with it, suggest beginning with fantasy about their partner in a romantic setting. More sexually explicit and varied fantasies can be encouraged as progress is made (McCabe, 2015), normalising the idea that fantasy about other people is sometimes inevitable.

Some couples enjoy sharing fantasies, but this can also be inhibiting. Generally, sexual fantasies are best kept private, not least in case a partner finds them funny. Sharing can often make them lose their effect anyway, as they're never as well described as they feel in fantasy. On the other hand, couples may enjoy discussing fantasies which have the potential to be acted out, thereby allowing bashful partners to be more sexually adventurous when 'not themselves'.

Mindful awareness

Mindful awareness is needed for all PST experiments and exercises; Sensate Focus is itself a form of mindful awareness (Weiner & Avery-Clark, 2017). Mindfulness techniques can be used to help clients both to relax and to let go of unhelpful thoughts. Help may be necessary in the form of discussion around how much they believe bodily signals, such as the idea that feelings of anxiety indicate there's really something to be anxious about. In reality, there's usually nothing to be worried about, but a situation triggers emotional memories from an earlier time which feel as though they belong in the present. For instance, feeling close to their partner may launch panicky feelings in people who've been let down by attachment figures/partners in the past. Memories associated with abandonment or hurt are often remembered emotionally rather than cognitively, so the person may not have accompanying thoughts to explain the way they're feeling. Any thoughts they do access may just be around something being wrong, which they may translate into negative feelings about themselves or the relationship. Psychoeducation around bodily feelings and memories can be helpful, as can improved personal awareness.

Clients can be encouraged to scan their bodies from top to toe at various times to notice different sensations and try to link these with emotions and thoughts. Suggesting scanning every time they stop at traffic lights, while watching television or even when on the loo can add prompts which may help them to become familiar with their bodies in different states. Practising first in the counselling room gives the therapist an idea of how easy they'll find this. Even some apparently comfortable clients, who claim to practise mindfulness and be proficient at yoga, find it difficult to tune into their bodies. Often, in the history taking, it will have emerged that they dislike being bored or alone, as this presents a risk of experiencing unpleasant memories, thoughts or feelings.

Mindfulness exercises can be set in-session, or clients can be encouraged to use mindfulness apps. It's important to check how their use is going though, just as it is with any other exercise set, and it's helpful if the therapist is familiar with the application being used. Where clients appear to be avoiding their use, it's possible they're afraid of an intrusive memory they fear will be activated on some level. With any fears of emotional disruption, it can be helpful to offer grounding techniques or guided imagery so clients have a resource to help regain emotional balance.

Noticing what they can see, hear, smell, taste and touch can provide helpful grounding as well, as mindful awareness in the here and now. Encouraging clients to anticipate what they'll enjoy at regular points in the day can also encourage mindful awareness, and consequently affect regulation (Siegel, 2007), as many people don't actively notice what they're doing at all. For instance, when they get up they may be urged to eagerly anticipate the lovely hot shower they're about to take, their delicious breakfast, playing with a pet or children. Looking forward to something, noticing what they enjoy, and acknowledging that they've enjoyed it can produce healthy and calming endorphins (Sapolsky, 2004). Indeed, anticipation can produce the same 'hit' as the actual event. Most of us are so familiar with our lives that we don't recognise what we like, so we don't bother looking forward to the pleasant aspects of our days or relishing them (Siegel, 2017). Yet mindful anticipation not only produces pleasure but promotes awareness and memory (Chiew *et al*, 2016), so it can improve the ability to engage positively with PST experiments.

Self-discovery

Many therapists suggest carrying out self-discovery experiments in the bathroom before Sensate Focus with partners. Having a bath or shower before joint experiments is both relaxing and addresses any potential hygiene issues. It also makes the most of time put aside for PST.

Many of the experiments are simple but can, nonetheless, be quite challenging or triggering, so detailed feedback should always be taken. Clients often say they don't need the experiments because they've done them before or 'do that anyway'. It needs to be explained that the experiments are not offered for their own sake; just doing them won't necessarily achieve much. It's how the person experiences them that's important, providing crucial personal learning as well as information for the PST process.

Simple self-focus experiments

- Touching different parts of the body with items which have different textures – a feather, cotton wool, a soft scarf, a rough brush – can increase sensory awareness and allow clients to be more mindful of their bodies.
- Being aware of different movements can be similarly useful. Rubbing the arms or legs, waving, bending, wiggling the toes, scratching, stroking and tossing the hair all produce different sensations. Encourage clients to be aware of the air around them as well as physical touch.
- Mindful noticing of the sensations associated with a bath or shower, including the temperature of the water, reactions of their skin, difference in touch between a hand, flannel, loofah, soap and anything else which touches them.
- Observing their own body in a full-length mirror, perhaps while towel drying, and noticing how different body parts respond to touch. This can provide information about the client's relationship with their body and tolerance of seeing it. Body dysmorphia and body-image issues sometimes emerge.
- Use of a hand mirror to explore the genitals and identify genital anatomy can be fascinating and educational. Squatting, supported by pillows or cushions, may be the most comfortable way to do this. Men can use a mirror to see beneath their scrotum and the perineal area, and to observe the difference made to this area when the penis is erect. Women can part the outer labia and explore the difference in the appearance of the vulva when they are aroused.

- Exploring the body can be offered alone or as part of a masturbatory programme.
- Showing photographs of a range of bodies and body parts can be helpful if clients consent to this, as many people believe their own bodies are different, deformed or ugly.
- Reading or a look at websites with helpful information or relevant blogs. Reading may be entirely educational, regarding sexual anatomy and/or sexual dysfunction, or it may be intended to offer a range of alternative viewpoints. Challenging unhelpful discourses through literature can be useful, as can relevant articles about sex and relationships. Erotic literature may be helpful where fantasy is difficult to achieve, but advice to access pornography should be offered judiciously. Though it may provide material for fantasy, it can also compromise the ability to fantasise. It's also not always possible to know the extent of someone's existing pornography use, which may be at the root of their problem.

More self-focus experiments will be given in relation to particular sexual problems as the book progresses.

Sensate Focus

For some clients, Pre-Sensate Exercises, or even just the history taking, offer all the help they need at the time, while others progress to Sensate Focus or skip the Pre-Sensate Phase and move directly to Senate Focus. Clients' comfort with the Pre-Sensate Exercises, ability to manage their anxiety and interest in moving on help to decide when to do so. Some couples are nervous about taking the next step, so it's always important to emphasise the experimental nature of the process.

Anxiety-free exploration and discovery was at the heart of Masters and Johnson's intentions in developing Sensate Focus exercises. They never properly explained their process for Sensate Focus, however, which has led to a variety of interpretations, some of which seem to contradict the spirit of Sensate Focus and encourage performance pressure. The point of Sensate Focus is not for clients to please their partner, or even consider them particularly. Rather, the intention is to focus entirely on subjective experience without worrying how the partner is responding or having expectations about personal arousal or pleasure, known as 'non-demand' experimentation. To this end, clients are advised not to talk during the sessions nor to offer feedback afterwards. In therapy, feedback will focus on their subjective experience and *not* how pleasing they found their partner's touch.

Preparation and planning

Giving couples the chance to think about and discuss what could be a problem can help make the early experiments go more smoothly. Even if they've missed something, having the conversations about what can be problematic normalises the idea that minor issues can crop up and assume undue importance in the moment.

Clients' first task in relation to Sensate Focus experiments is to find the time to do them. In order to not feel hurried, couples need a clear hour or two at a time of day when they won't be interrupted. They shouldn't drink or take recreational drugs before the exercise as it dulls response and causes sleepiness. A big meal or vigorous sport can also make people uncomfortable, sleepy or hyped up. Finding time is, consequently, difficult for most people, with some realising that tiredness and lack of time in their lives is what's stopping them from being sexual, not the quality of their relationship or a sexual 'problem'. Indeed, even going forward when therapy ends, timetabling sex or intimate time and sticking to it may be the only way some couples are able to be close.

Though some therapists encourage couples to take turns initiating the experiments, this can be disastrous. Fear of rejection deters some couples or they may just be anxious about how the experiments will go. Just fixing a time for them and turning up is simplest. Initiation of close encounters can be worked on much later in the therapy if it proves necessary. Diarising times during a therapy session, at least initially, means you can explore at the next meeting how the couple managed. Agree that, if they do miss their times, they need to set another immediately.

It often feels like a breakthrough when couples appreciate they have to work to make the experiments happen. It's common to underestimate the effort involved in change of any sort, and any kind of effort or obstacle provides a reason not to change. The more anxious clients are the more likely they are to find reasons why change isn't working. This is why it's so important to point out potential difficulties and encourage couples to be realistic about what's possible.

Sensate Focus experiments involve exploring and touching the partner's body, so it's best if the couple are naked. How each partner feels about this is important to explore in advance. Some couples won't have been naked together for a while, and may feel exposed or embarrassed about their bodies, so discuss what each partner thinks may be difficult for them. It's then possible to instil confidence by planning the management of difficulties. If clients are very anxious about nudity, discuss what they think would be possible. Initially, wearing a T-shirt or vest and pants may be reassuring.

Ensure partners agree not to coerce about removal of clothes. Sometimes one partner's insecurity makes them critical of the other, so both need to understand how sabotaging this can be and to be as supportive as possible. Remind them that PST couples are discouraged from talking during the session or debriefing afterwards. This can be difficult to achieve and tolerate, so it requires considerable therapeutic support. It's necessary so that each partner is able to focus on themselves rather than worrying about the other partner's experience or what they meant by something they said. Some partners still manage to communicate distaste or displeasure by grimacing or tutting during the experiments. Once again, mentioning that this can happen, and that this form of sabotage often occurs when someone is worried about getting something wrong themselves, makes it less likely to occur or less damaging if it does.

It should be explained to the couple that they aren't expected to become aroused during the experiments, or even necessarily enjoy them, but that they should just notice their response if they do. Some couples believe they should make the most of an erection or arousal if it happens, or sometimes one partner feels let down by the other's arousal or their own 'failure' to respond. Once again, anticipating such feelings makes them less likely and more manageable if they occur. Advise couples to notice any distractions, but to return to focusing on their own experience.

Part of the contracting process should include who's going to choose where the sessions occur, prepare this area and be first to do the touching. It's helpful if they take turns doing this, but there is some general planning needed first, such as agreement to keep mobile devices out of the room. Pets shouldn't be in the room, but it can obviously be hugely off-putting if they're whining behind the door. Keeping them safely occupied may require some thought.

Having the curtains open can be wonderfully liberating for some people and nerve-wracking for others. Whether or not to lock the door can also be an issue. Even if no one is home or likely to turn up, being locked in whilst naked can be massively distressing for some people, while others will only feel comfortable with locked doors. It's also important that the room is warm enough, which needs to be thought about in advance. It's quite common for couples to plan experiments for times when their heating is normally switched off, so forethought is needed to ensure the room has warmed up sufficiently. Similarly, the partner who's managing each experiment needs to ensure there's hot water for a shower beforehand.

Once couples have timetabled their experiments and decided who will 'manage' each one, they need to agree how the venue will be negotiated. Some couples just decide from the start that they'll use the bedroom, but others like to be creative or find the bedroom is associated with feelings of failure. Couples can either be very good at communicating arrangements or feel so awkward about it that they text or leave a message. Though this isn't ideal, don't push them to communicate face-to-face if they're more comfortable this way. The more relaxed they feel in the early stages, the sooner they'll be able to start communicating personally. For some couples, any talking creates pressure. Fortunately, commenting on the way the area has been prepared for an experiment is discouraged. Even positive remarks can create pressure to achieve or exceed next time. Consequently, the experiment manager should be advised to prepare the area the way they want it, rather than trying to please their partner.

Wincze and Weisberg (2015) like the idea of making each experiment a distinctive occasion by special preparation of the room, with touches like romantic music, scented candles and low lighting. However, others (Weiner & Avery-Clark, 2017) think this increases performance pressure and is suggestive of romance rather than experimentation. Even if they don't communicate their disappointment, if one expects a romantic setup they may be crushed if their partner just straightens the bed and removes the balled up tissues. Moreover, sometimes much more effort goes into room preparation than the experiments themselves. Generally, it's helpful to explain all this to clients so that the area preparation becomes as much a part of the experiment as the exercises; that is, something they can't get wrong as it's just an experiment.

Both members of the couple are advised to bathe or shower before the experiment as this allows time to relax, change gear and perhaps to carry out some self-focus exercises. Couples tend to feel more positive and confident when clean, too. While one showers, the other prepares the room and they can then swap. While the manager showers, the other partner should simply relax, perhaps practise some mindfulness or guided imagery, and not be tempted to tidy or answer a couple of e-mails. When the other partner returns, they both remove towels or bathrobes, unless they're wearing vest and pants for the experiment, which now begins.

Sensate Focus I

It can be helpful to begin with a few moments of gazing to create a connection. Then, with Partner 2 lying on their front, Partner 1, the experiment manager, explores Partner 2's body, avoiding breasts, buttocks and genitals. They should be curious, examining areas where they wouldn't normally venture, such as behind the ears, backs of the knees and between the toes, as well as more familiar parts of the body. They should also touch and caress the body, with bare hands only (no oils, creams, lotions or objects), using different pressures. The partner being touched shouldn't object to the exploration unless there's a good reason – it's triggering, painful, irritating or ticklish, for instance. Often, one of the couple will protest about something like having their feet explored because they don't like their own feet. This sort of objection may come up in feedback, when it's worth pointing out that both partners are on the same side and not setting out to discomfort each other. Managing feelings at these times should be seen as just like any other distraction and learning experience; notice it and reengage with the sensations being experienced rather than thoughts.

After at least five minutes of touch, Partner 2 turns onto their back so that Partner 1 can explore their front, again avoiding breasts, buttocks and genitals. After at least another five minutes, they can swap roles so Partner 2 will now explore Partner 1's body. Afterwards, they should have a non-sexual cuddle. The next time they do the exercise, the roles are reversed and Partner 2 becomes the experiment manager. They may find it helpful to make private notes about their own experience afterwards as an *aide memoire* for the next therapy session. Ideally, they'll do the experiments at least three times between therapy sessions.

Early feedback

Each subsequent session should include detailed feedback from the couple's experiments and setting of further exercises. There's no point in setting experimental exercises unless you take detailed feedback which will inform your choices about the next set of exercises, rather than trying to stick rigidly to a pre-determined treatment plan. When taking feedback, be curious about *everything*. How many times has the couple managed to do the experiments? What got in the way? What did they each find most difficult or easiest about the process? What were the differences between each time they did the experiment? How do they account for this and what have they learned? It's helpful to briefly catch up with what else is going on in the couple's lives and how this is affecting the process. Other content will depend on what seems necessary for the clients' experience or stage of treatment, discussed further in the chapters about specific problems.

Keep the attention on what particularly interested clients about touching their partner rather than how they felt being touched, to avoid increasing performance pressure. Ask, for instance, about the temperature of the skin, what sort of touch was used in different areas, how these felt and how they would describe different textures in different parts. Ask what doing this was like for them, keeping the focus on the experience of being toucher rather than touchee. Don't allow criticism or blame. If this happens, emphasise what a stressful process this can be and that there is no right or wrong – whatever happens provides learning. Some partners are highly critical of themselves, which is as much to be discouraged as blaming one another. See if they can feedback their feelings of discomfort or doubt rather than defaulting to self-blame. It's difficult to give up worrying about getting things right, but clients can be encouraged to notice this, be curious about it and redirect their attention rather than focusing on what they think was wrong. Couples sometimes even jointly declare that they did badly. They often giggle in the first session or two, for instance, and think this shouldn't have happened, but it's a really common response to the oddness of the situation and their natural anxiety.

Sometimes clients say the experiment was dull, because they already know each other's body so well and the exercise was nothing new. The more they say they're bored and don't see the point of an exercise, the more they may need to stay with it longer, until they're really able to treat it as experimental. Sometimes, complaints like this happen when clients find it uncomfortable to be so close and quiet in the experiment, though they're unlikely to acknowledge this. If they also grumble about the sex ban, you may need to discuss the effect they think this is having and how they're managing this. Emphasise their resilience and resourcefulness rather than focusing on their complaints – this means commenting on how well they're doing *in spite* of how hard they're finding it. The bottom line, if they continue to complain, is that PST is their choice and they're free to quit.

Complaints about the exercises can create the temptation to rush clients through each stage in order to encourage them and suggest progress, but this is not how progress is measured in PST. Clients' attitude about the exercises and engagement is far more important, so this is the progress that needs attention. It can take some time for clients to accept the idea of focusing on their own experience rather than their partner's, for instance. Normalise this and feel confident in repeating exercises. They won't be the same if the couple approach them with a different attitude, resisting the temptation to judge or become exasperated. However difficult they found the experiment, couples should experience a sense of achievement from feedback, leaving each session with a sense of hope.

Couples may continue with the same experiment(s) for many weeks before they're ready to progress. Moving on should be negotiated, so that clients feel involvement and ownership, but this doesn't mean allowing them to decide what to do next all by themselves. You should set the next experiment on the basis of what they seem able to manage and then check what aspects they see as problematic. Varying the experiments offers a new experience which builds on learning so far.

Sensate Focus I with additions

Additions to Sensate Focus are intended to be incorporated into the experiment, not be a replacement. Indeed, each new activity throughout the PST process is intended to be added. Differences and extra elements in Sensate Focus should be spread over several sessions, rather than added all at once. For instance, the couple may use lotion, body butter, oil or cream to assist with the touch, though they should be clear that touch must be confined to the skin rather than the muscle layers below. Each partner chooses their own addition, though they may need to discuss in advance how to protect furniture from oils and whether either of them has any allergies. Emphasise the importance of learning from variations; if they used body butter in one experiment, they could try lotion the next time. Another change could be for each partner to collect a box or bag 'of wonders'. This would be items with different textures, such as a scarf, cotton wool, flannel, feather, kitchen roll, contrasting fabrics such as silk and denim, a loofah or towel. Couples should be discouraged from using all the items in one session but spread them over different occasions, still avoiding breasts, buttocks and genitals.

When they're getting the hang of giving detailed feedback, managing not knowing their partner's experience and focusing on their own, you may introduce small kisses, licking and blowing gently across the skin, though this remains sensual rather than sexual; breasts, buttocks and genitals are still off-limits. Sometimes, it's appropriate to offer gentle blowing first, so the couple appreciate that this addition is about noticing sensations and not trying to arouse.

Sensate Focus II Interim

At some point, it becomes evident that the couple is complying with instructions, enjoying the PST process and demonstrating learning. They may, for instance, comment that concentrating on their own experience creates intimacy rather than detracting from it. When it seems there is little more to learn from Sensate Focus I, the next phase involves touching as before, but this time *including* breasts, buttocks and genitals. Just as the first two phases will have helped desensitise the couple to the anxiety of naked touch, and improved their management of self-sabotaging thoughts and worries, the Interim Phase gives the opportunity to tolerate genital touch with no demand for performance or response. Hence, the Interim Phase was originally known as the Non-Demand Phase, because there was no expectation of arousal or attempting to arouse, but now we tend to think of Non-Demand more in terms of reducing personal pressure.

The couple follow the same process as before, setting up the room, showering and touching non-sexual areas first. Touching breasts, buttocks and genitals is still not aimed at arousal, but at exploration for the partner's own interest, so couples are told just to be curious. It's common to feel a little awkward whilst being scrutinised, so do discuss this beforehand. When taking feedback, it's important to enquire about any distracting thoughts or feelings and how these were managed. It may be helpful to negotiate 'stop' signals in advance too; agreement that it's okay to move a hand away can instil confidence. At this stage, though, it's not appropriate to move hands when a partner wants more of a particular touch or desires touch in a particular area. Building up longing may be something the couple have never experienced. If mentioned in feedback, frustration should be framed as very positive desire.

Some couples are only too ready and delighted to move on, but many are wary and afraid of losing the closeness they've built up so far. Genital touch may feel associated with failure and performance, which is why this phase has so much learning to offer. Couples discover they can continue sensual touch without diving towards the genitals straight away. As the emphasis is on interest and discovery rather than arousal (and failure), many couples find they're becoming aroused and are quickly ready to move on to the next phase.

Sensate Focus II

Following the Non-Demand genital touching, Masters and Johnson used Sensate Focus II to introduce deliberately arousing touch. Some therapists still do this, but it works best if couples continue to keep their focus on personal interest. Simply advise them to let their arousal develop naturally and to notice if they seem to be trying to suppress it or if something was particularly arousing. As usual, it can be helpful for them to make personal notes after each experiment.

As before, the couple set up the room, shower and take turns to touch one another, initially only in non-erogenous areas before moving on to some potentially arousing touch. It's important to keep emphasising this touch is for personal interest. Though arousal is possible, if not likely, they shouldn't be seeking orgasm from their partner but remaining interested in the ebb and flow of their arousal. If orgasm happens, it doesn't necessarily signal the end of the experiment. Each partner should refocus and continue. Therapeutic response to orgasm should not be overly ecstatic nor viewed as a mistake. Be curious about how the clients experienced this, reiterating that this is great, but not required. Check how the other partner is feeling if only one climaxed, and try to reduce expectations. Often, an orgasm will happen in only one of three sessions, demonstrating that an intimate and successful experience doesn't need to include 'outcomes'.

In subsequent sessions, you may introduce variations and additions, such as oral sex or incorporation of sex toys. This is not a mutual phase, so deep kissing is usually avoided. In many ways, this is a shame as kissing is so intimate. A compromise is for the couple to kiss each other as part of turn taking. It's difficult to kiss deeply without reciprocation, but this brief mutual exchange should be employed judiciously and within the boundaries of the programme. Kissing can also be set as homework separately from Sensate Focus. Some couples find this provokes considerable anxiety, especially if it's something they rarely do. Indeed, it's surprising how little couples kiss, beyond the occasional peck on the cheek, yet intimate kissing can be bonding, comforting and arousing. Unfortunately, it can produce just as much performance anxiety and avoidance as intercourse, often due to hygiene concerns, time constraints and worries about where it's going (Campbell, 2015). Agreeing to time-boundaried kissing for its own sake can be liberating though. When a couple know it's coming they can make sure their breath is fresh and relax in the comfort of its limitations.

Feedback at this stage may include much more discussion of managing arousal, the difficulties of maintaining boundaries and the effect on the general relationship. It's always helpful to ask about the couple's lives and stresses and to monitor the effects of PST on the relationship, but this stage may create additional issues. The couple may be able to imagine an end to the process and a life which includes regular sex and intimacy. This may be a surprise and may make each partner feel differently positioned, and often more confident. This self-assurance can generalise into other areas. Consequently, it's quite common to find that, around this time, clients seek promotion, decide to retrain, take up new hobbies, retire or spend more time with family. Though, often, the relationship will have become closer and more trusting, changes can be unsettling, so some couples experience a little wobble during this phase or the next one.

Sensate Focus Plus

Though the couple are still not attempting to arouse, they *are* encouraged to take responsibility for their own arousal. They can proceed as before but now, during their turn at touching, they take their partner's hand and lead them to areas they wish to be touched. It's important that they first complete the early part of the exercise, with touching for their own interest. There may be times when one partner doesn't want arousing touch and doesn't lead the partner into erogenous areas or even direct touch. This has to be respected (see Chapter 13). Talking about this possibility and normalising it should be part of the task-setting process. When this happens, it can provide excellent learning for the future, demonstrating that it isn't essential for both partners, or even either partner, to be aroused during sex. This reduces the need for rules about what needs to be achieved during sex, which can then always be a non-demand experience.

It may, however, also be helpful to discuss management of extreme arousal in this phase. Many couples masturbate together at the end of the experiment, some choose to do this separately and some just let their arousal subside. Some want their partner to 'make' them climax. Though sometimes this may be appropriate, it may reduce the emphasis on each partner's responsibility for their own experience. Be aware, though, that some people find it difficult to climax during individual sessions or masturbation, especially if they've been brought up to believe sex is an exclusively couple activity. Nonetheless, asking for what they want happens more comfortably when both partners know they don't have to perform for the other – either by helping them to orgasm or climaxing themselves. As this phase progresses, some couples find it fun to try an experiment where one partner asks or tells the other what to do throughout – which can, of course, result in orgasm. This is not for everyone, as it can cause anxiety, but for some couples this is an enjoyable variation. It's still necessary to maintain emphasis on the experimental nature of the exercise though.

Feedback in the middle stages

It's important to feel the work is building, continuing the process of room preparation, showers, gazing and non-genital touch as the work develops. However, as the work progresses, clients spontaneously begin talking about their pleasure and enjoyment of the process. Not asking about this in the earlier stages keeps feedback as positive as possible, which reduces anxiety and instils hope. This allows space for each partner's experience, confident that there are no expectations. Goals are just about learning from the latest experiment, managing to be in the moment, in the body and not in the head, immersed in personal experience.

It's worth revisiting the history taking and formulation regularly, but especially as the work is moving along and clients can clearly see how far they've progressed. Clients don't need to be orgasmic, though they often are, and will by the later stages have accepted the idea of focusing on their own experience and taking responsibility for their own pleasure. They may have found this is allowing them to observe their partner's experience without anxiety, or with anxiety significantly reduced, and shouldn't be feeling the need to perform to some sort of standard, either to please their partner or to satisfy themselves that they're normal. Couples often report feeling closer and are beginning to experiment by themselves.

Sensate Focus Mutual Phase

At some point in the PST process many couples spontaneously begin mutual touching, often saying, 'It just feels right now'. From this time on, they generally have control of the pace and direction of the process, even when therapy continues and what happens is agreed with the therapist. Other couples remain scrupulously dedicated to the instructions of the programme and wait for mutual touching to be suggested. This is usually done when the couple are clearly doing well and feeling confident. They don't have to be orgasmic to be satisfied.

For this phase, couples proceed as before, beginning with non-genital touch but touching each other simultaneously. Some choose to start with individual turn-taking touch and gazing to make the initial connection, allowing intimacy and arousal to build. The experimental nature of this phase cannot be over-emphasised, and couples should be warned that anxiety may return. On the whole, though, the therapist's stance should be encouraging and celebratory, noting how much the couple have already changed.

Containment

'Containment' was how Masters and Johnson referred to putting the penis in the vagina. Given that many couples' goals are entirely focused on intercourse when they present, it's surprising how many become much less interested in this as therapy goes on. Some even fear that resuming penetrative sex will spoil the intimacy they've been enjoying. Whether they're interested in penetration or not, this phase is about genital-to-genital contact – again, assuming this is what they want. In straight couples, rubbing the vulva and clitoris with the (erect or flaccid) penis may be enjoyed by both partners. Frottage, where the man lies on top of the woman, and rubs his penis along the vulval area, is a variation. A comfortable position is for the woman to sit between the man's legs, well supported by pillows, with her bent legs on either side of his body so that she can easily caress her vulva with his penis.

Frottage is an option for gay men too, who may rub penises whilst standing or lying together. The penis can also be used to explore the testes, perineal and anal areas, though a condom should be worn for this. Women may enjoy rubbing the mons areas together and scissoring or 'tribbing' – when the genitals touch by adopting a 'V' scissors position.

Couples interested in penetrative sex often report they have spontaneously had some sort of intercourse during genital touching, or used fingers or sex toys to penetrate. Try not to suggest you expect this, however, as any expectation causes anxiety. Be interested in how they found this and what they learned, being as pleased as you can if this indicates progress, but avoid overdoing your delight.

Some couples feel all their problems are over at this point and wish to end therapy. This is a positive outcome. Though you may be tempted to point out everything that could still go wrong, instead be pleased for them and make clear that the door remains open if they encounter any glitches. Book a follow-up anyway.

For many couples, this is the beginning of the next stage of the PST process. Some may want to backtrack a little while others will be keen to experience full intercourse as soon as possible, if they haven't done this already. Those experiencing genital touch without 'slip-ups' will be feeding back their outcomes and you'll be discussing where to go next. The prospect of intercourse may still be terrifying, so they may need considerable reassurance that the emphasis remains on experimentation. They begin the experiments as usual with room preparation, showers, individual and mutual sensual and sexual touch, and use of the penis to stimulate the vulva and clitoris, with the woman sitting astride the man. This is followed by the woman lowering herself onto the penis. Insertion may need to be graduated, beginning with only the penis tip, then waiting for a moment before withdrawing. Some women like to use Kegels to see how that feels, but the man should not move or thrust. If either partner is very anxious, this may be enough experimentation for one day. Other couples may want to continue with other touch and then repeat the exercise. Either on this occasion or next time, if all has gone well, the woman can proceed to lowering herself fully onto the penis and just allowing it to rest in her vagina with no movement or thrusting this time.

Some couples repeat this stage many times before they both feel confident and comfortable enough to incorporate movement. Usually, as the woman is on top, she moves until she tires or either one decides this is enough. Orgasm is not necessary, but not a problem if it happens, and does not have to signal the end of the experiment, as the couple can continue with touch if they wish.

Anal sex is discussed on page 111 but don't assume gay men will all want to have penetrative sex or that lesbian women won't. Sometimes a difference of opinion emerges about this – for straight couples, too – and help may be needed in negotiating a way forward.

Creative Phase

By the Creative Phase, couples should be feeling much more confident and better able to manage their own feelings. They usually find their relationship is considerably more intimate, that their communication has improved and that they've experienced sex in a way they never felt possible. The therapist now takes much more of a back seat, assuming the role of cheerleader, celebrating the couple's progress and the experiments they're now choosing. At this stage, they're experimenting with lovemaking and the way life is going to be in the future. This is likely to include elements like finding/making time for sex; experimenting with different positions for penetration, manual and oral sex; enjoying flirting, simmering and erotic 'moments'; and finding ways to say and accept 'no' safely. They may be trying new ways of making love, sex toys, games/role play and discovering their body's capacity for pleasure in new ways.

Insertive sex in general may be something a couple is nervous about approaching, especially if it's new to them. Different kinds of penetration may be of interest, using fingers or hands and sex toys as well as the penis. Women may enjoy penetrative sex using strap-ons or double-ended dildos, as may some straight couples where the woman penetrates the man. The therapist's role may simply be one of providing information and advice about safety in response to clients' interest, rather than explicitly setting experiments. Indeed, clients often feel they're ready to continue experimenting without therapeutic help, but sometimes the therapist needs to encourage this. There can be some residual fear that they'll backslide without support, or they may just feel uncomfortable telling their therapist they're ready to end PST. Before they finish, it's important for them to imagine any blips or return to previous behaviour, what might contribute to this and how they'll manage it.

Feedback in the later phases

Well before there's any genital touch, you need to start discussing contraception and safer sex. Some couples have assumed intercourse was such a remote possibility that they haven't considered contraceptive choices at all. Safer sex applies to straight and female couples as well as gay men, particularly if either of the couple has an infection or is inclined to develop urinary tract infections, vulval sensitivity or skin problems. Use of dental dams and condoms can help with oral sex.

Much of the therapist's work now involves guiding conversations to address future issues raised by the feedback, such as how to maintain the progress that's been made and the way the couple see their future plans affecting their lovemaking. Check whether there's anything still bothering either of them, or whether they want information or advice to develop their ideas.

Follow-up

In the spirit of CBT, couples should always be offered a three-month follow-up appointment to report on how they're doing. This is often entirely celebratory, a delightful opportunity to review the process and great outcome – but there may still be some issues about which the couple need advice or reminders. Then wish them well for the rest of their (sex) lives!

References

Campbell, C. (2015) *The Relate Guide to Sex and Intimacy*, London: Vermilion.

Campbell, C. (2018) *Love & Sex in a New Relationship*, Abingdon: Routledge.

Chiew, K.S., Stanek, J.K. & Adcock, R.A. (2016) Reward anticipation dynamics during cognitive control and episodic encoding: Implications for dopamine. *Frontiers in Human Neuroscience*, November 10. www.frontiersin.org/articles/10.3389/fnhum.2016.00555/full. Accessed May 5, 2019.

Kasemy, Z., Desouky, D.E. & Abdelrasoul, G. (2016) Sexual fantasy, masturbation and pornography among Egyptians. *Sexuality & Culture*, 20, 626–638.

Kowalik, M. (2018) Why feminists enjoy rape fantasies. *Quadrant Magazine*, 62;10, 66–68.

Maier, T. (2013) *Masters of Sex*, updated edition, New York: Basic Books.

Maltz, W. (2012) Healing the sexual repercussions of sexual abuse. In: Kleinplatz, P.J. [ed] *New Directions in Sex Therapy*, Hove: Routledge, 267–284.

McCabe, M.P. (2015) Female orgasmic disorder. In: Hertlein, K.M., Weeks, G.R. & Gambescia, N. [eds] *Systemic Sex Therapy*, second edition, New York: Routledge.

Newbury, R., Hayter, M., Wylie, K.R. & Riddell, J. (2012) Sexual fantasy as a clinical intervention. *Sexual & Relationship Therapy*, 27;4, 358–371.

Ogden, P. & Fisher, J. (2015) *Sensorimotor Psychotherapy*, New York: W.W. Norton.

Sapolsky, R.M. (2004) *Why Zebras Don't Get Ulcers*, third edition, New York: Holt Paperbacks.

Schnarch, D. (1991) *Constructing the Sexual Crucible*, New York: W.W. Norton.

Shapiro, F. (2018) *EMDR Therapy*, third edition, New York: Guilford Press.

Siegel, D. (2007) *The Mindful Brain in Human Development: Reflection and Attunement in the Cultivation of Well-Being*, New York: W.W. Norton.

Siegel, D. (2017) *Mind: A Journey to the Heart of Being Human*, New York: W.W. Norton.

Stockwell, F.M.J. & Moran, D.J. (2014) A relational frame theory account of the emergence of sexual fantasy. *Journal of Sex & Marital Therapy*, 40;2, 92–104.

Weiner, L. & Avery-Clark, C. (2017) *Sensate Focus in Sex Therapy: The Illustrated Manual*, New York: Routledge.

Wincze, J.P. & Weisberg, R.B. (2015) *Sexual Dysfunction: A Guide for Assessment and Treatment*, third edition, New York: Guilford Press.

Chapter 7

Desire and arousal

Many clients don't appreciate the difference between arousal and desire, perhaps because they trigger one another and, for some people, seem to be experienced simultaneously. The major difference clients might need to appreciate is that arousal is beyond voluntary control. As Masters and Johnson (1970) were so fond of pointing out, arousal is a 'natural' and automatic physiological response to bodily or mental stimulation, whereas desire is more subjective. Both arousal and desire are, hence, more complex than most of our clients appreciate or imagine. Indeed, the concept of desire can be sexually disabling, as there are so many associated expectations around desire that we all absorb without even noticing. Though there *are* clinical reasons for low desire, performance pressure of many types underlies much of so-called low desire, especially as the issue of desire has now begun to replace traditional sexual performance as evidence of adequate sexuality (Vigoya, 2012).

Masters and Johnson (1966) didn't even include a desire phase in their Human Sexual Response Cycle, derived from laboratory experiments with human volunteers. Identifying four phases of arousal/excitement, plateau, orgasm and resolution, their findings about what happens to the body during each have been elaborated, debunked and queried over time. Nonetheless, this original four-stage model has been part of the psychoeducational package routinely offered to many clients, though a straightforward description of the cycle may conflict with clients' actual experience. For instance, arousal may be experienced many times in a day dependent on available triggers, but the idea of a cycle feeds the expectation that arousal must be pursued to a conclusion rather than enjoyed for itself. The Male Sexual Drive Discourse (Hollway, 1984) argues that men are constantly ready and able for sex, motivated by an unstoppable biological urge. This can lead men to believe they'll be ill if they don't ejaculate often, as well as suggesting they should want and be able to have sex at any time.

Presenting the Human Sexual Response Cycle as a truth about what is normal can feed into such unhelpful beliefs. Masters and Johnson, for instance, state that vaginal lubrication and a partial erection are the early signs of arousal, but this isn't the case for everyone. Men can feel highly aroused with no erection and women can be aroused with no lubrication. Rather than seeing their experience as variations of normal, those whose erections/lubrication are less reliable due to age or illness could easily give up hope upon learning their bodies aren't behaving as scientists expect.

Though men may notice some muscular contraction just before orgasm (known as the 'point of inevitability'), for women the plateau may simply be the point when the body stops changing as a response to stimulation. Arousal doesn't go away at this point, and orgasm doesn't necessarily follow once it's been reached. It's also perfectly possible for women to orgasm before reaching the plateau. There are huge subjective variations in the way arousal is experienced, with some people having virtually no sensations of arousal before they climax.

Orgasm is also presented as the end of arousal and 'sex', with a resolution phase following rapidly. For men, the return of the body to its homeostatic state is commonly accompanied by a refractory period characterised by the inability to have an erection again for a period of time which lengthens as they age. Some men, though, can have more than one orgasm in a day – or even an hour – and may experience further erections very quickly. Many certainly report the return of arousal, even without erection. Women's refractory period is extremely brief. Typically, the clitoris is super-sensitive following orgasm, making direct touch uncomfortable or irritating. Though some women prefer not to be touched at all after climaxing, indirect touch may be comfortably tolerable immediately; indeed, the sensitivity of the clitoris may make further orgasm rapid. Those who do have further orgasms may find these are more or less intense than the first. But this is a range of experience, much more complex than that which Masters and Johnson chose to present. Though they did sometimes acknowledge that women's sexual response was more complex than men's, with three distinct pathways, the impression given overall was that the male model was *the* model and this unnuanced version persists. Where there is acknowledgement of difference, it often seems to settle around the idea that men's sexual problems are more likely to be functional, such as erectile difficulties, whereas women's are more often seen as psychological in origin (Spurgas, 2013). Giving clients 'scientific' information collected in the 1960s can, therefore, be less useful to them than emphasising the vast range of sexual responses which can be different at different times in peoples' lives.

Loving someone and wanting to demonstrate this physically may have nothing to do with a reflexive sexual response associated with attraction. Both women and men are hugely affected by contexts other than their own bodies, and their sexual behaviour may have nothing at all to do with what they want or desire. It may be a great deal more about what they feel they *should* be doing. Many men believe in a biological imperative to impregnate as many women as possible which, combined with other tropes about masculinity, may underlie their 'desire' or high sex drive. Such men may see their erection as demonstrating desire and arousability, as well as social behaviours such as sexual banter, 'pestering' their partner for sex and interest in sex. Men are under pressure to perform being male, and loss of desire may be a side-effect of this.

As well as living up to the stereotypical male image, men feel required to have sensitivity and to 'give' their partners orgasms, creating response pressure in partners as well as more performance anxiety in the man. Less-reliable erections, which are a normal consequence of ageing, may be experienced as terrifying by a man who needs objective appraisal of his masculinity and sexual worth. Indeed, a man's ability to perform may be crucial to his overall sense of well-being. Sex may be both a release from everyday stress and a way to express it. Erection and ejaculation are often seen as 'necessary' for fertility, for good physical and mental health, and for the sexual well-being of partners, not to mention the man's personal image and masculinity.

None of this addresses the experience of non-straight, non-binary men and, moreover, relies on women to also adopt a clichéd approach to sex, being more interested in relationships and homemaking than biological drive, and more willing to give the man responsibility for their sexual pleasure (Brooks & Elder, 2012). Relationships with men or non-binary women may be freeing or have added complexity. Ultimately, however, all close relationships have the potential to threaten men's well-being if they deviate in any way from the man's perception of how sex and maleness should be performed. Though there are clinical reasons for low desire, performance pressure of many types may contribute. Indeed, women's responsiveness is often seen as an indicator of optimum sexual functioning (Spurgas, 2013). DSM-5 diagnostic criteria requires a lack of sexual *interest* from women and a lack of *desire* from men, suggesting women's cognitive choice to engage in sex rather than the physical urge experienced by men.

Kaplan's (1977) Triphasic Model – desire, excitement, orgasm – led to the inclusion in DSM-III (APA, 1980) of hypoactive sexual desire as a dysfunction, desire now becoming one more requirement of proper, normal sex. While Kaplan recognised that desire could be both spontaneous and responsive, the Triphasic Model focused on spontaneous desire. Much later, Basson (2000) identified spontaneous desire as occurring in early relationships, with responsive desire more common the longer the relationship lasted. She noted that sex was not just about satisfying a biological urge for most women, and that women respond with desire once they receive appropriate stimulation, be that visual, imaginary or physical. However, Basson originally viewed responsive desire as applying to everyone, not just women (Brotto & Luria, 2014), and it's interesting to ponder why men's desire continues to be viewed as so proactive. Her richer exposition of women's sexual response, focusing less on genital changes and emphasising the non-linear nature of women's arousal, was badly needed. Yet the focus seemed to settle once again on women as emotional and intimacy-driven at best and sexual commodifiers at worst, having sex to improve their partner's mood when they want a new washing machine, for instance. While women do value intimacy, more closeness doesn't automatically result in more intimacy/sex being sought (Durr, 2009) and, anyway, men value intimacy too (Pascoal *et al*, 2012).

Perhaps responsive desire in men has been so little explored because they're less likely to be honest about it (Štulhofer *et al*, 2013). Even though discourses about men's sexual readiness and insatiability inevitably affect self-report, both studies and clinical experience suggest men in long relationships also have responsive desire. Significantly, this apparently has no effect on the quality of sex or intimacy compared with men who have no desire (Štulhofer *et al*, 2013). Perhaps the expectation that men are more prepared to initiate sex has created the hostile pursuer:distancer dynamic which often presents clinically and in which obtaining and avoiding sex can become the relationship's motif. On investigation, the negative attention given to pursuit/avoidance may serve as the couple's only direct interaction in everyday life. Supplying evidence that they remain a couple may be a powerful unconscious reason to maintain this dynamic.

Discrepancy of desire

Initial conversations with couples about their loss of desire usually deliver a host of misunderstandings and misconceptions, with low libido commonly a result of sexual suppression. What's the point of desiring your partner when you expect rejection? Couples often present with discrepancy of desire, one claiming to have high desire while the other is not so interested. While not a DSM dysfunction, this *is* a problem for the couple, and one which responds well to PST. Commonly, the high-libido partner pursues the other, who mostly rejects the advances. This dynamic may be satisfying to some couples, as the high-libido partner evidences their sexual interest by pursuit, without the need to follow through, and the low-libido partner can claim they would be sexual if only their libido were higher. Couples often present for sex therapy either to 'fail' and justify their no-sex position, when they want to start a family or when no sex is affecting their self-image. Often, both partners are resentful, with each feeling misunderstood by the other.

Rebuffing sexual overtures can easily happen when timing is off, something couples don't always understand. Sometimes the story that men are always ready for sex motivates a partner to make moves because they feel they should or to prove they're desirable rather than because they want sex at that moment. Because being pushed away is wounding, they pursue more, with each partner feeling increasingly hurt and misunderstood until rejection becomes a habit, and eventually – after years – the pursuer gives up. This repetitive pattern can be broken by a little exploration. Sometimes, poor timing can be a bid to recapture what a partner sees as the sexual spontaneity of the early relationship. Pouncing on a partner while they're removing a sizzling pan from the oven is clearly not well-timed, but timing can be more subtle. For instance, someone may reject advances because they feel they have coffee breath, they're sweaty, need the loo, have mountains of work to do or are just plain exhausted. These *reasons* are often perceived as *excuses*, an example of how partners make up their minds about what's going on without checking their understanding.

Improving communication, including finding ways to say 'no' to advances and scheduling reliable couple time, can transform a couple's relationship. Conversations about what's actually possible, given a couple's schedule, and what sort of intimacy would be acceptable and achievable, can make a huge difference. Some couples need permission to acknowledge how difficult their lives currently are and to accept that a delicious kiss or chaste cuddle may be more comforting and satisfying than trying to cram in a session of intercourse twice a week.

A common version of the pursuer:distancer dynamic is when one partner believes sex demonstrates that they're loved and the relationship is okay, while the other wants to feel loved and that the relationship is okay before having sex. The pursuer doesn't appreciate that coercive sex isn't loving; they're just desperate to tick the sex box. The more they pursue, the more the other partner feels unloved and commodified. Hypothesising about this possibility with couples often brings forth awareness of each other's response and motivation. Realising that sexual pursuit is actually a bid for reassurance can make a huge difference to couples who may then feel more able to communicate their needs more honestly. Many partners feel unable to show their vulnerability, having underlying fears that any form of need will put-off their partner or that they aren't lovable enough to have their needs met. Pre-Sensate and Sensate Focus experiments provide space for such couples to slowly gain confidence and tolerate intimacy without fear.

Hypoactive Sexual Desire Disorder (HSDD)

It's often partners who push men with low desire to seek help (Hall, 2015). Because it's often present in combination with other problems, such as erectile difficulty, HSDD is often seen as a result of this rather than a condition in its own right, and has been relatively poorly researched as a result (Wincze & Weisberg, 2015). However, it's also possible that shame about their lack of desire causes some men to blame a more acceptable issue. For instance, since the introduction of PDE-5 inhibitors such as Viagra to treat erectile dysfunction, this can be seen as a more 'normal' problem than low desire. It's also common for unhelpful sexual discourses – such as the idea that men are always ready for sex – to be the cause of distress rather than genuine interest in a sexual relationship. There can, in addition, be a hidden loss of sexual interest in the primary partner which may or may not involve sex elsewhere. Factors such as these make assessment especially important, as there may be concealed issues, such as an affair, excessive pornography use or a preference for masturbation.

Therapists will be interested in what makes a man think he has low desire, when it started, how it's affecting the relationship, how he accounts for it and what he sees as a positive outcome of treatment. This can often be unrealistic and driven by ideas about how, as a man/partner, he should be behaving sexually. Discrepancies with the partner's answers will be revealing. Asking about solutions the couple have tried sometimes reveals one partner bearing all the responsibility for the problem.

Sometimes, issues with the partner are contributing to low desire. These include:

- Conflictual relationship
- Partner expressing sexual disappointment or criticism
- Man no longer finds the partner attractive

- Menopausal symptoms affecting partner's interest in sex or interrupting sex
- Concern about the partner's welfare, especially if there is sexual pain, recent surgery, illness or pregnancy
- The partner has had an affair
- The partner has revealed previous sexual abuse
- The partner's restrictive belief system
- Unrealistic expectations, such as denial of normal ageing, expecting sex to be the way it was at the beginning of the relationship.

Testosterone may be over-prescribed (Finkle *et al*, 2014). If medical investigations reveal low testosterone levels (hypogonadism), testosterone replacement may be helpful, but there's no benefit to prescribing testosterone when levels are within a normal range (Corona *et al*, 2011), and it can increase the risk of cardiovascular disease (Finkle *et al*, 2014). Medication for inflammatory bowel disease can lower testosterone, and it's a normal result of ageing (Wincze & Weisberg, 2015).

Understandably, almost all medical conditions can lead to low desire. Depression is common, and selective serotonin reuptake inhibitor (SSRI) antidepressants can also contribute to low libido. Indeed, low desire can turn out to be entirely iatrogenic. Recreational drugs such as alcohol, cocaine and ketamine dampen both desire and arousal. Antihypertensives, statins, epilepsy and prostate medication are among prescribed drugs implicated in affecting libido. When it's impossible to change medication, understanding the cause of low libido can be sufficient for the individual to choose to be sexual or to work out with his partner which intimate or sexual behaviours are possible.

Treatment for HSDD

Important early interventions include a complete sex ban, including masturbation, which considerably relieves pressure and allows space for desire. Early interventions could include psychoeducation and discussion around 'normal' desire and sexual functioning, ageing, unhelpful beliefs, recognition of resilience and resources, and realism about what's possible within the client/couple's circumstances. Some men/couples benefit from planning the way they want their sex lives to be in the future and consideration of how they express themselves sexually on a day-to-day basis, including elements such as their choice of clothes, flirting and awareness of their bodies (Campbell, 2015: 31–44).

Whether to start Pre-Sensate rather than Sensate Focus experiments will depend on anxiety levels, but some sort of couple exercise should be prescribed from formulation onwards to demonstrate belief in the couple's potential. Barring unexpected emergencies or information, Sensate experiments should be adhered to once begun. Difficulties with timing and anxieties are part of the process and not a reason to desist.

Sometimes it's the partner who sabotages Sensate Focus, having initially been the one to insist on therapy. Often, the other partner's libido will drop when the man's desire starts to return, which may reflect shared fears of intimacy, merger and rejection, leading to unconscious collusive turn-taking (Willi, 1986). For some couples, the relationship is so close that there isn't enough difference to encourage desire (Perel, 2007). This is addressed by Sensate Focus experiments which facilitate the development of differentiation (Bowen, 1978), as partners are required to tolerate loss of validation from the other and focus on self-interest.

Neither desire nor positive anticipation are necessary for Sensate experiments, but they do need to be scheduled and undertaken regularly, ideally two or three times a week. Mindfulness exercises can be helpful in focusing on bodily experience, as can logging negative thoughts and their triggers. Self-focus exercises should include Kegels to improve bodily awareness, mindful awareness, fantasy and use of erotica, though avoid internet porn and masturbation, as the aim is to notice and build desire rather than dispose of it!

Zilbergeld's (1999) simmering exercises encourage clients to notice their arousal and keep returning to it, allowing themselves to enjoy sexual feelings without pressure. They may enhance them if they want to with fantasy or Kegel exercises before letting arousal fade away. They're advised to try to recall the feeling and fantasy later, once again enjoying it and letting it fade. Remembering sexual moments with their partner is also encouraged, along with flirting, messaging, sexting, touching, kissing and cuddling just for its own sake. Simmering can be framed as an outcome for all PST clients, as the ability to notice arousal without pressure to perform can swiftly lead to the development of desire.

Sexual interest/arousal disorder

Sexual interest in women often wanes once they start a family. Sleepless nights, coupled with painful stitches, breastfeeding (which can lower libido), altered body image and understandable preoccupation with a new baby, can contribute to loss of interest in sex. When both partners are tired, they may resort to separate rooms in order to get enough rest, and there is even less incentive to be sexual. Fear of another pregnancy may be a disincentive and, ironically, hormonal contraceptives can affect sexual interest. Medical conditions, such as diabetes, other sexual problems or the menopause can also affect arousal. The absence of a mid-cycle peak of sexual interest when they ovulate makes some women feel they've lost libido altogether, particularly if they enjoyed the intensity of their sexual interest around ovulation.

The first drug on the market to treat low desire in pre-menopausal women was flibanserin (Addyi). Originally an antidepressant, 100mg tablets are taken at bedtime. In eight-week trials, women experienced one additional satisfying sexual experience per month. This seems a trivial outcome, especially as the manufacturers acknowledged a placebo effect (Pevzner & Klein, 2016). At the time of writing, a second drug, Vyleesi, is about to become available in the USA. Administered by subcutaneous injection 45 minutes before sex, its FDA detractors question its efficacy and say it may be unsafe (Cha & McGinley, 2019).

Testosterone is sometimes prescribed as Intrinsa patches to boost sexual interest, especially following surgical menopause. Hormone replacement therapy may be used to manage menopausal symptoms, and treatment of endocrine disorders, such as hypothyroidism, may be helpful. However, relationship disturbance, negative self-belief and lack of knowledge may be combining to maintain the problem (Weeks & Gambescia, 2015: 125–151). Indeed, it's not uncommon to find lack of knowledge about their bodies, insufficient sexual stimulation and poor communication are contributing to low arousal and lack of sexual interest.

It's important in PST to establish that the woman does, in fact, want to be sexual and to be clear about what she wants from therapy, rather than what her partner wants. Frequently, too, relationship issues or simply resentment about domestic responsibilities can be aversive (see Chapter 18). These may be caused or exacerbated if the partner believes sex is being withheld; coercion and pestering is often part of the couple's recent history.

Low desire in either gender can be therapeutically construed as adaptive and protective. For instance, sexual avoidance may be framed as 'waiting for the right time' rather than 'having poor experiences due to tiredness, illness or stress'. It follows that motivation for exercises may be low. To improve this, acknowledge the bravery involved in attempting PST, and celebrate all attempts at change. Building in rewards such as a sensual picnic to follow Sensate Focus, watching a movie in bed or snuggling up for an early night may also influence compliance, though it's important this doesn't create extra tasks or responsibility for the woman.

Women can benefit from a treatment process similar to that for HSDD, but more work is often needed to manage negative thoughts and beliefs and to create effective communication. It can be difficult for some women to focus on their own needs and to make time for experiments. Relaxation and guided imagery exercises may assist in changing gear from mother/employee to partner/lover. Self-focus exercises should include experiments with fantasy, masturbation and sex toys. Introducing role play in the experimental phase of Sensate Focus may be liberating.

Individual and short-term clients

The PST programme usually helps the relationship overall, building general and sexual confidence, intimacy and relationship satisfaction. It's much more difficult to monitor improvement when partners aren't involved in PST. To maintain momentum, individual clients should ideally be seen weekly, whereas couples can be seen less often – optimally, fortnightly. In short-term work, longer gaps between sessions may be necessary, perhaps as far apart as monthly or every six weeks. Where possible, e-mail or telephone messaging between sessions is helpful. Though far from ideal, short-term clients may need to be given a series of experiments – for example, Sensate Focus I and Sensate Focus I with additions. Wincze and Weisberg (2015) argue that 'sexual arousal and interest benefit from novelty, risk and unpredictability'. Consequently, experimentation is important to help futureproof the sexual relationship and should not be rushed.

Erectile Difficulties (ED)

Most of the time, hormones keep the penis flaccid. Put simply, erection occurs when extra blood enters the penis under pressure, squeezing shut the veins which return blood from the penis. Various medical conditions, drugs and psychological factors can interfere with this process, leading to ED. Cardiovascular disease accounts for up to 80 percent of organic causes (Simopoulos & Trinidad, 2013). Other contributory conditions include:

- Peyronie's disease, in which there is a bend in the penis, often following trauma, making erection painful
- Endocrine conditions, such as metabolic syndrome, diabetes and hypogonadism
- Medication, especially antidepressants, drugs for cardiovascular conditions and recreational drugs, such as heroin and methadone; chronic alcohol abuse causes liver and testicular damage which can, thus, result in low testosterone
- Neurological conditions, including multiple sclerosis, Parkinson's disease, dementia, stroke and spinal cord injury
- Iatrogenic causes, such as genital radiotherapy, some prostate and bowel surgery
- Prostate surgery usually causes a period of ED, at least initially.

Medical treatment

PDE5 inhibitors like Viagra (sildenafil) have revolutionised the medical treatment of ED, with many men self-treating now that it's available over the counter. It works within 30–60 minutes and lasts four to six hours. Levitra (vardenafil) can act more quickly than Viagra, and Cialis (tadalafil) may be quicker still, lasting up to 36 hours. Spedra (avanafil) works within half an hour and lasts six hours. Side-effects of PDE5 inhibitors include flushing, a stuffy nose, headache, tummy ache or they don't work, though some users don't realise sexual stimulation is also necessary. Trying a different drug may overcome side-effects; a daily dose may be prescribed if the drug doesn't work. Taking folic acid may help, particularly in men with diabetes (Madani *et al*, 2013).

If PDE5 inhibitors really don't work, or are contraindicated, there are drugs which can be directly applied to the penis. Intracavernosal injections, for instance, are particularly used for when there's spinal cord injury. Individuals are taught to inject a vasodilator directly into the erectile tissue of the penis. Erection occurs within a few minutes, regardless of arousal, and lasts about half an hour. Alternatively, the medicated urethral system for erection (MUSE) involves inserting a vasodilator into the urethra after passing water using a plastic applicator. Handling the penis and walking around, if that's possible, facilitates absorption. An erection should occur within 15 minutes, though it may be short-lived.

Penile prosthesis is a last resort whereby flexible rods or inflatable tubes are surgically implanted into erectile tissue. The penis never becomes fully erect, but vaginal intercourse should be possible with a semi-erection. They are especially helpful in conditions such as Peyronie's disease but, if they need to be removed for reasons such as infection, physiological erection is no longer possible. At the time of writing, numerous new products to treat ED are in the pipeline, ranging from gels and sprays applied directly to the penis to the use of shockwaves.

PST

By the time they attend therapy for ED, most men have tried PDE5 inhibitors. Even when they work successfully, many men don't like relying on a drug and want to be able to function 'normally'. When a clinical cause for ED has been identified and treated, there are often still psychological maintaining factors, such as performance anxiety.

Men may be shocked to find themselves experiencing ED, though it seems to affect most men at some point. It's rarely a lifelong condition, but can occur suddenly or gradually. Sudden onset of ED often follows a single incident, such as failure to get an erection while drunk or very tired, which leads to performance anxiety. Gradual progression may be related to ageing or have a clinical cause, such as cardiovascular disease or diabetes, so all ED clients should see their GP. It's important to obtain a very thorough history and be clear about precipitating and maintaining factors. Availability of PDE5 inhibitors has made the prevalence of ED very evident, which is reassuring to some men, but many feel considerable shame about it – some even fearing they'll lose their partner as a result. PST plus PDE5 inhibitors may be necessary where there are organic causes of ED.

The approach to treatment may depend on whether the problem is seen as constant or situational, such as only occurring with a partner. If someone's still having erections in the morning and with masturbation, there's probably no organic reason for ED, though this should still be checked. The aim of treatment is to lower performance anxiety through a stepped approach to sustainable erection, as well as cognitive restructuring to normalise erectile difficulties. However, erection as an initial goal is usually unhelpful. Couples often collude in erection monitoring, making thoughtless or unkind comments and ruminating on unhelpful ideas which just feed their fears. It's, therefore, important to take the therapeutic focus away from erections and intercourse and direct it towards other forms of pleasure and ways of building intimacy.

The relationship and way the ED is thought of by the couple is crucial. Many believe men should be able to have hard, spontaneous erections without stimulation. They're also often unaware that additional stimulation may be needed to maintain erections as men age and that erections may become less firm. Equally, many straight couples still believe women should be sexually satisfied through intercourse or that only intercourse is 'real' sex. Emphasise that unreliable erections shouldn't be seen as a reflection of a man's sexual interest or arousal and that intercourse is possible even with a less firm erection. Sometimes the ED has disappeared or become manageable by the time of formulation, as the assessment process and the improved understanding and communication it promotes offer more sense of control.

Men with ED and their partners often develop low desire/interest in sex when the problem has existed for some time, with avoidance being less stressful than 'failure'. Partners' contribution to anxiety and ability to support is significant, so it's helpful to work with the couple. Once the PST process is underway, and progress is being made, the man can be offered wax and wane exercises to improve erectile confidence. This shouldn't be suggested until the couple are becoming more mindful and able to focus on their own interest. Spectatoring is common, when a person observes their performance during sex, so this needs to be overcome before any focus on erections occurs. Wax and wane should be offered as an optional experiment to improve erectile confidence rather than a cure for ED. Not all clients wish to try this at all, and some want to wait a while. Advising couples not to talk about progress outside sessions removes scrutiny and pressure if the exercise *is* tried. Feedback in sessions should be met with positivity and encouragement from the therapist, whereas couples can worry each other with speculation.

Wax and Wane experiment

Stimulating the penis is set as a self-focus exercise. Feedback is initially taken more about the man's feelings during the exercise, and ability to focus without negative thoughts, rather than what the penis is doing. When the man reports consistently getting an erection, he's asked to notice the arousal and then let the erection subside. He can then repeat the exercise twice more before ejaculating if he wants to. Therapists explain that doing the exercise may be difficult initially, and encourage the use of mindful refocusing to help. For very anxious clients, just getting the erection and letting it go may be enough for the first experiment. If there's also early ejaculation, the client can be encouraged to stimulate to the point of inevitability (see page 78) before allowing the erection to subside. Variations include masturbating with an oiled hand, experimenting with different kinds of touch or wearing a condom. Positivity and advice about managing refocusing is vital.

Once the experiment has been completed several times, and the client is expressing confidence about the process, the experiment can be included from Sensate Focus II onwards. This allows the couple to develop strategies for regaining the erection together. Advise them that the experiment isn't about the erection but about how the couple manages the process, and plan with them how they want to proceed. Initially, the man may want to do the experiment himself with the partner present, or he may prefer to share the exercise. It's helpful, at some point, to have the partner touch. As confidence grows, different kinds of touch can be used. Later, the couple may want to incorporate oral sex or genital to genital contact.

Towards the end of treatment, as the couple's confidence increases, they may be keen to experience and experiment with the erection, including penetrative sex. In cases where the client has a history of losing his erection at the point of penetration, use of PDE5 inhibitors for a while may be helpful to offer extra confidence. The medication can then be gradually reduced and ultimately withdrawn.

PiV containment in ED

Experiments with intercourse are liable to reignite anxiety, so the client needs to be reasonably confident about being able to maintain an erection and to have previously practised Wax and Wane solo and with his partner, including penile stimulation of the vulva and clitoris. The partner needs to be aroused or well lubricated. It often helps to have the woman on top, and stimulate the man to erection while he tries to concentrate on the *sensations* he's experiencing, rather than the erection and what's happening. When she feels the erection is sufficient for penetration, the woman can guide his penis inside her. Neither should move for 30 seconds, then the woman dismounts and lovemaking continues in other ways. This can be repeated several times, with the man spending increasing lengths of time inside the vagina, but without movement. This allows both partners to just enjoy the closeness and feeling of the penis inside the vagina.

The next time, the woman can tighten and release vaginal muscles at the second or subsequent attempts, but the man is still told not to thrust and to focus on the sensations he's experiencing. Kegels may be sufficient to cause orgasm, which is framed as a great reason to lose an erection. However, the couple may want to try the exercise a few times to work out how much stimulation is needed for the man to climax.

When the couple feel comfortable with these exercises they may try allowing the woman to move on the penis, stopping and starting to maximise pleasure. Subsequently, and as their confidence increases, the couple should try different positions, incorporating activities they enjoy. If the erection is lost, they should immediately switch to other sexual activities and resume intercourse experiments later if they both feel comfortable doing so. The couple should be aware that older men may need constant stimulation in order to maintain erection to orgasm.

Feedback from the experiment should consistently make clear that the emphasis is not on the erection but on what is learned from the experiment. Don't start by asking, 'So! Did you keep your erection this time?' but rather, 'What did you both learn from the experiments this time?' If there's considerable anxiety but a strong wish to attempt PiV sex, just inserting the tip of the penis may be a good way to begin. With no pressure to continue, this may just offer the couple insight into how relaxed or tense they both are, or it may be an experience they both wish to extend. If the woman stimulating the man to erection causes stress or prompts more spectatoring, it may be beneficial for him to manage his own erection. However, in reality, couples are often much more comfortable together and trusting of each other by this stage. Most are considerably less focused on the importance of penetration, as they will have been enjoying satisfying sex for some time. If one partner still feels intercourse signifies something that's missing from the relationship or 'needs' intercourse to prove something – such as love or masculinity – or if anxiety remains very high, the programme may have been rushed and more time needs to be spent attending to fears and unhelpful beliefs.

Experiments with the penis flaccid in advance of containment experiments can demonstrate to the couple that an erection is not absolutely necessary anyway. These are essential when there's little or no chance of physiological erection. Using the flaccid penis to stimulate the woman's vulva and clitoris often results in her orgasm, especially when the nipples are stimulated too. When setting this experiment, frame it as potentially fun learning rather than the aim being orgasm. The newness of the experiment or self-consciousness may mean it takes times to feel like fun to the couple. Once it does, though, they learn that the flaccid penis can be very 'useful'!

Another experiment, known as 'stuffing', involves the woman folding the flaccid penis into her vagina and holding it there, which can be comfortably achieved sitting astride the man. It's helpful to mention this as a possibility some time before actually setting it as an experiment to see how the clients react. Some hate the idea while others just go away and try it. Both partners need to feel confident and comfortable with this. It can add a layer of intimacy or be a disaster which adds to feelings of difference, so do proceed with caution.

Anal containment

A hard penis is necessary for anal penetration, so this wouldn't normally be set as an experiment in the Containment Phase unless it had previously been part of a couple's sexual repertoire. The anus can be prepared by penetration with tongue and fingers. Experiment initially with just the tip of the penis and plenty of water-based lube. Resistance is normally felt as the anal sphincter reflexively closes, so it's usual to rest the penis for a few moments so that the receiver's body has time to relax before any movement.

Experiments can be set modelling the vaginal containment process, resting the penis in initial stages and moving on gradually to movement. The difference is that in vaginal containment the man remains still, whereas it's the receiver who doesn't move in anal penetration experiments. Dental dams should be used if there's mouth to anus contact, and condoms should be worn for penetration. Lube may need to be reapplied as it can be absorbed by the anus.

Other ED interventions

Intense focus on penile performance can be treated by asking the man to create a narrative about what's happening from the point of view of the penis, Kleinplatz (2012: 107–108) suggests. Giving the penis a voice can reveal the anxiety and lack of attention to sensory experience many men go through. Fraser and Solovey (2018) point out that men often attempt intercourse using PDE5 inhibitors without first understanding the effects on their body. Encouraging experimental masturbation with a drug like Viagra can help the client to learn about the way his body responds, offering a more confident approach to its use in partnered sex. Weiner and Avery-Clark (2017: 76) suggest use of a code word when the man begins to become anxious during exercises to signal a need to change what's happening, refocus and reconnect.

Addressing their shame can be an especially effective way of working with individual clients who are extremely anxious about getting sex right and for couples where the relationship is compromised by criticism and conflict (DeYoung, 2015). Finally, plenty of discussion around the meaning of desire, arousal and erections, and their expectations, is crucial since it's easy to miss erroneous beliefs. Pointing out that erection is a physiological response, and that it isn't actually possible to control, can be very liberating. Remind clients that they probably struggled with unwanted erections when they reached puberty and that, though embarrassing, they probably saw this as natural – though this may turn out to be the origin of sex anxiety. Difficulty with erections is also natural when ageing, distracted, tired, drunk or stressed, for instance. Looking at the person's life and the pressures they're experiencing is sometimes all that's needed to start freeing them from their fears.

References

American Psychiatric Association (1980) *Diagnostic and Statistical Manual of Mental Disorders*, third edition, Washington, DC: APA.

Basson, R. (2000) The female sexual response: A different model. *Sex & Marital Therapy*, 26, 51–65.

Bowen, M. (1978) Toward the differentiation of self in one's family of origin. In: *Georgetown Family Symposia: A Collection of Selected Papers 1971–1972*, Washington, DC: Georgetown University Family Center.

Brooks, G.R. & Elder, W.B. (2012) Sex therapy for men: Resolving false dichotomies. In: Kleinplatz, P. [ed] *New Directions in Sex Therapy*, second edition, Hove: Routledge, 37–50.

Brotto, L. & Luria, M. (2014) Sexual interest/arousal disorder in women. In: Binik, Y.M. & Hall, K.S.K. [eds] *Principles and Practice of Sex Therapy*, fifth edition, New York: Guilford Press.

Campbell, C. (2015) Your sexual image. In: *The Relate Guide to Sex and Intimacy*, London: Vermilion, 31–44.

Cha, A.E. & McGinley, L. (2019) FDA approves new female Viagra despite skepticism, *Washington Post*, June 21.

Corona, G., Rastrelli, G., Forti, G. & Maggi, M. (2011) Update in testosterone therapy for men. *Journal of Sexual Medicine*, 8, 639–654.

DeYoung, P. (2015) *Understanding and Treating Chronic Shame*, New York: Routledge.

Durr, E. (2009) Lack of 'responsive' sexual desire in women: Implications for clinical practice, *Sexual and Relationship Therapy*, 24;3–4, 292–306.

Finkle, W.D., Greenland, S. & Ridgeway, D.K. (2014) Increased risk of non-fatal myocardial infarction following testosterone therapy prescription in men. *PLoS One*, 9;1. www.ncbi.nlm.nih.gov/pubmed/24489673. Accessed May 24, 2019.

Fraser, J.S. & Solovey, A. (2018) The process of change in brief sex therapy. In: Gree, S. & Flemons, D. [eds] *Quickies: The Handbook of Brief Sex Therapy*, third edition, New York: W.W. Norton, 70–98.

Hall, K. (2015) Male hypoactive sexual desire disorder. In: Hertlein, K.M., Weeks, G.R. & Gambescia, N. [eds] *Systemic Sex Therapy*, second edition, New York: Routledge, 55–71.

Hollway, W. (1984) Women's power in heterosexual sex. *Women's Studies International Forum*, 7;1, 63–68.

Kaplan, H.S. (1977) Hypoactive sexual desire. *Journal of Sex and Marital Therapy*, 3;1, 3–9.

Kleinplatz, P.J. (2012) Is that all there is? A new critique of the goals of sex therapy. *New Directions in Sex Therapy*, Hove: Routledge, 102–118.

Madani, H.M., Asadohlahzade, A. & Mokhtari, M. (2013) Assessment of the efficacy of combination therapy with folic acid and tadalafil for the management of erectile dysfunction in men with type 2 diabetes mellitus. *Journal of Sexual Medicine*, 10;4, 1146–1150.

Masters, W. & Johnson, V.E. (1966) *Human Sexual Response*, New York: Little Brown & Co.

Masters, W. & Johnson, V.E. (1970) *Human Sexual Inadequacy*, New York: Little Brown & Co.

Pascoal, P.M., Narciso, I. & Pereira, N.M. (2012) Emotional intimacy is the best predictor of sexual satisfaction of men and women with sexual arousal problems. *International Journal of Impotence Research*, 25, 51–55.

Perel, E. (2007) *Mating in Captivity*, London: Hodder.

Pevzner, H. & Klein, S. (2016) The hot little sex pill that couldn't. *Prevention*, 87–93.

Simopoulos, E.F. & Trinidad, A.C. (2013) Make erectile dysfunction: Integrating psychopharmacology and psychotherapy. *General Hospital Psychiatry*, 35;1, 33–38.

Spurgas, A.K. (2013) Interest, arousal, and shifting diagnoses of female sexual dysfunction, or: How women learn about desire. *Studies in Gender and Sexuality*, 14, 187–205.

Štulhofer, A., Carvalheira, A.A. & Træen, B. (2013) Is responsive sexual desire for partnered sex problematic among men? Insights from a two-country study. *Sexual and Relationship Therapy*, 28;3, 246–258.

Vigoya, M.V. (2012) Sexuality and desire in racialized contexts. In: Aggleton, P., Boyce, P., Moore, H.L. & Parker, R. [eds] *Understanding Global Sexualities*, New Frontiers, London: Routledge, 218–231.

Weeks, G. & Gambescia, N. (2015) Definition, etiology and treatment of absent/low desire in women. In: Hertlein, K.M., Weeks, G.R. & Gambescia, N. [eds] *Systemic Sex Therapy*, second edition, New York: Routledge, 125–151.

Weiner, L. & Avery-Clark, C. (2017) *Sensate Focus in Sex Therapy*, New York: Routledge.

Willi, J. (1986) *Dynamics of Couple Therapy: Understanding the Potential of the Couple-Therapist Triangle*, New York: Hunter House.

Wincze, J.P. & Weisberg, R.B. (2015) *Sexual Dysfunction: A Guide for Assessment and Treatment*, third edition, New York: Guilford Press.

Zilbergeld, B. (1999) *The New Male Sexuality*, New York: Bantam.

Chapter 8

Orgasm

Orgasm is hugely misrepresented. If you believe what you see in the movies, it's an easily and simultaneously acquired essential of intercourse which generally seems expected to signal the end of lovemaking. The written media, meanwhile, tell us that getting it and giving it are necessary skills. Scientific descriptions usually define it as a peak of arousal, involving involuntary muscular contractions, feelings of release and altered perception (Levin, 2004). None of these ideas seem particularly helpful if you're anxious about orgasms or not having them when you want to.

That there's no universal definition of orgasm (King *et al*, 2011), and that many people are unsure if they've even had one, makes orgasm a mysterious and much pursued event. This brings clients to sex therapy, eager to correct their 'deficiencies'. The relevant disorders identified by the DSM are:

- Female orgasmic disorder (anorgasmia)
- Premature (early) ejaculation
- Delayed ejaculation.

Female Orgasmic Disorder (FOD)

Where once female orgasm was seen as undesirable, its lack is now often seen as dysfunctional (Butler & Byrne, 2010). Masters and Johnson (1970), though arguing that all orgasms were clitoral, helped set that ball rolling by positioning orgasm as a learned skill which can and should be controlled. The goal-orientated language often used by sex therapists endorses this; we *attain*, *reach* or *achieve* orgasm, rather than just have one. It was Freud (1905), however, who promoted the idea of 'vaginal' orgasm as superior to 'clitoral' orgasm. Research into the female orgasm subsequently focused on climax during intercourse rather than on how it was achieved, with penis-in-vagina (PiV) intercourse seen as 'proper' sex (Frith, 2015). Consequently, much research into incidence of orgasm has assumed that respondents were climaxing as a result of intercourse rather than investigating how orgasm was caused. Self-stimulation was doubtless among other ways of causing orgasm (Armstrong *et al*, 2012) which were not being recorded.

Shere Hite (1967) was the first person to conduct in-depth research with thousands of women into their sexual behaviour and preferences, establishing for the first time that nearly three-quarters of women rarely, if ever, have vaginal orgasms. Later research (Lloyd, 2005) supported the view that only a quarter of women reliably climax during intercourse.

So-called vaginal orgasm requires appropriate anatomy and enough stimulation to ensure the small, potentially arousable area on the anterior wall of the vagina (Hines, 2002) is engorged enough to respond during intercourse (Laan & Rellini, 2011). However, both this area – sometimes known as the G-spot – and form of stimulation remains highly controversial (Greenberg *et al*, 2017) and speculative (Levin, 2003). It may be absent, deeply buried, non-responsive or non-existent. Nonetheless, the *possibility* of its existence has led to expectations that women ought to be able to climax with stimulation of this area and that partners should be able to make them do so (Frith, 2015). Indeed, this possibility triumphs over evidence, so female orgasm during intercourse continues to be sought. Despite debunking the myth of the vaginal orgasm, sex therapists and sex manuals nonetheless encourage couples to experiment with different positions to enhance clitoral stimulation during penetration. Consequently, couples with healthy, satisfying sex lives still often believe they're failing if they don't both orgasm during PiV sex.

Even when orgasm is not required *during* intercourse, women are nevertheless required to be orgasmic at some point, preferably phenomenally, multiply and noisily (Potts, 2002). However, women's wish to orgasm, experience of orgasm and enactment of orgasm differs, not just between women but in the same woman at different times. What's more, their experience of what's arousing can change from moment to moment, causing confusion for partners, especially if asked to stop touch that seemed to be working well. There's a danger they can then exclude this from their repertoire of sexual techniques, often causing the woman to believe *the partner* doesn't like it. Indeed, Schnarch (1992) argues most couples have 'deficit sex', employing only the small remainder of sexual activities left once others have been excluded through perception of the partner's dislike.

Even when adequacy of stimulation is an acknowledged issue, women often still blame themselves for failure to climax (Fahs, 2011). Many experience response pressure, whereby they need to climax in order to demonstrate the sexual prowess of their partner (Nicholson & Burr, 2003). Indeed, research suggests that about 48 percent of women have faked an orgasm, compared with only 18 percent of men (Muehlenhard & Shipee, 2010). Interestingly, women who have sex with women orgasm during partnered sex more regularly than women who have sex with men (Douglas & Douglas, 1997).

While about 10 percent of women have never experienced orgasm (Graham, 2010), and 40–60 percent don't experience orgasms reliably, only about half the women who have orgasm difficulties say it distresses them (Laan & Rellini, 2011). Very few women are concerned about climaxing too soon, which may be related to post-orgasm clitoral sensitivity. Advice to pause direct touch for a few moments is often sufficient to manage this, and further orgasms may be possible if clitoral stimulation is restarted. Another way to manage this is to ensure the women climaxes just before penetration, which may then produce further orgasms, as the whole genital area – including clitoral tissue – will be engorged and sensitive.

A few women present for PST having never experienced orgasm or having difficulty climaxing with partnered sex. Many, however, just complain it takes them too long to climax or about the quality of their orgasm, citing reduced pleasure or intensity. There's some evidence that changes in hormone levels post-menopause may affect quality of orgasm, but it's often younger women who seek help. Either partner may initiate concern about the quality of the woman's orgasm, so it's important to check whether *she's* dissatisfied. She may even be experiencing the tyranny of expectations about her ability to have multiple orgasms, again often wished for by the partner. It's also thought that some women *expect* to develop sexual problems as they age (Nobre & Pinto-Gouveia, 2009). Their beliefs about sex and their body can be hugely inhibiting to all women, who may experience spectatoring during sex as they monitor their response. The overarching goals for treatment should, thus, focus on 'satisfying sex' rather than specifically mentioning orgasm.

Assessment

It's important to assess attitudes towards sex and orgasm in both partners, who may have negative beliefs which make it challenging to accept themselves as sexual. Women who have difficulty climaxing seem to be more passive during sex, have a more traditional female script and have poor knowledge of both sex in general and their own bodies (Laan & Rellini, 2011). Some don't like sex, have fears about letting go or issues with intimacy which stall orgasm; some actively dampen down their arousal.

As well as the history and nature of the problem, you should ask about any medical conditions or treatment. A number of drugs can affect orgasm, including SSRI antidepressants, hormonal contraception, antipsychotics, chemotherapy, antihypertension medication, alcohol and some recreational drugs. Pain and limited mobility may cause distraction during sex, and neurological and endocrine problems are highly implicated in arousal difficulties. Sometimes a recent issue is distracting, such as changes to the body due to surgery, pregnancy and childbirth, or incontinence.

It's surprising how often clients just assume issues are untreatable or don't make the association between their attitude to the medical issue and its effects. You also need to know what's been tried to achieve orgasm and how long is spent in stimulation, though poor technique is rarely the only cause of anorgasmia.

Treatment

Psychoeducation about female arousal and orgasm may be helpful to both partners, and both sexual and general communication will improve as they progress through Sensate Focus experiments. Learning that it's associated with rhythmic vaginal contractions, and that the clitoris is sensitive afterwards, usually helps women identify the experience, which some then describe as disappointing compared with the hullabaloo. Thus, the discrepancy between choreographed romantic sex portrayed in the media and the clumsier, messier reality makes seeking orgasm seem like just one more way to fail at lovemaking (Frith, 2015). Cognitive restructuring around beliefs, sexual scripts and expectations is, therefore, essential.

Kegel exercises improve genital awareness and can sometimes be used to tip women from arousal to orgasm. Kegels can also sometimes produce further orgasms if used just after the first climax. Women who have difficulty recognising bodily feelings in general will benefit from exercises which focus on the body and mindfulness.

Self-care and curiosity about their bodies is especially helpful when women have low self-esteem. Discussion of what contributes to feeling sexual can lead to spontaneous experiments with, say, flirting, wearing sexy clothes, getting a new hairstyle or manicure, enjoying smelling nice and feeling clean. Other self-focus exercises, including fantasy, are especially important, with particular attention paid to feelings and beliefs about self-touch and masturbation. Some women have such negative attitudes towards masturbation that self-stimulation is impossible; hand-on-hand stimulation may be acceptable, however.

When setting masturbatory experiments, emphasise the importance of adequate time and privacy. Gentle exploration, perhaps using a mirror, with no expectation of arousal, is a good start to a masturbatory programme, linking experiments to fantasy, mindfulness and self-awareness. If experimenting with arousal, encourage initial focus on the breasts, as nipple stimulation can be rapidly exciting. Early experimentation with a vibrator will also help to demonstrate that arousal is possible, though direct clitoral stimulation may be too intense initially. Never prescribe an orgasm. Experimentation with erotica and sex toys, such as different shapes and sizes of vibrator, using different levels of vibration and different types of touch, can rapidly produce orgasm. When this happens 'accidentally', it can hugely enhance confidence even if orgasm is not a new experience.

Don't encourage incorporation of sex toys into partnered experiments until the woman feels really confident to do so. Avoid mutual touch until a late stage in treatment, when satisfactory arousal/orgasm is established. Bear in mind, though, that some women are not interested in orgasm and only participate in PST to please their partner. This needs to be negotiated with the partner so that response pressure is removed and the woman's position is validated. Indeed, the woman's attitudes towards partnered stimulation always need exploration – don't assume this will be successful just because the woman is orgasmic with self-stimulation. It remains important throughout to investigate the woman's thoughts about what she experiences and to look out for expressions of distaste or negativity in either partner. Remain aware that the partner's attitude can have a major impact on the woman; for example, some men feel vibrators threaten their masculinity.

An orgasm ban can remove considerable pressure, so they can be a helpful intervention once genital touch begins or, indeed, during self-focus. That orgasm isn't required may even reduce anxiety sufficiently for a woman to engage in self-focus in the first place. Fantasy and role play can be especially helpful when she finds it difficult to let go as herself. Though shared role play may be used at some point, some women can find it helpful during Sensate Focus, masturbation and sex to fantasise that they're a different person in a different situation. Some women who've been brought up to believe sex is wrong or a woman's duty may choose fantasies involving force. Though they would never want to experience non-consensual sex in real life, the fantasy can relieve shaming feelings of choosing sex. Pretending to orgasm and acting this out, both alone and with a partner, can help overcome self-consciousness or may provide a trigger to orgasm, as can tensing and relaxing or holding and releasing breath (Heiman & LoPiccolo, 2009).

Discussing what they've learned through self-focus, as well as showing their partner how they like to be touched, may be difficult for self-conscious women, though many are proud to celebrate their progress and quickly develop a more sex-positive attitude. Help to explore embarrassment and negative thoughts may require an individual session at some point. Ultimately, it's hoped women will feel responsible for their sexual pleasure and comfortable with this.

Creative stage

Many sex therapists encourage couples to experiment with different positions to find the best way to achieve clitoral stimulation during intercourse. However, if they're including intercourse in their repertoire, it may be more helpful to just suggest trying different positions to see what they enjoy, rather than creating pressure by implying orgasm during intercourse is expected. They may, of course, ask about this themselves or look for other ways to provide clitoral stimulation during penetrative sex. Being on top allows the woman to position herself for optimal clitoral contact, while the partner is free to stimulate her breasts. Alternatively, the partner can stimulate both breasts and clitoris, or the woman can stimulate her own clitoris or breasts.

Some women find particular positions or bodily touch unexpectedly arousing, so any kind of experimentation is to be encouraged. Indeed, continue experiments with other forms of partnered and self-stimulation and, if desired, gradually phase out vibrator use. It can be used until just before orgasm, continuing with fingers and stopping use of the vibrator earlier and earlier.

Premature (early) ejaculation (EE)

Though many men would like to last longer before ejaculating, the majority who bring this problem to sex therapy don't meet DSM criteria of ejaculating within a minute of penetration three-quarters of the time, most being well within the normal range for ejaculatory response of one to 10 minutes (Brewer & Tidy, 2017). A belief that men should be able to control when they orgasm and that they should last longer is encouraged by pornography use (Wincze & Weisberg, 2015: 46–52). Nonetheless, attention is justified by feelings of dissatisfaction which are severe enough for a couple or individual to seek treatment. There's often considerable distress, with both performance anxiety and more general worry characterising their whole lives. Many couples benefit from psychoeducation, reassurance and confidence building, so it's helpful to proceed to history taking and beyond even when PE doesn't meet DSM criteria.

About 20–30 percent of men *do* meet DSM criteria (Porst, 2007), genuinely needing little or no stimulation in order to ejaculate. This has often been a lifelong problem. Recent development of EE is often associated with erectile difficulties, where the man ejaculates quickly to avoid losing his erection or over-stimulates in order to have a firmer erection. ED can also develop as a result of EE, especially when partners are upset by it or lack understanding.

EE assessment

Once again, the way the couple view the problem, and have tried to manage it, is important to know. Many men/couples have dogmatic beliefs about sex; often, only intercourse, ejaculation and orgasm are considered 'real' sex. There's also often a belief that men must not ejaculate until their partner has been 'satisfied', so partners have to speed up their orgasm. Over-focusing on a partner's pleasure, or hurrying because someone feels their partner doesn't enjoy sex, can lead to a habitual problem. It's, thus, important to know if EE also occurs when masturbating or only with a partner.

Sometimes EE develops as a result of habitually rushing masturbation due to fear of discovery – whilst sharing a bedroom, for instance. Many men with EE have grown up in an atmosphere where sex is considered dirty, selfish or generally negative. There can also be psychological consequences to genital surgery in childhood or there may be a history of sexual trauma (Maltz, 2012). Some people see EE as retribution for their sexual thoughts, arousal or behaviour (Richardson *et al*, 2005). Be on the alert for known or unconscious fears of pregnancy too.

Do check solutions that have been tried, as they are often disruptive to intimacy and pleasure, commonly including holding back, distraction, multiple condom use, frequent masturbation, refusing touch, use of alcohol/cannabis and avoiding sex altogether. Sexual avoidance can exacerbate relationship problems, with partners wondering if the man's having an affair (Brewer & Tidy, 2017).

Most men don't discuss their EE with anyone, so it grows in proportion until they feel as though they're the only person ever to experience this, and it can affect all their relationships. They can, for example, lose some of the pleasure associated with friendships as they feel unable to participate in conversations about sex. Single men may avoid new relationships, preferring casual sex (Brewer & Tidy, 2017), while those with partners report associated relationship problems. For instance, focus on their sexual performance sometimes leads to neglect of other aspects of their relationship (Phillips, 2014). Partners frequently find it difficult to discuss their own needs, and worry about hurting feelings, simply expecting to be disappointed and sometimes blaming themselves (Brewer & Tidy, 2017). On the other hand, partners can be angry and critical, complaining that the man is selfish, and exacerbating shame in them both.

A medical checkup may be helpful to rule out treatable causes or offer explanations for the EE. It's often associated with high testosterone levels, for instance, which some men find reassuring (Corona et al, 2011). Endocrine conditions, such as diabetes and hyperthyroidism (Carani et al, 2005), have also been implicated. There's an association with high alcohol and opiate use, and with pelvic pain and urological problems (Betchen, 2015). Some over-the-counter cold remedies, are also implicated. There are many more theories about the clinical causes of EE which remain unproven. There does, however, seem to be a possibility that the condition runs in families (Waldinger et al, 1988) and may not improve with age (Althof, 2014).

Medical treatment

Use of daily SSRI antidepressants can bring improvement within a matter of weeks (Waldinger, 2003), and PDE5 inhibitors are sometimes prescribed for life-long PE. Dapoxetine (Priligy) can be taken one to three hours before sex, but is contraindicated with PDE5 inhibitors and has side-effects of dizziness, headaches and nausea. Local anaesthetic cream is sometimes tried, though it can be messy. Anaesthetic sprays containing lidocaine are less messy, but can cause skin irritation and numbing. They must be washed off before oral sex and should be used with a condom for intercourse.

Psychosexual treatment

The emphasis of treatment should be on the whole sexual experience rather than focusing on ejaculation, with goals aimed at feeling more in control and relaxed. Psychoeducation is crucial for both partners, as is cognitive restructuring around unhelpful beliefs. Partners may have loss of desire or orgasm difficulties themselves if sex has become problematic or disappointing.

The PST process and Sensate Focus is often beneficial to both partners, reinstalling a sense of intimacy and confidence in the relationship and each partner's ability to be sexually expressive. Interestingly, men with EE often try to hurry the PST process, and need encouragement to take it slowly. Couples shouldn't move on from Sensate Focus I until both partners are clearly comfortable to concentrate on their own experience rather than worrying about the other.

Stop:start experiments

Many men have difficulty recognising when they are reaching the point of inevitability, beyond which ejaculation is unavoidable, so this self-focus exercise is aimed at offering more control. It should, nonetheless, be framed as experimental and not introduced until the client's anxiety about the process is beginning to reduce.

When feeling relaxed, the client should masturbate to a high state of arousal, close to the point of inevitability, and then stop. After waiting a short while, and allowing the erection to diminish a little, masturbation begins again – once again, stopping just before the point of inevitability. This process can be repeated three or four times before allowing climax. Many men find it difficult to recognise the point of inevitability at first and ejaculate unexpectedly, making it impossible to repeat the process. Advising them to anticipate this, and taking feedback about what they learned, is most helpful. They should also be advised to change the way they masturbate from their normal method, which they know will produce results, to a much slower, more unhurried method. To begin with, this slower approach can be so pleasurable that they ejaculate even sooner, but they still eventually find it easier to recognise the point of inevitability and become able to stop before reaching it.

Only once the man feels confident about the technique should it be attempted with the partner. Initially, the couple should just agree to a signal to stop any touch when he feels he's becoming very aroused. Once they have progressed to Sensate Focus II and beyond, they can proceed as the man did whilst masturbating if they both wish to. Again, a slower, more sensual approach may make it easier to recognise the point of inevitability, allowing the man to give the stop signal well in time. The couple should experiment with manual and oral stimulation and expect 'control' to vary. As control and confidence improves, and anxiety diminishes, the man or his partner can stimulate the vulva and clitoral area with the penis and become used to the sensations this produces.

Containment

If the couple wish to have intercourse, they should first experiment with placing the penis at the vaginal entrance. Penetration is prohibited until the man can recognise the point of inevitability in this position. It's as well not to tell him this is what you're waiting for, but to frame repeating the exercise as allowing confidence to build. Just inserting the tip of the penis and allowing it to rest is the next stage, which may alone result in ejaculation. Once again, the novelty – and consequent anxiety – of the experience may be responsible, and this shouldn't be regarded as a setback. Subsequently, it often works well to practise just allowing the penis to rest in the vagina after insertion, without any thrusting or movement of the partner's pelvic floor at all. Once the man is used to being inside the vagina, movement can begin, with the usual signal for the partner to stop when the man is close to the point of inevitability. The couple may want to experiment with different positions to see which are least likely to lead to EE at this stage

A similar process works for anal sex but needs to incorporate condom use, plenty of lube and preparation for the receiving anus. Resting the penis inside the anus after initial penetration is always a good idea to give it time to relax and accommodate the penis.

Men can be encouraged to practise 'edging' by enjoying high stimulation which brings them close to orgasm followed by periods of less arousing behaviour; for instance, a few short bursts of intercourse may be possible before he ejaculates. This basically continues the stop:start exercise in the couple's regular sex life but with a normalising rationale. Another approach may be to simply slow down stimulation, rather than stop it altogether, when approaching ejaculation (Betchen, 2009).

Ongoing difficulties

As a last resort, the man or partner can squeeze the shaft of the penis firmly for about 30 seconds just before reaching the point of inevitability. This reduces the erection and prevents orgasm. However, this can be painful and requires the man to be confident about recognising the point of inevitability. More importantly, if it doesn't work, or if the erection is completely lost, a potentially intimate experience has been interrupted for nothing, so it must be framed as a learning experience if clients wish to attempt it.

Treatment is likely to progress slowly when anxiety remains high in either partner or the other partner is unsupportive. Men usually believe their partner is upset by their EE, and they may indeed be very critical, but some actually dislike penetrative sex and were happier when the affected partner withdrew from intimacy. Equally, men often come to counselling at the request of their partners, rather than choosing to do so themselves, and aren't really motivated to change.

Individual clients

Stop:start and other self-focus experiments can be very helpful to individual clients, but there's no guarantee any learning will transfer successfully to partnered sex. Other work concentrates on psychoeducation, mindful awareness to improve focus and avoid negative thoughts, mood management and reduction of performance anxiety. Work on the client's resilience and resources may improve overall confidence and confidence in sexual performance. As with couples, negative attitudes towards intimacy, unhelpful beliefs and cognitive distortions also need to be addressed.

Delayed ejaculation (DE)

At the opposite end of the spectrum, DE is said to occur when, despite adequate stimulation, a man is unable to ejaculate and experience orgasm, or finds this difficult, at least three-quarters of the time. It has been described as the least common and least understood of male sexual problems (Perelman, 2014), but it may be significantly under-reported. It's more common in younger men in longer relationships and *may* be less common among gay men (Jern *et al*, 2010). Some couples view it as the man having good 'staying power' or it just isn't a cause of distress. PST may be sought when the couple want to have a baby and ejaculation is necessary.

It's thought that lack of confidence and/or anxiety distracts the man from erotic cues. However, there have been many theories about men being angry and with-holding, fearing defiling the woman with their sperm, fear of vaginas, fear of pregnancy, shame, sexual guilt, previous sexual abuse and poor relationship. It's also possible that some men may not be particularly aroused, despite their erec-tion, and find it difficult to climax as a result. Self-consciousness is also inhib-iting, so that even one episode of DE can produce performance anxiety. Men and women consequently fake orgasm to avoid embarrassment or end stressful or unenjoyable sexual encounters.

DE assessment

Both partners may become injured or exhausted by lengthy intercourse, so an agreement about how long it's reasonable to continue may be urgently needed. Find out exactly what's happening and upsetting each of the couple. Partners may feel unattractive or worried there's an affair. Focus on pregnancy or the partner's (missing) orgasm may make the man even more anxious about performance. Sometimes a man *is* ejaculating, but is concerned about the volume or strength of the ejaculate and/or the pleasure he's experiencing may have changed (Perelman, 2014). The history and circumstances of the problem are important to ascertain.

Failure to ejaculate may be situation-specific – such as during intercourse – occasional or constant, even occurring during masturbation, though this general-ised type only occurs in about a quarter of those affected (McMahon, 2013). DE can be associated with some neurological conditions, including spinal cord injury and multiple sclerosis, diabetes, pelvic surgery or urological disease. It's impor-tant to have clinical investigations to rule out organic causes of DE, though there are sometimes obvious clinical factors, such as prostate surgery which can cause retrograde ejaculation (see Chapter 11) and orgasm still occurs. Medication can be implicated, including antidepressants, antipsychotics, antihypertensives, antiadr-energics and antiulcer medication. Recreational drugs have also been associated with DE, especially amphetamines, cocaine, cannabis and alcohol.

A thorough exploration of the relationship and level of attraction is needed. There may be covert issues with sexuality, an affair, relationship conflict or the relationship may feel unsuitable or taboo for some reason. Ask about the way the couple make love and whether the man is getting adequate stimulation before intercourse. The presence of an erection doesn't necessarily mean the man's aroused.

There may be a great deal of unhelpful thinking. For instance, he may find it difficult to let go or lose control in other areas of life as well and be highly focused on getting things right. There are often limiting discourses around pleas-ing partners and how a 'real man' should be. A perceived lack of vaginal tightness or other changes in a partner's body following weight gain, surgery, menopause, pregnancy or childbirth may be involved. The man may also be self-conscious about his own body. Performance anxiety, especially when accompanied by the partner's criticism, may significantly inhibit arousal.

Sometimes, dormitories, shared bedrooms or fear of discovery encourage boys to hurry masturbation and/or to get used to using unusual methods, such as squeezing or rolling the penis or rubbing it against the bed. Indeed, an idiosyncratic masturbatory style, which is not easily reproduced by the partner, is probably the most common reason for DE (Perelman, 2014). Many men are too embarrassed to convey their masturbatory preferences to their partner anyway.

As well as enquiring about frequency and method of masturbation, do find out if it's accompanied by pornography use. The images being viewed may be so unusual that it's unlikely they can be reproduced, even in role play. Repeated extraordinary fantasy can make real-life sex seem a bit dull. Some men get used to using internet porn regularly for relaxation and stress relief so that partnered sex becomes much less exciting. If it seems there's dependency on porn, it may be necessary to refer for treatment before attempting PST (see Chapter 15).

DE treatment

Frequently, men with DE find it difficult to concentrate on their own pleasure and fear being selfish. Their focus on orgasm can also be hard to shift. A non-judgemental, accepting approach is especially important for those who've found masturbation more satisfying than partnered sex. For them, a complete sex ban is important to allow space to explore non-demand intimacy rather than performance, and to let deeper intimacy and mutuality develop. In this case, the ban on masturbation and pornography may be more important than banning partnered sex, though the break will allow both partners to reconnect with sensuality and their relationship. Cognitive restructuring, including exploration of discourses and sexual scripts, may be important for both partners to develop a compassionate and non-judgemental approach to their sexual expression, a process which begins during history taking.

The Sensate Focus programme should be taken slowly. Masturbatory experiments should be avoided before Sensate Focus II when there is evidence of arousal with the partner. Meanwhile, Kegel exercises may help to improve genital awareness, and exercises focusing on mindful awareness of feelings and senses may be helpful. A different, more conventional stroking motion can be encouraged if masturbation is later introduced as part of the man's self-focus programme. The use of lube and/or condoms may help to change the masturbation technique. Internet pornography should still be avoided, trying to make fantasy as realistic as possible. It's important to take detailed feedback about the way this and partnered experiments are being experienced. Sometimes men are ashamed to admit they're not feeling aroused or that they've continued to use pornography.

Many couples enjoy the sense of connection and intimacy developed in Sensate Focus and both become less focused on orgasm. If there's still distress late in the process, yet the man feels close to climax, orgasmic triggers may be needed, such as holding and releasing the breath or tensing and relaxing muscles. Intercourse shouldn't be attempted until ejaculation and orgasm are being reliably experienced in other forms of partnered sex, unless the couple are now satisfied with the idea of sex without ejaculation/orgasm. Accepting that this isn't necessary every time may also be liberating prior to reinstating intercourse.

Unless the partner has issues which require a tentative approach, progress to full intercourse may proceed more rapidly than with other sexual problems. However, there should be considerable arousal before intercourse, as some couples continue to see any sexual excitement or an erection as evidence that intercourse is appropriate.

Perhaps the most important conversation with couples affected by DE will be aimed at dispelling the idea that sex is only good enough if it concludes with intercourse and orgasm. Reminding couples that a satisfactory experience can be had without either may not be needed as the PST process progresses, yet some couples hang onto the belief that sex isn't complete without intercourse and ejaculation. Usually, this is due to remaining self-blame, either about failure to climax or to be a sufficiently arousing partner. In this case, it may be necessary to slow the process further and spend more time on feedback and the clients' ability to appreciate what *is* working well.

References

Althof, S.E. (2014) Treatment of premature ejaculation. In: Binik, Y.M. & Hall, K.S.K. [eds] *Principles and Practice of Sex Therapy*, fifth edition, New York: Guilford Press, 112–137.

Armstrong, E.A., England, P. & Fogarty, A.C.K. (2012) Accounting for women's orgasm and sexual enjoyment in college hook-ups and relationships. *American Sociological Review*, 77;3, 435–462.

Betchen, S.J. (2009) Premature ejaculation: An integrative, inter systems approach for couples, *Journal of Family Psychotherapy*, 20;2–3, 1–30.

Betchen, S.J. (2015) Premature ejaculation. In: Hertlein, K.M., Weeks, G.R. & Gambescia, N. [eds] *Systemic Sex Therapy*, second edition, New York: Routledge, 90–106.

Brewer, G. & Tidy, P. (2017) Premature ejaculation: Therapist perspectives. *Sexual & Relationship Therapy*, 32;1, 22–35.

Butler, C. & Byrne, A. (2010) Culture, sex and sexuality. In: Butler, C., O'Donovan, A. & Shaw, E. [eds] *Sex, Sexuality and Therapeutic Practice*, Hove: Routledge.

Carani, C., Isidori, A.M. & Granata, A. (2005) Multicenter study on the prevalence of sexual symptoms in male hypo- and hyperthyroid patients. *Journal of Clinical Endocrinology & Metabolism*, 90, 6472–6479.

Corona, G., Jannini, E.A. & Lotti, F. (2011) Premature and delayed ejaculation: Two ends of a single continuum influenced by hormonal milieu. *International Journal of Andrology*, 34, 41–48.

Douglas, M. & Douglas, L. (1997) *Are We Having Fun Yet?* New York: Hyperion.

Fahs, B. (2011) *Performing Sex: The Making and Unmaking of Women's Erotic Lives*, Albany, NY: SUNY Press.

Freud, S. (1905) Three essays on the theory of sexuality. In: Strachey, J. [ed] *Complete Works of Sigmund Freud*, standard edition, London: Hogarth Press.

Frith, H. (2015) *Orgasmic Bodies*, Basingstoke: Palgrave Macmillan.

Graham, C.A. (2010) The DSM criteria for female orgasmic disorder. *Archives of Sexual Behavior*, 31, 256–270.

Greenberg, J, S., Bruess, C.E. & Oswalt, S.B. (2017) *Exploring the Dimensions of Human Sexuality*, sixth edition, Burlington, MA: Jones & Bartlett.

Heiman, J.R. & LoPiccolo, J. (2009) *Becoming Orgasmic*, London: Piatkus.

Hines, T.M. (2002) The G-spot. *American Journal of Obstetrics and Gynecology*, 187, 520.

Hite, S. (1967) *The Hite Report*, New York: Dell.

Jern, P., Santtila, P., Johannson, A., Alanko, K., Salo, B. & Sandnabba, N.K. (2010) Is there an association between same-sex sexual experience and ejaculatory dysfunction? *Journal of Sex & Marital Therapy*, 36;4, 303–332.

King, R., Belsky, J., Mah, K. & Binik, Y. (2011) Are there different types of female orgasm? *Archives of Sexual Behavior*, 40, 865–875.

Laan, E. & Rellini, A.H. (2011) Can we treat anorgasmia in women? The challenge to experiencing pleasure. *Sexual & Relationship Therapy*, 26;4, 329–341.

Levin, R.J. (2003) The G-spot – Reality or illusion? *Sexual & Relationship Therapy*, 18;1, 117–119.

Levin, R.J. (2004) An orgasm is . . . who defines what an orgasm is? *Sexual & Relationship Therapy*, 19;1, 101–107.

Lloyd, E.A. (2005) *The Case of the Female Orgasm: Bias in the Science of Evolution*, Cambridge, MA: Harvard University Press.

Maltz, W. (2012) Healing the sexual repercussions of sexual abuse. In: Kleinplatz, P.J. [ed] *New Directions in Sex Therapy*, second edition, Hove: Routledge, 267–284.

Masters, W. & Johnson, V.E. (1970) *Human Sexual Inadequacy*, New York: Little Brown & Co.

McMahon, C. (2013) Taxonomy of ejaculatory disorders and definitions of premature ejaculation. In: Jannino, E., McMahon, C. & Waldinger, M. [eds] *Premature Ejaculation: From Etiology to Diagnosis and Treatment*, Milan: Springer-Verlag, 53–69.

Muehlenhard, C.L. & Shipee, S.K. (2010) Men's and women's reports of pretending orgasm. *Journal of Sex Research*, 47;6, 552–567.

Nicholson, P. & Burr, J. (2003) What is 'normal' about women's (hetero)sexual desire and orgasm? A report of an in-depth interview study. *Social Science and Medicine*, 57, 1735–1745.

Nobre, P.J. & Pinto-Gouveia, J. (2009) Cognitive schemas associated with negative sexual events: A comparison of men and women with and without sexual dysfunction. *Archives of Sexual Behavior*, 38, 842–851.

Perelman, M. (2014) Delayed ejaculation. In: Binik, Y.M. & Hall, K.S.K. [eds] *Principles and Practice of Sex Therapy*, fifth edition, New York: Guilford Press, 138–155.

Phillips, R. (2014) Premature ejaculation and female sexual satisfaction. *Nature Reviews Urology*, 11, 304.

Porst, H., Montorsi, F., Rosen, R.C., Gaynor, L., Grupe, S. & Alexander, J. (2007) The premature ejaculation prevalence and attitudes (PEPA) survey: Prevalence, comorbidities and professional help seeking. *European Urology*, 51, 816–824.

Potts, A. (2002) *The Science/Fiction of Sex*, Hove: Routledge.

Richardson, D., Wood, K. & Goldmeier, D. (2005) Premature ejaculation: Does county of origin tell us anything about etiology? *The Journal of Sexual Medicine*, 2, 508–512.

Schnarch, D. (1992) *Constructing the Sexual Crucible*, New York: W.W. Norton.

Waldinger, M.D. (2003) Rapid ejaculation. In: Levine, S., Risen, C. & Althof, S. [eds] *Handbook of Clinical Sexuality for Mental Health Professionals*, New York: Brunner/ Routledge, 257–274.

Waldinger, M.D., Rietschel, M., Nothen, M. M., Hengeveld, M.W. & Oliver, B. (1988) Relevance of methodological design for the interpretation of efficacy of drug treatment of premature ejaculation: A systematic review and meta-analysis. *International Journal of Impotence Research*, 16, 1–13.

Wincze, J.P. & Weisberg, R.B. (2015) Premature (early) ejaculation. In: *Sexual Dysfunction*, third edition, New York: Guilford, 46–52.

Chapter 9

Sexual pain

There are numerous clinical reasons for genital pain, including interstitial cystitis, urinary tract infection, atrophic vaginitis, pelvic inflammatory disease, endometriosis, candida, childbirth and vulvodynia. In some of these, pain is independent of sex and may be intermittent or constant, while some conditions only cause pain during arousal and/or intercourse. Negative beliefs and/or fears about sex, tampon use and childbirth often develop as a result of horror stories told by relatives and friends. They can lead to anxiety, inability to relax and muscle tension.

Pain inevitably has psychological consequences. It makes sense to avoid doing something that hurts, to fear being hurt and to, thus, be hypervigilant for signs of pain. It's also natural to feel exhausted and depressed by the management of pain. Psychosocial help with this is entirely appropriate. However, because these ways of responding to pain are treated as pathological, many people are offered psychiatric or psychosexual referrals rather than referral to the appropriate medical professional – gynaecologist, urologist, dermatologist or pain specialist. It's important to encourage clients to continue to seek medical investigation, if only for reassurance. It's pointless and unethical for us to use approaches which help clients to tolerate unnecessary pain and disruption to their lives and self-image when clinical solutions may exist.

Chronic pelvic pain

Pain in the lower abdomen and pelvis, lasting for more than six months with no apparent organic cause, is considered chronic pelvic pain. Pain can be intermittent or continuous and can change in relation to physical and mental fatigue, depression and anxiety (Kaya *et al*, 2006). Some women experience pelvic pain associated with arousal, which is highly aversive and can result in dyspareunia and vaginismus. *Mittelshmertz* is pain associated with ovulation. As this may be the time when some women feel desire, the mid-cycle pain may seem like punishment for desire or caused by desire.

About one-fifth of men experience pelvic or genital pain, usually in the perineum or penis, but it may appear anywhere in the pelvic area and genitals and may come and go. Ejaculatory pain and erectile dysfunction are common, as are

urinary symptoms. Sufferers often seem to be high achievers in stress
tions (Luzzi, 2003). Though urinary tract or prostate inflammation/infe
be implicated, diagnosis may be difficult. Many men experience years o1
or intermittent pain, despite no history of trauma and no evidence of in1
Dyspareunia is often associated with tight foreskin, leading to balanitis, a sore,
itchy penis.

Genito-pelvic pain/penetration disorder

This diagnosis first appeared in DSM 5, encompassing both vaginismus (difficulty
with penetration) and dyspareunia (painful intercourse), as they are so closely
connected. It involves:

- Difficulty with vaginal penetration when PiV sex is attempted
- Genital or pelvic pain during attempts at intercourse
- Fear of pain as a result of penetration
- Tensing or tightening of the pelvic floor muscles during intercourse attempts
- The development of vulvodynia, also associated with prescribed hormones,
  such as in the contraceptive pill or HRT, and use of creams for thrush.

Vulvodynia is a condition in which chronic burning pain is felt in the vulval area,
near the entrance to the vagina. Provoked vestibulodynia is burning pain around
the vaginal entrance brought on by some sort of touch, such as tampon insertion,
caressing or intercourse. Nerve endings in the area multiply and are more sensitive. Sometimes there are pelvic floor abnormalities, though these may develop
as a result of the condition. Discomfort caused by touching the area gently with a
cotton bud is highly suggestive of vulvodynia.

People tend to do better when partners are understanding and caring, stopping
intercourse/touch as soon as there is any pain (Rosen et al, 2014). Significantly,
partners of women with vaginismus are often extremely supportive, are not pushy,
and may have problems like early ejaculation or erectile difficulties themselves,
though it's unclear whether these develop as a result of the partner's pain. Nonetheless, women often present individually, seeing the issue as solely their problem,
possibly having struggled with it for many years before the current relationship.
However, therapy is much more likely to be successful when both partners are
involved (Meana et al, 2015).

Often, the person doesn't believe their pain can be controlled. Their anxiety
then distracts them away from pleasure and towards hypervigilance (Desrochers et al, 2009). Any suggestion of pain may cause panic, so sexual avoidance
is common (Vlaeyen & Linton, 2000) and partners may avoid or hurry sex.
Ironically, though the partner with pain may appreciate this, it can create additional tension as well as making them feel undesirable or a nuisance. This can
affect self-image, leading to generalised depression and anxiety (Desrochers
et al, 2009).

Assessment

Many more people are thought to experience genital and pelvic pain than ever report it. They may think there's no help available or be embarrassed to seek treatment. Consequently, there's a high chance of pain being presented 'accidently' when taking a PST history. You'll need considerable detail about the pain in order to have any idea about the way it interferes with sex and any underlying associations this may have. For instance, someone who experiences deep genital pain on arousal, and was brought up on negative stories about sex, may be much harder to treat than someone with a clearly physical reason for pain, such as recurrent infection or scarring. You'll need descriptions of how the pain feels (burning, stabbing, aching, gripey, for instance), where it is and what triggers it. For example, does it only show up during intercourse, during any kind of touch, when aroused, after sex, during tampon insertion or genital examination?

Clients can present with a feeling that PST is their last resort or they may have little faith in the process, having been let down many times before. It's important to ascertain what they want from PST and what they see as the main problem. It may be that the most important change would be to the relationship itself, which they may feel has suffered. Sometimes, self-doubt is the major issue, or a feeling of not being understood. For some, *any* improvement in sex and intimacy would be welcome.

You need to know how the issues have been managed so far, whether one or both feel they're more responsible for the problem, whether it feels out of control, how they've coped with this, and their attitude to the problem and each other. Ask about any times when the pain isn't there, what helps/makes matters worse, whether they have any exacerbating medical conditions or have had previous treatment.

As with other sexual problems, sexual pain can act as an intimacy regulator or legitimise avoidance of unwanted sex. Indeed, there are numerous reasons why people may, consciously or unconsciously, have an investment in continuing the problem (Meana *et al*, 2015). There may even be an unrevealed history of physical, sexual, or psychological abuse contributing to sex and intimacy issues, though this is by no means always the case.

It's understandable that vaginismus would develop in response to pain, but it can also develop on its own, often when there's been a health issue involving the genital area, such as being catheterised, bad experiences trying to use tampons, a tough hymen or someone becoming sexually active before they were ready.

Medical treatment

Medical opinion should always be sought to rule out pathology and see what help is available, though women may have numerous gynaecology referrals with no resolution. Others may have had bad experiences, such as a lack of understanding about their pain. In cases of vulvodynia or other skin conditions, a dermatologist may be more helpful than a gynaecologist.

Locally applied anaesthetic cream, such as Lidocaine, may be useful, and it's also beneficial during flare-ups of herpes. Botulinum toxin (Nazik *et al*, 2014) and electrostimulation are among other therapies with reportedly good results. Physiotherapy may help women to regain control of the pelvic floor. However, they need to be sufficiently relaxed to allow examination.

PST treatment

Daily vulval massage, which involves gentle, light, rotational touch using a lubricated finger, is often suggested. Women who're afraid that any touch will be painful benefit from self-focus exercises involving genital exploration, introduced gradually, with the extent of touch appropriate to their level of tolerance. Sitting well-supported with knees bent, they can begin by just observing the vulva using a hand mirror. Initially, they may notice the vulva seems very tense but, given time, they'll relax. Gently touching the area around the vaginal entrance whilst contracting and relaxing the pelvic floor shows them the muscles which tighten when they 'guard' during penetration attempts.

Clients may want to keep a diary of their thoughts and feelings during these experiments. Not only does this provide a record of progress, but also demonstrates fears and unhelpful thinking which can be addressed in therapy. They may also wish to keep a pain or arousal diary, logging the type and quality of pain, how it was provoked, whether and how it resolved, plus thoughts that preceded, accompanied and followed the pain. When this sort of detail demonstrates a pattern of thoughts and behaviours, clients can see for themselves what needs to change. They may identify their own experiments and be more likely to collaborate in experiment setting.

Whilst it's useful to identify the muscles involved in vaginismus, Kegel exercises only exacerbate the problem. **Reverse Kegels** can be helpful, however, using the following steps:

- Advise clients to lie down and begin deep breathing, as this helps to relax the pelvic floor
- As they breathe, they should notice the feeling of their body against the floor or bed, being particularly aware of their lower back
- When this feels comfortable, they can push the lower back downwards towards the floor, trying not to tilt the pelvis or move the spine
- This should be repeated five times, whilst visualising the muscles of the pelvic floor stretching with each in-breath.

Take feedback about how the experiment goes and any thoughts and feelings experienced. It can be varied by increasing the time spent doing the exercise, building up the number of times it's done and standing, leaning against the wall or sitting. Some people will be able to start with far more than five pushes, but just a handful may be as much as very anxious clients can manage. Introducing these differences individually, and later in a variety of combinations, helps to suggest progress and prevent boredom. This is very slow work.

When the client is comfortable with looking at and touching her genitals, they may wish to try inserting a lubricated finger. Start with just the tip of the little finger and progress gradually to larger fingers and more than one finger. Eventually, they may feel comfortable transferring this into joint exercises and borrowing their partner's fingers. They should initially insert the fingers themselves and only allow the partner to try this when they feel entirely comfortable about doing this themselves. The exception would be when the client has a deep aversion to self-touch or there's a religious or cultural prohibition to it. In this case, they may prefer their partner to do all the touch experiments. If so, they may be comfortable guiding the partner themselves. An alternative is to use vaginal trainers, which are washable silicone tubes of different sizes to use instead of fingers. There are also contoured overnight trainers which can be left in whilst asleep. Though many women are reassured by the ability to insert the trainers, others find them off-putting, so it's generally helpful to suggest fingers first.

Partners should also be doing self-focus experiments. Even if they have no apparent sexual problem – though they often do – they can do mindfulness exercises, Kegels, their own looking and touching exercises, and keep their own logs of thoughts and feelings. Sensate Focus should be started gradually if the couple haven't been sexual recently, trying Pre-Sensate exercises to begin with. These may not include touch at all initially, but may start with communication exercises or ways to express sexuality. Women with vaginismus often enjoy non-penetrative sex and are regularly orgasmic, however, so they may enjoy Sensate Focus from the beginning whilst both partners simultaneously experiment with self-focus.

Containment

If the client has been able to introduce fingers into the vagina and wants to attempt intercourse, this should be treated as experimental and, as usual, taken slowly. They should first be comfortable and relaxed having a penis touch the vulva and able to maintain arousal when it nears the vagina. Early experiments should just involve the tip of the penis. If the woman is astride, they can control depth of entry. The partner should be instructed not to thrust, but to stay as still as possible. This allows the woman control of shallow movement or full penetration and no movement.

The aim on the first occasion should be just to insert the tip so she can assess this and consider what she'd like to try next. If she wants to proceed with insertion at any stage, she should be advised to pause before any movement begins. This allows the vagina to relax and accommodate the penis.

If the couple feel a containment experiment goes badly, focus on what's been learned and how to utilise this information. In reality, most couples are highly satisfied with their progress long before containment is considered, so they usually approach it with a high level of confidence. This is all the more likely if you're realistic about the potential for anxiety whilst focusing on the gains already made.

Keep in mind that women with genital pain often have difficulty describing feelings (Ciocca et al, 2013), so they may need prompting or encouragement to help them express themselves. Some therapists have a bowl of descriptive words – laminated on card – to assist with this. The most important quality the therapist can have is patience. Often, the slower the start to this sort of work, the more rapid the progress. Therapeutic ruptures need to be addressed as soon as possible, as damage to the therapeutic alliance is particularly likely to disrupt trust and progress. Though many partners are kind and understanding, they also need support and encouragement and to understand the potential damage of complaining about the speed of treatment.

Anal sex

Some couples require assistance with difficult anal sex. Though it's relatively common among men and women, and should not be assumed to be painful (Hollows, 2007), it's nonetheless thought that 10–15 percent of men who have anal sex with men experience pain. Fear of pain, injury, infection or faecal accidents are among the psychological barriers to relaxation – which is crucial, as the external sphincter is liable to tighten on entry attempts. High arousal, anal foreplay to promote relaxation and sufficient water-based lubrication are essential for successful penetration (Damon & Rosser, 2005). It helps to be comfortable with the insertion of fingers, and some people like to wear a butt plug for a few hours beforehand to allow the rectum to relax.

As with vaginal penetration, the penis should rest for a while after insertion to allow for relaxation. Ensuring penetration is slow and gentle may be more achievable with the recipient on top. Initial mild discomfort is common, but actual pain is a reason to stop. It's usually caused by muscular tension, which makes the anal sphincters contract more in response to thrusting.

Clients shouldn't have anal sex if they have haemorrhoids, sores or warts around the anus, as pain and infection are more likely. If anal penetration with a penis or strap-on isn't possible, they can still enjoy anal play using fingers, tongue and sex toys. Sex toys should be well washed between use, a dental dam used for oral sex, and a well-lubricated finger cot is advisable to facilitate comfortable digital penetration. Condoms should always be worn for penetration, and clients mustn't switch from anal to vaginal sex without changing their condom and/or washing.

Persistent Genital Arousal (PGA)

Thought to be a sub-type of vulvodynia, PGA is experienced as uncomfortable, unwanted genital sensation that persists for an extended period of hours, days, months or longer, and may be continuous or come and go (Jackowich *et al*, 2018). Congestion, tingling and wetness is usually felt in the vulval area but may also be in the pubic bone or anal area, sometimes accompanied by genital contractions or feelings of imminent orgasm (Goldmeier *et al*, 2014). It's usually unrelated to subjective feelings of sexual desire and isn't relieved by orgasm. Throbbing spontaneous pain may also occur in the vulva, vagina and clitoris (Leiblum *et al*, 2007). It may be triggered by intercourse, orgasm, clothing or there may be no stimulus at all. Sometimes it's triggered by the initiation or withdrawal of antidepressants (Leiblum *et al*, 2007). Some people have episodes of multiple orgasm which they can't bring to an end.

Though PGA is more common in women, it can affect men too (Kruger & Hartmann, 2016; Kamatchi & Ashley-Smith, 2013). Men seem more likely to seek medical solutions, whereas women may consider PST instead/as well. Men may present for PST because their GP hasn't heard of PGA. Clients frequently haven't heard of it either and may feel embarrassed and isolated by it. Consequently, they often present by themselves, with partners sometimes unaware there's a problem.

Psychoeducation and a containing, normalising approach are hugely important. Cognitive restructuring around the effect of the condition on life and self-image can be helpful, along with mindfulness and distraction techniques (Goldmeier *et al*, 2014), guided imagery and relaxation. Sufficient sleep makes coping and anxiety management easier, but some people are kept awake by needing to urinate or restless leg syndrome, both of which seem to be associated with PGA (Pink *et al*, 2014).

Medical interventions are normally aimed at alleviating anxiety and neuropathic pain, so Pregabalin is often the drug of choice as it does both (Kamatchi & Ashley-Smith, 2013). Alternatively, antidepressants and tranquillisers may be prescribed. More extreme interventions include ECT, use of TENS or a periclitoral nerve block with Botulinum toxin (Nazik *et al*, 2014).

Relationship work

All the conditions involving sexual or genital discomfort and pain can affect relationships. Often, partners don't understand the debilitating and disabling effect of the pain or how anxiety provoking it can be. Sometimes they think their partner is just trying to avoid sex or that the pain isn't as bad as they 'pretend', particularly if the partner has, until recently, endured pain without complaint to please them or to make themselves feel more normal. Concern about a partner's pain can be highly aversive and sometimes the person with pain feels so undesired and different that relationship conflict develops. The PST programme gives the couple a chance to reconnect with intimacy and to experiment with what works for them sexually using the skills of a supportive therapist.

This chapter has discussed pain which originates or occurs in the genital and pelvic area. Chapter 10 considers female genital cutting and its effects on sex.

References

Ciocca, G., Limoncin, E. & Di Tommaso, S. (2013) Alexithymia and vaginismus: A preliminary correlation perspective. *International Journal of Impotence Research*, 25, 113–116.

Damon, W. & Rosser, B.R. (2005) Anodyspareunia in men who have sex with men: Prevalence, predictors, consequences and the development of DSM criteria. *Journal of Sex & Marital Therapy*, 31;2, 129–141.

Desrochers, G., Bergeron, S., Khalifé, S., Dupuis, M-J. & Jodoin, M. (2009) Fear, avoidance and self-efficacy in relation to pain and sexual impairment in women with provoked vestibulodynia. *Clinical Journal of Pain*, 25;6, 520–527.

Goldmeier, D., SadeghiNehad, H. & Facelle, T.M. (2014) Persistent genital arousal disorder. In: Binik, Y.M. & Hall, S.K. [eds] *Principles and Practice of Sex Therapy*, fifth edition, New York: Guilford Press, 263–279.

Hollows, K. (2007) Anodyspareunia: A novel sexual dysfunction? An exploration into anal sexuality. *Sexual and Relationship Therapy*, 22;4, 429–443.

Jackowich, R., Pink, L. & Gordon, A. (2018) Symptom characteristics and medical history of an online sample of women who experience symptoms of persistent genital arousal. *Journal of Sex & Marital Therapy*, 44;2, 111–126.

Kamatchi, R. & Ashley-Smith, A. (2013) Persistent genital arousal disorder in a male: A case report and analysis of the cause. *British Journal of Medical Practitioners*, 6;1, a605. www.bjmp.org/content/persistent-genital-arousal-disorder-male-case-report-and-analysis-cause. Accessed June 20, 2019.

Kaya, B. *et al* (2006) Anxiety, depression and sexual dysfunction in women with chronic pelvic pain. *Sexual & Relationship Therapy*, 21;2, 187–296.

Kruger, T.H.C. & Hartmann, U. (2016) A case of comorbid persistent genital arousal disorder and premature ejaculation: Killing two birds with one stone. *Journal of Sex & Marital Therapy*, 42;1, 1–3.

Leiblum, S.R. (2007) Persistent genital arousal disorder: Perplexing, distressing and unrecognised. In: *Principles and Practice of Sex Therapy*, New York: Guilford, 54–83.

Luzzi, G. (2003) Male genital pain disorders. *Sexual & Relationship Therapy*, 18;2, 225–325.

Meana, M., Maykut, C. & Fertel, E. (2015) Painful intercourse. In: Hertlein, K.M., Weeks, G.R. & Gambescia, N. [eds] *Systemic Sex Therapy*, second edition, New York: Routledge, 191–210.

Nazik, H., Api, M., Aytan, H. & Narin, R. (2014) A new medical treatment with Botulinum toxin in persistent genital arousal disorder: Successful treatment of two cases. *Journal of Sex & Marital Therapy*, 40;3, 170–174.

Pink, L., Rancourt, V. & Gordon, A. (2014) Persistent genital arousal in women with pelvic and genital pain. *Canadian Journal of Obstetrics and Gynaecology*, 36;4, 324–330.

Rosen, N.O. *et al* (2014) Impact of male partner responses on sexual function in women with vulvodynia and their partners: A dyadic daily experience study. *Health Psychology*, 33;8, 823–831.

Vlaeyen, J.W. & Linton, S.J. (2000) Fear-avoidance and its consequences in chronic musculoskeletal pain: A state of the art. *Pain*, 85, 317–332.

Chapter 10

Female genital cutting

Female genital cutting (FGC) refers to 'deliberate injury to the female genital organs for non-medical reasons' (WHO, 2019). FGC is common in more than 30 countries and currently thought to affect more than 200 million women and girls, with three million cut every year (WHO, 2019). Nine out of 10 women and girls in Djibouti, Egypt, Guinea, Mali, Northern Sudan, Sierra Leone and Somalia undergo the procedure (Yoder & Kahn, 2008). FGC is also practised in other parts of Africa, the Middle East and Asia. Though illegal since 1985, it still sometimes happens to UK girls, some of whom are taken abroad to be cut (Berg & Dennison, 2013), with about 137,000 affected women in England and Wales alone (Macfarlane & Dorkenoo, 2015). It's therefore important to ask all women with heritage from the countries where cutting is practised about any surgery or procedures to the genitals, especially as some present for PST without mentioning cutting. Couples may not use English phrases to describe FGC and may not know there are different types of the procedure. It can be helpful to laminate drawings of the different types to help the woman/couple to establish what's been done. The support group Daughters of Eve (www.dofeve.org) has pictures, and is a phenomenal resource for clients.

As well as sexual difficulties, reasons for seeking help may include pain, infection, body image and feeling different. It's important to establish what the woman/couple wish to achieve and whether they already know about the available options. It's helpful to develop a relationship with local gynaecological/urological/plastic surgery/specialist FGC services in order to offer effective information and appropriate referral. Sometimes sex therapy is offered as part of a multidisciplinary approach in specialist clinics.

Women may want to consider their options and seek surgical repair before considering PST, and you can be helpful in discussing what's available. You may see someone who's already had some reparative surgery who doesn't mention this unless asked. It's then helpful to contact the surgeon to find out what's been done and what's now possible.

The client's wishes determine whether, when and where it's appropriate to refer. They may present for treatment of medical conditions and not wish to have PST. Women with Type III cutting may, for instance, need surgery to free their genitalia, treat and prevent health problems. Some women have painful fibrosed nerve tissue (neuromas) at the clitoral site, which requires surgical removal (Abdulcadir *et al*, 2017; Berg & Dennison, 2013).

Box 10.1   *Types of female genital cutting*

- Type I (clitoridectomy) involves removing all or part of the external clitoris.
- In type II (excision), all of the clitoris, the labia minora and, sometimes, the labia majora are cut away.
- Type III (infibulation) narrows the vaginal opening by cutting and sewing the labia to form a seal. The clitoris and inner labia are not always removed, but the procedure has major health implications as the remaining opening is often so small that even urination is difficult and trapped menstrual blood can cause pain and infection. The woman may need to be cut to have intercourse and will need to be cut to give birth.
- Type IV refers to any other procedures causing damage to the female genitals, including pricking, piercing, cutting, packing, scraping or burning.

Many women wish to have clitoral reconstruction in order to feel normal or because they believe it's necessary for sexual stimulation. However, many opt not to have surgery following counselling/PST (Merckelbagh *et al*, 2015). For those who do, this is a relatively simple half-hour procedure which can be performed under local anaesthetic, though general anaesthetic may be preferred to prevent retraumatisation.

As well as the medical consequences of removing sensitive tissue and the long-term compromise to hygiene caused by some versions of the procedure, the psychological trauma associated with genital cutting is immense. Cutting is often sanctioned or performed by trusted family members, which may considerably exacerbate distress, resulting in post-traumatic stress disorder, anxiety, somatization, phobia and low self-esteem (Buggio *et al*, 2019). Assessment of trauma is crucial; trauma therapies such as EMDR may be helpful before decisions are made about treatment paths.

When clients decide not to proceed with any treatment, it's important for therapists not to push their own solutions or behave as though they know more about the client's situation than they do. Some affected women are, understandably, very angry about what's happened to them and resist the idea that they can have anything like a 'normal' life as a result. Nonetheless, the options they have should be discussed and the door left open should they wish to access support in future. Sometimes, they may just want someone to talk to.

Sexual pleasure

The outcome of treatment to improve sexual response depends on the type of cutting, age of cutting, how 'well' this was done and the current condition of the genitals. It's been established that, as clitoral tissue remains following cutting, women are capable of desire, arousal and orgasm (Abdulcadir *et al*, 2016). The clitoral stump may be adequate to provide sexual stimulation unless there's very severe scarring in the area (Catania *et al*, 2007), and stimulation of the vulva, G spot and cervix may also produce arousal and orgasm.

It's important to offer hope and to explain the potential for sexual pleasure, but it's vital to listen to the woman's concerns and what she wants; sexual pleasure may be highly important or of no interest at all. Her beliefs about what's happened, sexual education and skilled lovemaking also influence satisfactory sexual response. A study of Egyptian women (Thabet & Thabet, 2003) found no loss of sexual function in those who'd undergone Type I cutting, but most studies support the view that cutting inevitably causes some sort of sexual dysfunction (Ismail *et al*, 2017). Women in countries where cutting is practised tend to report difficult, painful sex, anorgasmia, loss of desire and sexual avoidance (Oyefara, 2015). This may be influenced by a lack of information about sex among women and their partners, and the idea that sexual interest is not necessary in women. Women in sex-positive countries which don't normally practise FGC are more likely to be optimistic about sexual pleasure and desire (Oyefara, 2015; Catania, 2007).

It's impossible to predict the outcome of PST, so it's important to be clear in assessment about the difference between the ability to have intercourse and sexual enjoyment. Couples may be more interested in one than the other. It's also important to help them accept what's happened rather than behave as though the woman hasn't been cut. What's possible will also depend on the pace she can tolerate.

Of course, treatment options need to offer the best fit for the client, but sex therapists can offer helpful psychoeducation to give women information and space to help them make appropriate choices. As well as information about possible treatment options, psychoeducation could include pictures of the vast variety of different vaginas, information about sexual technique, lubrication, sexual response and sexual hygiene. Clients can be encouraged to experiment with arousal and to enjoy stimulating their nipples as well as exploring genitals.

Where PST is sought, women may need more individual counselling and support; if possible, partners should be involved and the usual PST process can be followed. Sensitivity is needed during history taking due to the risk of retraumatisation, and careful contracting may be needed to plan and merge history taking with relevant psychoeducation. It's often appropriate to do this before surgery or whilst considering surgery; self and Sensate Focus experiments may be appropriate later.

Therapy can be highly empowering for women. It's important for them to determine the pace of therapy and for therapists to explain the importance of maintaining sex and intercourse bans, privileging the woman's experience of what's comfortable and possible. Partners, if they attend, may have little knowledge about FGC and may be highly anxious about hurting the woman. Their anxiety offers potential for them to develop a sexual dysfunction as a result. More care may be needed to assess sexual knowledge and explore sexual and social discourses with both partners. You may need to ascertain their comfort in discussing the issues together and separately, and contract accordingly.

Cultural issues

Factors such as religion, social class and education are not necessarily helpful in predicting whether someone has been cut. For instance, despite officially being illegal, some middle-class Egyptian women *choose* to be cut before marriage (Van Bavel, 2018). Given that nearly 90 percent of Egyptian women have been cut, this may not be that surprising. Though uncut women, living in a place where this doesn't happen, may see cutting as barbaric and abusive, those living among people who believe it's essential may not agree. Women from families who've moved away or who were 'sent home' to be cut feel more unusual and dissatisfied than those living in a community where the 'benefits' of cutting – and disadvantages of not being cut – are more obvious.

Regulated health and social care professionals must report to police if they're told by a girl under the age of 18 that she's been cut or if there are physical signs on a girl under the age of 18. Child protection and safeguarding responsibilities still apply if someone else talks about another person being cut, even though there isn't the same duty to report. Once again, we need to keep our curiosity active to seek the couple's views and elicit their trust, rather than imposing our own opinions about something that has already happened.

Pricking

Cutting is a cultural, rather than religious, practice which actually predates even Islam and Judaism (Ismail *et al*, 2017). Currently, its prevalence is thought to be growing in some places, despite improved literacy and health education about its dangers (Oyefara, 2015). It's mainly performed as a custom which confers social acceptability and marriageability, though the idea that it enhances men's sexual pleasure has been disputed by men. It's widely and increasingly opposed and has, in some places, been replaced with a ritual 'pricking' of the clitoris. This is often performed as a medical procedure, using sterile equipment and local anaesthetic, unlike traditional cutting which is often done using shared 'equipment' which may be as rudimentary as a broken bottle.

Pricking shouldn't cause scarring and there should be minimal pain, as it's only intended to produce a single drop of blood (Isa *et al*, 1999). As it's considerably less invasive than traditional cutting, supporters hope that, if it became an acceptable alternative to cutting, cultural wishes may be satisfied and the more radical practice may end (Arora & Jacobs, 2016). Yet pricking is banned in Europe and North America. The American Pediatric Association agreed to perform pinprick procedures in 2010, but quickly changed its mind (Belluck, 2010). Campaigners against pricking argue that, as it's recognised by the WHO as Type IV FGC (WHO, 2008), it still represents a practice that denigrates female sexuality and has potential psychological implications. There are also fears that claims to be performing pricking may mask a far more radical procedure (Wahlberg *et al*, 2017). Nonetheless, genuine support for pricking does seem to be growing, especially in migrant communities and areas where there have been health education campaigns about FGC (Wahlberg *et al*, 2017; Belmaker, 2012).

Another view is that male circumcision and labiaplasty are considered acceptable, whereas a procedure involving women of colour is not (Van Bavel, 2018; Johnsdotter & Essén, 2016). Though this view seems valid, opponents of male circumcision are also growing (Nunn, 2019). In the USA, where boys are often circumcised shortly after birth, there's a mounting movement against the practice, insisting that medical arguments in favour of circumcision cannot be justified, and citing cases where lasting damage has been caused. Indeed, it seems rates of male circumcision are falling generally. In 2018 an attempt was made to ban male circumcision in Iceland, which failed following lobbying from religious groups (Demurtas, 2018). The UK male circumcision rate is already thought to be as low as five percent, and it's only one percent in Scandanavia (Barkham, 2012). Many men express some sort of dissatisfaction or problem with their circumcision when asked, arguably making it advisable to enquire about genital procedures in all clients.

Medically unnecessary genital procedures will continue to provoke controversy. Meanwhile, we have a duty to inform ourselves about them, their consequences and ways we can help. More about ways to manage clinical issues and sexual functioning is discussed in Chapter 11.

References

Abdulcadir, J., Botsikas, D. & Bolmont, M. *et al* (2016) Sexual anatomy and function in women with and without genital mutilation: A cross-sectional study. *Journal of Sexual Medicine*, 13, 226–237.

Abdulcadir, J., Tille, J-C. & Petignat, P. (2017) Management of painful clitoral neuroma after female genital mutilation/cutting. *Reproductive Health*, 14;22. https://reproductive-health-journal.biomedcentral.com/track/pdf/10.1186/s12978-017-0288-3. Accessed December 15, 2019.

Arora, K.S. & Jacobs, A.J. (2016) Female genital alteration: A compromise solution. *Journal of Medical Ethics*, 42;3, 148–154.

Barkham, P. (2012) Circumcision: The cruellest cut? *The Guardian*, August 28. https://www.theguardian.com/world/2012/aug/28/circumcision-the-cruellest-cut. Accessed December 15, 2019.

Belluck, P. (2010) Group backs ritual 'nick' as female circumcision option. *New York Times*, May 7, A16.

Belmaker, R.H. (2012) Successful cultural change: The example of female circumcision among Israeli Bedouins and Israeli Jews from Ethiopia. *Israel Journal of Psychiatry & Related Sciences*, 49;3, 178–183.

Berg, R.C. & Dennison, E. (2013) A tradition in transition: Factors perpetuating and hindering the continuance of female genital mutilation/cutting (FGM/C) Summarized in a systematic review. *Health Care for Women International*, 34, 837–859.

Buggio, L., Fachin, F. & Chiappa, L. (2019) Psychosexual consequences of female genital mutilation and the impact of reconstructive surgery: A narrative review. *Health Equity*, 3;1, 36–46.

Catania, L. *et al* (2007) Pleasure and orgasm in women with Female Genital Mutilation/ Cutting (FGM/C). *Journal of Sexual Medicine*, 4;6, 1666–1678.

Demurtas, A. (2018) Ban on circumcision in Iceland to be dismissed in Parliament. *The Reykjavík Grapevine*, April 26. https://grapevine.is/news/2018/04/26/ban-on-circumcision-to-be-dismissed-in-parliament/. Accessed July 21, 2019.

Isa, A.R., Shuib, R. & Othman, M.S. (1999) The practice of female circumcision among Muslims in Kelantan, Malaysia. *Reproductive Health Matters*, 7;13, 137–144.

Ismail, S.A., Abbas, A.M. & Habib, D. (2017) Effect of female genital mutilation/cutting; types I and II on sexual function: Case controlled study. *Reproductive Health*, 14;1. www.ncbi.nlm.nih.gov/pmc/articles/PMC5577780/. Accessed June 23, 2019.

Johnsdotter, S. & Essén, B. (2016) Cultural change after migration: Circumcision of girls in western migrant communities. *Best Practice & Research Clinical Obstetrics & Gynaecology*, 32, 15–25.

Macfarlane, A.J. & Dorkenoo, E. (2015) *Prevalence of Female Genital Mutilation in England and Wales: National and Local Estimates*, London: City University.

Merckelbagh, H.M. *et al* (2015) Assessment of multidisciplinary care for 169 excised women with an initial reconstructive surgery project. *Gynecoligie, Obstetrique & Fertilitie*, 43, 633–639.

Nunn, G. (2019) Foreskin reclaimers: The 'intactivists' fighting infant male circumcision. *The Guardian*, July 21.

Oyefara, J.L. (2015) Female genital mutilation (FGM) and sexual functioning of married women in Oworonshoki Community, Lagos State, Nigeria. *African Population Studies*, 29;1, 1527–1541.

Thabet, S.M.A. & Thabet, A.S.M.A. (2003) Defective sexuality and female circumcision: The cause and the possible management. *Journal of Obstetrics and Gynaecology Research*, 29, 12–19.

Van Bavel, H. (2018) FGM: Zero tolerance to what? *SOAS Blog*, February 5. www.soas.ac.uk/blogs/study/fgm-zero-tolerance/. Accessed June 14, 2019.

Wahlberg, A., Johnsdotter, A.S. & Selling, K.E. (2017) Factors associated with the support of pricking (FGC type IV) among Somali immigrants – Across-sectional study in Sweden, *Reproductive Health*, 14;92, 1–10. www.academia.edu/34241927/Factors_associated_with_the_support_of_pricking_female_genital_cutting_type_IV_among_Somali_immigrants_a_cross-sectional_study_in_Sweden. Accessed May 24, 2019.

WHO (2008) *Eliminating Female Genital Mutilation: An Interagency Statement*, Geneva: World Health Organization.

WHO (2019) *Female Genital Mutilation*, Geneva: World Health Organization.

Yoder, S. & Kahn, S. (2008) *Numbers of Women Circumcised in Africa: The Production of a Total*, DHS working papers, 39, Washington, DC: United States Agency for International Development.

Chapter 11

Physical obstacles

How we feel about ageing and body challenges inevitably affects our ability to be sexual. PST can help to both change negative thinking about physical obstacles and seek solutions. Couples may come to PST seeking help with specific health-related concerns, a sexual health problem or have a health issue that needs to be addressed in relation to sexual functioning. For instance, someone with a chronic illness may come to PST because of their partner's loss of desire, but addressing the effect of their illness on the relationship and its practical restrictions will be part of the treatment. Some need practical advice about issues like positioning, use of aids, hoists, pillows and sex toys.

Immediately following a life-changing diagnosis, couples may find comfort in sex or feel it's inappropriate, not a priority or even dangerous. Some reduce or cease sexual activity following a heart attack, for instance, due to fear of another attack (d'Ardenne, 2004). In reality, the risk is extremely low and sexual activity can be gradually resumed (Stevenson & Elliott, 2007: 319). Sometimes risk is an excuse when a man is anxious about erectile dysfunction (Kloner *et al*, 2003) associated with cardiovascular disease, which may be exacerbated by medication (Sainz *et al*, 2004). Conditions affecting the nervous system, such as multiple sclerosis and Parkinson's disease, neuromuscular disease and brain injury, such as stroke, are all associated with sexual dysfunction and low libido. Physical limitations, such as difficulties with mobility, positioning and sensation, exacerbate sexual problems and may lead to depression and/or loss of motivation. Some people who are older, ill or have a disability are seen as asexual, which may both mean they aren't offered help with sexual problems and feel reluctant to seek help in case this is seen as inappropriate. Older clients may feel there's stigma attached to seeking counselling anyway (Agronin, 2014, 2018), but many benefit particularly from psychoeducation around normal ageing and from permission-giving conversations.

Chronic illness

Whether you first meet the individual or couple during the initial period of adjustment or after years of managing the condition(s), feelings of sadness and loss are natural and may need expression before a couple can start considering their strengths. Exploration of ways they've been affected can reveal their resilience, as well as allowing them to feel heard and understood. It helps to have these conversations individually, during the history taking, and with the couple together. Inhibitions, problems and fears can only be addressed once they've been identified. Some partners may feel they aren't entitled to express concerns, so their physical and emotional health may suffer as a result, particularly when they've become exhausted by caring (D'Ardenne, 2004). As with all clients, it's important to find out what they've already tried and to celebrate their efforts.

All contexts of oppression and liberation for both partners, not just those related to ability, may reveal altered power dynamics (D'Ardenne, 2004). Sometimes the partner with the 'problem' can be oppressively demanding or the able partner's behaviour may become inadvertently or deliberately abusive (Ward et al, 2010). This can emerge in sexual demands or avoidance, which need sensitive assessment. A life-threatening illness or experience can make both partners reassess their future, becoming more experimental and less inhibited.

Often, psychoeducation and permission giving, normalising and validating conversations which encourage creativity (Enzlin, 2014) are all that's needed. However, many clients have fixed, negative views and biases around illness, ability and ageing, as do many therapists. Explaining that all sexual relationships need to adapt as they pass through different stages may be normalising. Examples could include pregnancy, times of work stress, when children are young, when other family members are sick or ageing, menopause and retirement.

Cheerleading around the prospect of sexual exploration and mystery may prove highly validating, as the couple come to see the issues as challenges to be overcome creatively and with support rather than just obstacles. It's important to remain curious, continually checking prejudices, assumptions and stereotyping in both oneself and the clients. Couples can be encouraged to identify ways they've found solutions to problems in the past and see if similar strategies will help now.

When clients are ability and goal-focused, PST offers ways of enjoying a wide range of sexual experience and moving away from outcome-oriented sex. They may, however, need practical advice and encouragement with ways to manage PST experiments and sex, such as timing to follow bowel and bladder care and pain medication. In men, indwelling urinary catheters can be folded back, covered with a condom and taped to the body. Women's catheters should also be taped back and care taken not to pull on them.

Ideally, partners shouldn't perform intimate tasks, as this makes it much more difficult for couples to feel like lovers (D'Ardenne, 2004). In any case, a change in ability can disrupt not just self-image but each other's sexual role. A previously passive partner may find it difficult to assume a more active, facilitating role, for instance. However, they can look at ways the other partner can take responsibility, especially in initiating sex. If the issue is self-consciousness, they may overcome this through role playing the kind of person who wouldn't be self-conscious or varying their sexual repertoire. For example, a woman who needed to be on top for intercourse found this very exposing, but the couple overcame this initial anxiety with play using blindfolds.

Some broad brush approaches to common issues are in the sections that follow.

Surgery

Any surgery can affect sexual functioning, if only because anaesthetics are tiring and needing surgery is worrying. Sex therapists often see people before surgery, when an illness has already taken its toll on a couple's relationship, so are in an excellent position to prepare them for what to expect and ways to manage difficulties. Afterwards, sex therapists can be a source of emotional support and practical advice about ways to maintain or regain sex and intimacy.

Prostate surgery

Benign prostatic enlargement (BPE) is the term used when the prostate grows and causes pressure on the bladder and ureter, creating difficulties with urination. These include frequency, especially at night, trouble starting to wee, interruptions to urine flow and incomplete emptying of the bladder. It's more common in older, obese men and those with diabetes or cardiovascular disease. Half of men have developed BPE by the age of 80. Often, this is a manageable nuisance, but some men develop complications such as incontinence or frequent urinary tract infections (Barnas et al, 2004). Drugs to shrink the prostate and slow urine production at night, as well as lifestyle changes, often help considerably. Surgery would only be considered in the most severe cases, which don't respond to more conservative treatment (Smith & Christmas, 1999). There are numerous procedures to shrink the prostate, remove it or reduce pressure.

Advice about sex and relationships should be offered to anyone undergoing prostate treatment as both prostate conditions and their treatment can affect sexual function. Erectile problems are common immediately following most of the treatments for prostate cancer, for instance, as they may cause nerve damage. Men are usually advised to do Kegel exercises. Arousing themselves promotes blood flow to the penis and improves their chance of any ED being temporary. They may be prescribed PDE5 inhibitors to encourage erections.

PST needs to be approached creatively to deal with the need for 'penis exercise'. For men who dislike solitary exercises with an unresponsive penis, partnered genital exercise may need to be incorporated at the end of non-genital Sensate Focus. Skipping straight to genital stages of treatment is like building a house without foundations. The early phase is when individuation, intimacy and confidence are built, and many couples particularly need this gentle reconnection with themselves as well as their partner post-surgery.

Some men develop significant body image issues. Sometimes this is related to ED and the feeling that their body is failing them, especially if they're also affected by incontinence or bowel issues. The penis may appear smaller or a different shape, and they may experience loss of libido. Orgasm may be different, too, and ejaculation may be absent or different, depending on the procedure. Sometimes there's no ejaculate, less ejaculate or they may ejaculate backwards into the bladder. This should not stop the man from having an orgasm, but the sensations may change. The orgasm may be less intense and they won't have a point of inevitability, so may climax earlier than previously.

Men are usually advised to resume partnered sex as soon as possible. This may be more of an issue for gay men, as anal sex can be painful, damaging or compromise post-operative investigations. Advice may vary depending on the procedure they've had. There could be risk to sexual partners with brachytherapy, for instance, where radioactive seeds are implanted in the prostate. For receptive partners, penetrative sex may be advised after anything from a week to eight weeks. Insertive partners may find ED particularly difficult, as a firmer erection is needed for anal penetration than PiV sex. Men who enjoyed stimulation of the prostate will no longer have this option.

Prostate Cancer UK has produced excellent information and advice about sex after treatment (https://prostatecanceruk.org/prostate-information/guides/). It also advises that trans women and male-assigned non-binary individuals may develop prostate cancer despite having had hormone therapies. It's therefore important that urinary disturbances, pelvic pain and bleeding are investigated with the prostate in mind.

Mastectomy

Surgery which alters body image or changes the body radically has the potential to be sexually devastating, especially if the consequences of surgery were unexpected (Moin *et al*, 2009). With many of the conditions that require body altering surgery, the individual or couple are struggling with adjusting to a life-threatening diagnosis and ongoing treatment and check-ups as well as recovering from the treatment itself. In the case of breast cancer, treatment can continue for years. Chemotherapy can result in vaginal dryness and women prescribed Tamoxifen long-term may experience a number of side-effects including loss of libido, hot flushes, mood swings and constipation.

Women may be required to make choices about the type of treatment they receive, including big decisions such as whether to have breast reconstruction. As this requires further major surgery, couples may be facing considerable disruption to their everyday lives if the woman goes ahead. Sometimes, a woman or couple just need support for what they're going through and help with ways to stay intimate or regain intimacy. This may not initially mean engaging in any sex at all for a while, but making time for the relationship and non-sexual cuddles and touch. Some couples, meanwhile, are ready to get cracking with PST, sometimes having felt disconnected for long periods. Many couples still feel close but are nervous about being sexual post-surgery.

The detailed history taking of PST facilitates assessment of relationship quality and sex before diagnosis and surgery, and gives both the opportunity to express their fears. Partners may be terrified of hurting the woman or of the wound itself, and may need ways to manage their fears separately and jointly. It isn't always helpful to insist they share concerns if these feed the other's worries. It may be more helpful initially to offer psychoeducation about the possibility that such feelings may be experienced and to facilitate general discussions about their management. Contained and supported conversations may allow fears to emerge organically. Indeed, responding to the clients' pace in PST should offer feelings of control that may have been lost since the diagnosis.

Therapy can facilitate creation of the couple's own experiments, such as showing a scar and then allowing the partner to touch it. However, if women and/or their partners don't wish to see or show the operation site, this should be respected. Any associated distress can be addressed and revisited as necessary. It's also important to recognise and celebrate the cooperation and closeness that can develop during treatment, with many women feeling well supported by their partners (Fasse *et al*, 2017; Andrzejczak *et al*, 2013).

Hysterectomy

Depending on the reason for hysterectomy, it may be greeted with relief or grief. When it brings an end to the discomfort of uterine prolapse or painful and heavy periods, it may provide the gateway to more satisfying sex. When it ends fertility earlier than desired, or is performed because of a life-threatening condition, it may be accompanied by anxiety and loss. If the ovaries are also removed, the woman may experience the sudden onset of menopausal symptoms. She'll be given hormone replacement therapy, but this varies in how long it takes to relieve symptoms. These will usually have settled by the time sex therapy is sought, but their effect may have been jarring and affected the woman's self-image.

Many women are frightened to resume sex after hysterectomy in case intercourse is painful, and partners may be frightened of causing damage. PST can be extremely helpful in rebuilding confidence and increasing feelings of safety. However, post-hysterectomy some women experience a marked alteration in the quality of orgasm. The feeling of uterine contractions during climax is now missing, which may be perceived as less pleasurable. For some post-menopausal women, though, this can improve orgasm as the contractions sometimes start to feel gripey and uncomfortable as women age.

Menopause

Menopause is said to have occurred when periods have been absent for at least six months, normally at around the age of 51. This is preceded by perimenopause, when women experience symptoms such as hot flushes, irregular and heavy periods, mood swings, headaches, fatigue and achiness. Initially, these may only occur during weeks when a period is missed but then increase in frequency and intensity, often continuing after menopause itself. As women age beyond menopause, the genital area becomes generally more delicate, with more risk of urinary tract infection, vaginal dryness and painful sex. Postmenopausal absence of oestrogen also increases the risk of osteoporosis and cardiovascular disease. Other changes include shrinkage of the uterus and vagina, loss of libido, and changes in orgasm and arousal. The clitoris and breasts may become less sensitive. In some women with a uterus, an unpleasant dragging sensation can occur during and after orgasm.

PST doesn't usually need any special adaptations, though the couple will usually benefit from psychoeducation about menopause and ageing in general. Some couples are delighted by freedom from periods and contraception, though single clients may need advice about condom use and the risk of sexually transmitted infections. Much research suggests that older couples have the most satisfying sex lives, even if they aren't having sex as often as they used to. More older couples are divorcing too, and embarking on new relationships where they discover sexual problems and seek PST.

Peri- and postmenopausal symptoms can make sex very unattractive. However, a woman's negative beliefs about the effects of menopause and ageing may be even more off-putting. Though lack of oestrogen is often blamed for loss of desire, testosterone is actually more responsible for libido. As testosterone doesn't begin to fall until 10–12 years after menstruation stops, women's perceived loss of interest in sex much earlier than this is unlikely to be all due to hormone changes. Unpleasant menopausal symptoms – especially night sweats, heavy periods and fatigue – may begin the process and be exacerbated by factors such as the development of responsive desire (see page 79), the psychological effects of fertility loss and body consciousness. Relationship problems or external issues, such as caring for elderly parents, worry about children, work stress and financial concerns, may all compromise desire. Most significantly, ovulation is when many women most notice physical sexual desire, so its absence may be perceived as a reduction in libido.

Medical solutions to menopausal symptoms include systemic hormone replacement therapy (usually delivered via patches), vaginal creams or pessaries and/or lubrication to combat dryness and itching, and anti-depressants to manage mood. A well-ventilated bedroom, spare cool pillow and cotton nightwear may be useful for troublesome night sweats. It may be helpful to keep a diary to see what exacerbates symptoms – anxiety, spicy food, caffeine and alcohol are often implicated in hot flushes. More importantly, partners may need to understand that snuggling up can also be a trigger.

Mobility issues

Some people with conditions like arthritis endure days of pain after sex. Pain may make it difficult to stay in one position for long, so Sensate Focus may need to be adapted accordingly and analgesia taken before and after experiments/sex. V-shaped cushions can be helpful in propping someone up or supporting areas of the body. If it's difficult to open the legs, intercourse may be preferred from behind or lying on one side.

With conditions like fibromyalgia, there may be particular sensitivity, with quite gentle touch perceived as painful. Tiredness is another major issue with many conditions. Experimentation is especially helpful to work out what's possible and what helps someone to feel more comfortable. Obese men may prefer intercourse in a chair with the partner on top, while obese women/recipient partners may benefit from bending their knees up and sliding down the chair so their bottom is at the seat edge. Use of a wedge behind them and support for their legs with pillows may be needed. Those with sufficient lower limb flexibility may want to place their legs round the partner's waist or over their shoulders.

Spinal cord injury (SCI)

Sexual dysfunctions can also affect people with existing physical issues, such as spinal cord injury, or they may come to PST wanting general help with being sexual. When someone presents shortly after an injury or diagnosis, they'll benefit from psychoeducation around what's possible and from experimentation. When the issue is long-standing, they'll be educating you about their condition and sexual behaviours.

Loss of genital sensation, incontinence, spasm, tremor, pain and loss of mobility may exist, as may loss of vaginal lubrication and erection (Stevenson & Elliott, 2007). Nevertheless, many people with SCI experience orgasm, some by conscious imagery, without any form of physical touch, while others climax with non-genital touch (Komisaruk & Whipple, 2012). When sensation is limited below the level of spinal cord injury, sensitivity above the level of injury can increase with resulting hypersensitivity. 'Zone' orgasms occur when a specific non-genital area is stimulated (Paget, 2001), including neck, fingers, toes, earlobes, underarms, knees, hips and thighs. Skin near the site of injury may also be hypersensitive and an area where stimulation can produce orgasm (Sipski et al, 1993). Orgasm resulting from stimulation of ears, lips, breasts and nipples has been reported in women (Comarr & Vigue, 1978). Stimulation of the anus and mouth – including during oral kissing and fellatio – produce orgasms which may begin in the mouth or throat and spread around the body (Otto, 1999). Referred sensation or sensation which bypasses the spinal cord (possibly via the vagus nerve) may be responsible for orgasm achieved when spinal fracture is complete. Many women enjoy cervical stimulation, for instance. Orgasm can also happen during sleep. In men who can't easily orgasm, use of a vibrator to stimulate the underside tip of the penis (frenum) may help.

In some people with injuries at T6 and above, sexual arousal and ejaculation can cause autonomic dysreflexia, a condition causing excessively high blood pressure, which needs urgent attention (Elliott & Krassioukov, 2005). If they orgasm, men with injuries from T11 to L2 only produce a trickle of semen and the rhythmic contractions of the pelvic floor associated with ejaculation are absent. Retrograde ejaculation into the bladder is common too.

Encourage experimentation with sexual positions. Some people prefer wheelchair sex, as most chairs have removable parts which make access to the body much easier than in a bed. There is a huge range of aids available to assist with positioning and wheelchair sex. There are also specialist sex toys for people with disabilities which make them easier to use for all those with limited movement.

Cognitive issues

Consent and capacity for consent are important issues for people with learning difficulties (McGuire & Bayley, 2011). Relationships which are loving and consensual are often supported by health professionals and care workers, so sex therapists may occasionally find themselves acting as advocates when family members oppose the relationships of someone with cognitive impairment (Evans et al, 2009).

Dementia

Consent and capacity are obviously also important when a partner is affected by a condition like dementia. Though both partners may long to be sexual together, the unaffected one may feel they shouldn't continue to look for sexual intimacy. It's important to normalise both desire and feelings of discomfort, so sex can be encouraged as long as it's sought and enjoyed by both partners. However, sometimes the unaffected partner may feel as though they're taking advantage or may start to feel more of a carer than a lover. Again, their feelings should be respected and validated, so they don't feel obliged to have sex when it no longer feels enjoyable or suitable. Sometimes, other intimate activities may be enjoyed by both, including many of the Pre-Sensate exercises.

There is sometimes inappropriate sexual behaviour following brain injury, such as a stroke, or the onset of dementia, particularly in men. Sometimes sex may be demanded constantly, there may be sexual disinhibition or sexual interest may decline. This may be off-putting for partners, as well as causing embarrassment, but is likely to change over time, becoming more or less troublesome. Sometimes, encouraging masturbation may be a solution. Though some partners may find this distasteful, others are grateful for permission to 'allow' this. Both partners may need support to express their grief at the changes in their relationship and sexual selves or encouragement to celebrate their continuing sexual relationship.

High-functioning autism

Autism can have considerable effect on sex and relationships. Up to half of couples affected by Asperger syndrome (AS) may not be sexual at all, though may wish to be and may seek help (Aston, 2001). Sometimes the couple present in crisis because the AS person seems to have loss interest in their neurotypical (NT) partner, having previously been completely devoted to them. A new interest, such as a baby, job or hobby may have become their passion, leaving their NT partner wondering what they've done wrong.

AS women are more likely to date younger men, while AS men are often more comfortable with older women. AS women may present as more socially adept but also more childlike than men and may be more vulnerable to abuse (Simone, 2010). However, AS partners may also appear more controlling themselves, as they attempt to meet their need for routine and predictability. This need for routine can lead to sexual boredom for the NT partner, whose efforts to spice things up may be missed or seen as criticism. Indeed, NT partners need to be absolutely clear about what they want and mean as nuanced behaviour, such as flirting, may be missed. AS partners have more problems working out what the other wants and means (Baron-Cohen *et al*, 1997). Likewise, therapists need to carefully and patiently check understanding, as it may take the AS partner longer to process information and respond (Thompson, 2008).

Sensory sensitivity is common, to the extent that touch can cause pain, or insensitivity may be associated with anorgasmia (Aston, 2009). Men may consequently find masturbation more reliably arousing than intercourse, which NT partners can find hurtful. An AS partner's aversion to body odours or fluids may also be upsetting (Aston, 2012). PST often has a hugely beneficial effect on the relationship, as the couple dynamic is explored and attempts are made to improve understanding and meet needs. It's particularly important that the early stages of the work aren't rushed, so that both the couple are able to genuinely feel the effects of their progress.

Cassandra Syndrome is the term for NT individuals who become worn down, particularly by feeling they're not listened to, which can lead to physical symptoms and mental health issues. For partner support, see www.different-together.co.uk/.

Infertility

Failure to conceive when they want to can make couples feel unsuccessful and unattractive, and affect how they feel about their sexual and gender image (Mechanick Braverman, 2004). To compound this, it's thought that negative sexual consequences are experienced in up to 60 percent of couples who receive infertility treatment (Wischmann, 2010). Sexual problems which existed before treatment also become more pronounced as treatment progresses (Daniluk *et al*, 2014). The longer couples remain in treatment, the worse the effects become (Daniluk & Frances-Fisher, 2009), with some couples still feeling affected decades later (Wirtberg *et al*, 2007; Schanz *et al*, 2011). It's no wonder infertility treatment has been described as 'mortifying and intrusive' (Piva *et al*, 2014).

Unexplained infertility may also often be accounted for by unrecognised sexual problems (Wischmann, 2013). Indeed, it's common for couples to seek PST in order to conceive, and they may not be really motivated to have sex. Sometimes they aren't actually all that motivated to have a baby either, but are under pressure from family to do so. It's also common to see couples who need help to restore their sexual relationship after infertility treatment (Hammer Burns, 2006). They may now be suffering from exhaustion, the mother's changed body and lack of time if the treatment was successful or the grief of adjusting to life without biological children if it wasn't. Couples often hide their real feelings from each other, especially when they're different (Vizheh et al, 2013). For instance, one may be relieved that trying to conceive is over, and they can get on with their lives, while the other is finding it much harder to accept being childless.

A common experience of having babies after a long period of infertility is that one or both may be ashamed to admit they aren't now enjoying being parents. When, for so long, the focus has been on achieving a pregnancy, the reality of a baby – or twins – may be a shock, arriving before the couple has had time to recover from the long years of trying to conceive.

It's helpful as a sex therapist to be aware of what couples have been through, or are facing if they present ahead of treatment. Women may experience decreased arousal and desire, orgasmic dysfunction and dyspareunia (Keskin et al, 2011). Infertility is considered a major risk factor for erectile difficulties (Shindel et al, 2008), particularly in the ovulatory part of the cycle, and ejaculatory disorders appear to be two to three times higher than in the general population (Wischman, 2010). Triggers for ED and performance anxiety include ovulation, previous abnormal semen analysis, tests requiring timed intercourse or masturbation, and masturbation in an infertility clinic (Quattrini et al, 2010). Having to masturbate causes extreme guilt in men from some cultures, which can inhibit sexuality as well as cause ED when masturbation is required (Bechoua et al, 2016). While some couples have more sex – particularly around ovulation – around two-thirds find their sexual contact is impaired (Piva et al, 2014). Women often feel overweight, uncomfortable and unattractive while taking fertility drugs, which further deters them from feeling or being sexual (Wischman, 2010). Some stop having sex, even around ovulation, or they find it's become all about making babies rather than making love (Collier, 2010). Anxiety and depression are common throughout treatment and may persist subsequently.

While cisgendered gay couples may not have clinical fertility issues, they will need some sort of assisted conception. Trans/non-binary couples and individuals may have extremely complex feelings about their fertility. Pregnant trans men, for instance, may experience genuine distress about their bodies changing with pregnancy, though this shouldn't be assumed. Experiences of discrimination may need to be processed for all these couples. Facilitating safe exploration of the experience of fertility and pregnancy in any couple may be full of happy memories of achievement and fulfilment, or packed with trauma, doubt and confusion. Often a mixture of emotions persists.

Sexually transmitted infection (STI)

There isn't space here to do much more than mention STIs. It's worth knowing, however, that they're on the increase in some parts of the UK. Though most cases are occurring among younger men who have sex with men, there are new cases in all age groups and genders. Though most clients won't test your knowledge of STIs, it's helpful to be aware of symptoms and to always advise checkups if someone has any unusual genital symptoms or has been having unprotected sex.

Herpes

Condoms may not always protect against herpes, as 'shedding' of the virus from the whole affected area can occur in people who are asymptomatic. It's also possible to pass cold sores to the genital area through oral sex. Most of the time, people infected with herpes aren't infectious except during an outbreak – when they produce painful blisters – but they usually also have occasional shedding episodes. Many, however, experience some tingling at such times, as they would just before an outbreak. Usually, the initial herpes outbreak is the worst and people are at their most infectious in the following couple of years. Some people meet their partners through herpes dating sites.

HIV infection

Human immunodeficiency virus is the infection which causes AIDS when left untreated and is permanent once acquired, making it likely that sex therapists will meet HIV-positive clients. Having said this, many people who've been infected are being treated with highly active antiretroviral medication and have an undetectable viral load. Acquiring the infection should not, therefore, be an issue for their partners if they comply with medication instructions, though some couples and individuals relax safer sex practices over time (Carballo-Diéguez et al, 2012). Where HIV status is unknown or positive and untreated, post-exposure prophylaxis (PEP) taken within 72 hours and continued for a month considerably reduces infection risk, as does pre-exposure prophylaxis (PREP). However, they're not routinely available in the UK at the time of writing, and individuals must be tested for HIV before PEP will be prescribed.

Sexual problems are known to be associated with positive HIV status (Cove & Petrak, 2004). All genders may experience low desire, with delayed ejaculation and erectile difficulties common and treated with testosterone and PDE5 inhibitors. It isn't clear how often sexual difficulties are psychological, due to the condition or a result of medication/recreational drug use (de Tubino Scanavino, 2011). Though medication may contribute to some sexual problems, it may actually improve libido (Carballo-Diéguez et al, 2012).

Some people develop abdominal fat and prominent veins on the limbs, which may make them self-conscious. Accelerated ageing associated with HIV may contribute to the high incidence of erectile difficulties in late youth and early middle-age (Shindel & Smith, 2011). Clinical investigation is consequently advisable, but PST may be helpful in exploring both partners' feelings about the way HIV affects their relationship and self-image and in (re)establishing intimacy and optimal sexual functioning. Again, adopt a non-judgemental positive approach, focusing on what works and encouraging exploration.

Post-orgasmic illness syndrome (POIS)

Clients with relatively unusual sexual problems present with a huge range of symptoms they assume are unique but are frequently more common than they assume. Persistent Genital Arousal (see page 111–12), for instance, is becoming more widely reported as it increasingly receives publicity. Another common complaint is a fishy smell after orgasm, which is caused by bacterial vaginosis.

A further fairly unusual complaint, POIS, causes flu-like symptoms soon after ejaculation. Specific symptoms vary but last up to a week, peaking at about the second day. There may be a history of spontaneous ejaculation with no arousal or early ejaculation (Waldinger, 2016).

POIS can be a lifelong condition, but is most likely to be seen in PST when it has been recently acquired. It's highly disruptive to sexual relationships, with both partners baffled by what happens. Reassuring them that this is a real condition, discussing initial adaptations to their sexual behaviour and urging them to seek a urological referral are positive first stages. POIS may be an allergy to the person's own semen, which can apparently be treated (Waldinger & Schweitzer, 2002), but a range of interventions have been used, including prophylactic medication and CBT.

Sexomnia

Since 2007 it's been recognised that some people initiate sexual behaviour or masturbate whilst genuinely fast asleep, so couples who mention this should always be taken seriously. While GPs may not have heard of the condition, they can help by referring the couple to a sleep clinic. Meanwhile, sleeping tablets or antidepressants are often helpful.

Sexomnia is a sleep disorder, but can cause considerable relationship distress. There have been occasional cases of people accusing partners of raping them, when it ultimately emerges *they* were initiating sexual behaviour in their sleep and the partner was merely responding (Markovic, 2012). Such behaviour can sometimes occur during periods of illness or stress, or it may be chronic, and can begin at any time of life. It should always be explained to clients that the affected partner potentially has a real disorder which needs medical investigation and treatment. It's not appropriate to try to treat the condition with PST alone.

Sexomnia is more common in people with other sleep disturbances, such as sleepwalking, tooth grinding and sleep apnoea (Martynowicz et al, 2018). The condition is also associated with epilepsy and obstructive sleep apnoea/hypopnea

(OSAH) – especially in people over forty – when muscles in the throat relax and interfere with breathing. Treating OSAH also fixes sexomnia (e Cruz & Soca, 2016). Sometimes lifestyle changes are all that's required, such as losing weight, avoiding smoking and alcohol, changing sedative medication or treating conditions that challenge breathing, such as a deviated septum (Schanz et al, 2011). Use of a continuous positive airway pressure device or mandibular advancement device are used when lifestyle changes are insufficient.

Whether or not your clients are affected by physical issues, most clients at some point experience challenges to the PST process, which are explored in Chapter 12.

References

Agronin, M.E. (2014) Sexuality and aging. In: Binik, Y.M. & Hall, K.S.K. [eds] *Principles and Practice of Sex Therapy*, fifth edition, New York: Guilford Press, 525–539.

Agronin, M.E. (2018) *The End of Old Age: Living a Longer, More Purposeful Life*, Boston: Da Capo Lifelong Books.

Andrzejczak, E., Markocka-Mączka, K. & Lewandowsk, A. (2013) Partner relationships after mastectomy in women not offered breast reconstruction. *Psycho-Oncology*, 22, 1653–1657.

Aston, M. (2001) *The Other Half of Asperger Syndrome*, London: National Autistic Society.

Aston, M. (2009) *The Asperger Couple's Workbook*, London: Jessica Kingsley.

Aston, M. (2012) Asperger syndrome in the bedroom. *Sexual & Relationship Therapy*, 27;1, 73–79.

Barnas, J.L., Pierpaoli, S., Ladd, P., Velenzuela, R., Aviv, N. & Parker, M. (2004) The prevalence and nature of orgasmic dysfunction after radical prostatectomy. *British Journal of Urology International*, 94;4, 603–605.

Baron-Cohen, S., Gleitman, L. & Carey, S. (1997) *Mindblindness: An Essay on Autism and Theory of Mind*, Cambridge, MA: MIT Press.

Bechoua, S., Hamamah, S. & Scalici, E. (2016) Male infertility: An obstacle to sexuality? *Andrology*, 4, 395–403.

Carballo-Diéguez, A., Remien, R.H. & Frasca, T. (2012) HIV serodiscordant male couples. In: Kleinplatz, P.J. [ed] *New Directions in Sex Therapy*, second edition, Hove: Routledge, 303–320.

Collier, F. (2010) When a couple wants a baby: What are the consequences on their sexuality? *Sexologies*,19, 143–146.

Comarr, A.E. & Vigue, M. (1978) Sexual counselling among male and female patients with spinal cord injury and/or cauda equine injury. Parts I and II. *American Journal of Physical Medicine*, 57, 107–227.

Cove, J. & Petrak, J. (2004) Factors associated with sexual problems in HIV-positive gay men. *International Journal of STD & AIDS*, 15;11, 732–736.

Daniluk, J.C. & Frances-Fisher, J.E. (2009) A sensitive way to approach your infertile patients' concerns. *Journal of Sexual & Reproductive Medicine*, 7, 3–7.

Daniluk, J.C., Koert, E. & Breckon, E. (2014) Sexuality and infertility. In: Binik, Y.M. & Hall, K.S.K. [eds] *Principles and Practice of Sex Therapy*, fifth edition, New York: Guilford Press, 419–435.

D'Ardenne, P. (2004) The couple sharing long-term illness. *Sexual & Relationship Therapy*, 19;3, 291–308.

de Tubino Scanavino, M. (2011) Sexual dysfunctions of HIV-positive men: Associated factors, pathophysiology issues, and clinical management. *Advances in Urology*, 1–10.

e Cruz, M.M. & Soca, R. (2016) Sexsomnia and REM- predominant obstructive sleep apnea effectively treated with a mandibular advancement device. *Sleep Science*, 9, 140–141.

Elliott, S.L. & Krassioukov, A. (2005) Malignant autonomic dysreflexia following ejaculation in spinal cord injured men sexuality and illness. In: Stevenson, R.W.D. & Elliott, S.L. [eds] *Principles and Practice of Sex Therapy*, fourth edition, New York: Guilford Press, 313–349.

Enzlin, P. (2014) Sexuality in the context of chronic illness. In: Binik, Y.M. & Hall, K.S.K. [eds] *Principles and Practice of Sex Therapy*, fifth edition, New York: Guilford Press, 436–456.

Evans, D.S., McGuire, B.E., Healey, E. & Carley, S.N. (2009) Sexuality and personal relationships for people with an intellectual disability. Part II: Staff and family carer perspectives. *Journal of Intellectual Disability Research*, 53;11, 913–921.

Fasse, L., Flahault, C. & Vioulac, C. (2017) The decision-making process for breast reconstruction after cancer surgery: Representations of heterosexual couples in long-standing relationships. *British Journal of Health Psychology*, 22, 254–269.

Hammer Burns, L. (2006) Sexual counselling and infertility. In: Covington, S.N. & Hammer Burns, L. [eds] *Infertility Counselling: A Comprehensive Handbook for Clinicians*, second edition, New York: Cambridge University Press, 212–235.

Keskin, U. *et al* (2011) Differences in prevalence of sexual dysfunction between primary and secondary infertile women. *Fertility and Sterility*, 96, 1213–1217.

Kloner, R.A. *et al* (2003) Erectile dysfunction in the cardiac patient: How common and should we treat? *Journal of Urology*, 170, S46–S50.

Komisaruk, B.R. & Whipple, B. (2012) Non-genital orgasms. *Sexual and Relationship Therapy*, 26;4, 356–372.

Markovic, D. (2012) Personal communication.

Martynowicz, H., Smardz, J. & Wieczorek, T. (2018) The co-occurrence of sexsomnia, sleep bruxism and other sleep disorders. *Journal of Clinical Medicine*, 7;9, 233.

McGuire, B.E. & Bayley, A.A. (2011) Relationships, sexuality and decision making capacity in people with an intellectual disability. *Current Opinion in Psychi*atry, 24, 398–402.

Mechanick Braverman, A. (2004) Psychosocial aspects of infertility: Sexual dysfunction. *International Congress Series*, 1266, 270–276.

Moin, V., Duvdevaney, H. & Mazor, D. (2009) Sexual identity, body image and life satisfaction among women with and without physical disability. *Sexuality & Disabilities*, 27, 83–95.

Otto, H. A. (1999) *Liberated Orgasm: The Orgasmic Revolution*, Silverato, CA: Liberating Creations.

Paget, L. (2001) *The Big O. Orgasms: How to Have Them, Give Them and Keep Them Coming*, New York: Broadway Books.

Piva, I., Lo Monte, G., Graziano, A. & Marci, R. (2014) A literature review on the relationship between infertility and sexual dysfunction: Does fun end with baby making? *The European Journal of Contraception and Reproductive Health Care*, 19, 231–237.

Quattrini, F., Ciccarone, M., Tatoni, F. & Vittori, G. (2010) Psychological and sexological assessment of the infertile couple. *Sexologies*, 19, 15–19.

Sainz, I., Amaya, J. & Garcia, M. (2004) Erectile dysfunction in heart disease patients. *International Journal of Impotence Research*, 16, S13–S17.

Schanz, S., Reimer, T., Eichner, M., Hautzinger, M., Hafner, H.M. & Fierlbeck, G. (2011) Long-term life and partnership satisfaction in infertile patients: A 5-year longitudinal study. *Fertility and Sterility*, 96, 416–421.

Schenck, C.H., Arnulf, I. & Mahwald, M.W. (2007) Sleep and sex: What can go wrong? A review of the literature on sleep related disorders and abnormal sexual behaviors and experiences. *Sleep*, 30;6, 683–702.

Shindel, A.W., Nelson, C.J., Naughton, C.K. *et al* (2008) Sexual function and quality of life in the male partner of infertile couples: Prevalence and correlates of dysfunction. *Journal of Urology*, 179, 1056–1059.

Shindel, A.W. & Smith, J.F. (2011) Sexual dysfunction, HIV and AIDS in men who have sex with men. *AIDS Patient Care and STDs*, 25;6, 341–349.

Simone, R. (2010) *Aspergirls*, London: Jessica Kingsley.

Sipski, M., Komisaruk, B., Whipple, B. & Alexander, C.J. (1993) Physiologic responses associated with orgasm in the spinal cord injured female. *Archives of Physical Medicine and Rehabilitation*, 74, 1270.

Smith, G.L. & Christmas, T.J. (1999) Potency preserving surgery. In: Carson, C., Kirby, R. & Goldstein, I. [eds] *Textbook of Erectile Dysfunction*, Oxford: ISIS Medical Media, 599–606.

Stevenson, R.W.D. & Elliott, S.L. (2007) Sexuality and illness. In: Leiblum, S.R. [ed] *Principles and Practice of Sex Therapy*, fourth edition, New York: Guilford Press, 313–349.

Thompson, B. (2008) *Counselling for Asperger Couples*, London: Jessica Kingsley.

Vizheh, M., Pakgohar, M., Babaei, G. & Ramezanzadeh, F. (2013) Effect of counselling on quality of marital relationship of infertile couples: A randomised controlled trial study. *Archives of Gynaecology and Obstetrics*, 287, 583–589.

Waldinger, M.D. (2016) Post-orgasmic illness syndrome. In: Levine, S., Risen, C.B. & Althof, S.E. [eds] *Handbook of Clinical Sexuality for Mental Health Professionals*, third edition, New York: Routledge, chapter 32.

Waldinger, M.D. & Schweitzer, D.H. (2002) Post-orgasmic illness syndrome: Two cases. *Journal of Sex & Marital Therapy*, 28, 251–255.

Ward, K.M., Bosek, R.L. & Trimble, E.L. (2010) Romantic relationships and interpersonal violence among adults with developmental disabilities. *Intellectual & Developmental Disabilities*, 48;2, 89–98.

Wirtberg, I., Möller, A. & Hogström, L. (2007) Life 20 years after unsuccessful infertility treatment. *Human Reproduction*, 22, 598–604.

Wischmann, T.H. (2010) Sexual disorders in infertile couples. *Journal of Sexual Medicine*, 7, 1868–1876.

Wischmann, T.H. (2013) Sexual disorders in infertile couples: An update. *Current Opinion in Obstetrics & Gynaecology*, 25, 220–222.

Chapter 12

Blocks and challenges

Managing blocks is the crucial skill at the heart of PST. History taking offers information to anticipate blocks or make sense of them once they emerge. If you think a particular block is likely, it can be helpful to present it to the couple as a generic issue that 'some people' experience. They may then recognise it themselves and manage it before it really gets started. The likelihood of blocks occurring supports the experimental nature of PST. If clients know you welcome the information glitches they provide, they're more likely to tell you about them. It's common for couples to turn up for a session very upset and disappointed about the way their Sensate Focus went (or didn't go), expecting to be in trouble, to find their therapist is actually full of ideas about what happened and ways to go forward. They frequently leave the session delighted rather than shamed.

The PST process described in this book is designed to help manage anxiety by overcoming potential blocks. For example, couples learn to tolerate not knowing what their partner is thinking. Anxious clients who have difficulty managing their emotions will find this particularly challenging and may avoid exercises, break the sex ban, complain about the PST process/therapist or talk to their partner when they aren't supposed to. However, warning the couple about what may be difficult is the beginning of managing the difficulty.

Once they start to enjoy the experiments without the pressure of wondering what their partner is thinking, and appreciate that PST works, couples are more likely to comply readily without their previous anxiety. The main block to this happening is often not the client's fears and anxiety but the therapist's. Many of us start PST practice after very little training and may not even really know what happens next in the PST process. We haven't seen it work and can't be sure we can make it work. Not until our fellow students, or we ourselves, experience some success will our own enthusiasm and faith in the process be conveyed to our clients.

When preparing the formulation, studying the history taking can help us develop ideas for the interventions which may be needed early in the work. It's still possible to be taken by surprise, of course, and can be quite troubling if the block is acute anxiety or panic during the sessions. During history taking it's also helpful to note whether the couple are at the same point in the change cycle (Prochaska & Norcross, 2018). Sometimes it's evident that one partner has brought the other to be fixed and has no interest in changing themselves. Rarely, both partners are already actively making changes. Interestingly, though they may already be sexual together, these are the couples most likely to embrace the sex ban and thoroughly enjoy the early non-genital intimacy building exercises. They may also have more sexual confidence than those who claim to have a high sex drive and a rich sexual history. Confidence building and incentivising reluctant partners helps them to catch up, and the therapist's understanding and patient confidence in them and the process will usually prove motivational.

Working with blocks is an invitation to creativity and the utilisation of whatever approach produces the best results (Hoyt & Bobele, 2019). CBT was the way Virginia Johnson chose to work with blocks in the early days of Sensate Focus, and is particularly helpful in PST as it addresses the associations between thoughts, feelings and behaviours. The addition of some systemic interventions makes CBT even more powerful, as it attends to the wider influences on clients and the dynamics of the relationship system. The systemic concepts of curiosity, neutrality, hypothesising and not-knowing are helpful in supporting this. Curiosity, for instance, involves looking further into clients' narratives, rather than just accepting what they say and taking it for granted everyone shares the meaning of what's been said. This leads to further questions, encouraging a position of neutrality (Cecchin, 1987). Neutrality isn't about being neutral, but about openness to a range of ideas, neither believing nor disbelieving, which supports couple balance and helps avoid the appearance of taking sides. Rather than making assumptions, the therapist creates hypotheses about what's going on for the clients, some of which appear in the formulation. As hypotheses are explored, they lead to the formation of new hypotheses.

In PST, psychoeducation or informed discussion can alter perception to the extent that change is virtually automatic, as context becomes reframed. Clients may be freed from unhelpful discourses or enabled to question prevailing ideas and scripts, an adaptation which is likely to continue beyond treatment.

Mentalising

Some psychodynamic awareness can also be helpful. For instance, it's useful to notice unconscious processes at work in the therapy, including the clients' transference towards you and your own relationship with their material. Hypotheses about the way the past is affecting the present, the couple fit or attachment style all bring additional dimensions to the work. The PST process encourages differentiation, a feature of Bowen Theory, related to an individual's ability to self-regulate, particularly in relation to their partners (Bowen, 1978). Indeed, research suggests the more differentiated partners are, the better their relationship (Rodríguez-González et al, 2016).

Partners with poor differentiation look for validation from one another. They may feel both need to share all their feelings and opinions for this to happen and have difficulty in accepting their partner's differences. This can cause problems from the outset of PST when they're immediately encouraged to focus on their *own* experience. Therapist modelling of a not-knowing and curious approach demonstrates to clients the advantages and possibilities differentiation creates, including greater flexibility and much better understanding of themselves and others. It also enhances, and is a feature of, the ability to mentalise – the skill of thinking about thinking and meaning making (theory of mind). This is compromised in poorly differentiated clients who either claim to 'know' what their partner is thinking, even if this conflicts with what they say they're thinking, or they expect others to know what *they're* thinking. They don't, therefore, see that it's ever necessary to share what sort of touch/sex they like, but are cross when their partner can't guess. Surprisingly, the process of not speaking about personal experience in experiments demonstrates the range of possibilities there could be and improves skills in non-verbal communication and personal responsibility.

Cognitive restructuring

In CBT, changing the way people think is called cognitive restructuring. Essentially, it demonstrates to clients that there are many ways of thinking, and that fixed, *knowing* ways aren't helpful. Many clients are desperate for certain, reassuring knowing. They think that if they know about things – what to expect, the essential nature of people and processes – they'll be in control and won't be disappointed. In reality, knowing removes control and causes not just disappointment but confusion and even panic when the world doesn't respond as expected. A knowing stance means reacting as though there's something wrong with the world – or other people – rather than wondering about one's own response or the motivation behind the other person's behaviour.

This sort of fixed knowing is behind much relationship conflict and distress. For instance, clients with a great deal of anxiety or negative thinking may be helped to catch Negative Automatic Thoughts (NATS). NATs are often so fleeting that the client only notices the feeling they produce, and may not realise they've had a thought at all. Catching thoughts offers the opportunity to challenge them. For instance, some people's thoughts are treated as beliefs and are never questioned. Indeed, they may be so longstanding that they haven't ever considered them. They may produce behaviour that clients assume is the same for everyone, so they benefit from the systemic intervention of questioning where reasons *originate*, such as family, media, culture or religion. Also using the CBT question of how *helpful* their beliefs are may assist them in re-evaluating some of their thinking. These aren't necessarily ideas they would have considered before.

Often, NATs are considered to be 'truths' rather than just acquired thoughts which have been subject to outside influences. We aren't born with our thoughts, and there's nothing wrong with having thoughts which are different to other people's. However, clients often assume that ideas and behaviours they've grown up with will be the same for their partner.

Sabotage

Therapeutic ruptures often occur in the context of poor mentalising, when the therapist's motivation is misunderstood. However, mistakes happen and ruptures need to be addressed whether they're due to misunderstanding, accident or neglect. Betchen (2009) argues that couples who seem eager and ready for PST still sometimes seem to sabotage the work, especially when success could mean an end to blaming. Sometimes the sexual problem is a way of managing a couple's intimacy and they may not have an alternative strategy to replace this when the problem improves. An astute therapist may suspect this at an early stage, but the couple themselves are often oblivious to their own dynamic and insist nothing but good can come from change.

PST may settle unconscious anxiety and collusion as the couple become more trusting and secure in the relationship. Indeed, it's surprising how much general change can occur in a relatively short time. Nonetheless, sabotage can occur at any stage, so that it appears clients are going backwards. It isn't always possible to predict what they'll find stressful or triggering. Sometimes one partner's reaction to the other's anxiety escalates it when it might otherwise have been easily dealt with. Blaming, frustration or loss of patience in a partner, coming out of the blue, needs investigation as this could be a sign that the apparently stressed partner is not really the one with the problem.

Sometimes it seems that clients are deliberately repeating behaviours they claimed to dislike and wanted to end. It's possible these had a protective function, helping the couple to avoid becoming too close, for instance. There's less chance of such unconscious collusion if it's anticipated and addressed within the programme. For example, couples may feel closer after Sensate Focus if they have a peaceful and bonding cuddle rather than just getting straight on with their day.

Initiation problems

Partners sometimes turn up in the early stages saying they haven't done the experiments because neither initiated them. Some sex therapy textbooks suggest telling couples to take turns in initiating when sessions will take place. While it's fair to ask couples to take turns in preparing the room/having first shower, asking them to initiate experiments can cause considerable pressure. If one partner has never initiated intimacy, and that's been okay, why would you impose change?

Initiation problems can be minimised with clear contracting. When setting exercises, it's helpful to agree and note times the couple plan to do the experiments. Agree that each partner should be in the place they're supposed to be at the agreed time – one should be preparing the room while the other showers. Even this can be sabotaged by one, say, beginning a task at the last minute. Explain that each partner needs to take responsibility for ensuring they're available, so nipping to the computer 'to just send a couple of e-mails' minutes before the experiment time isn't a good idea. Ask sabotaging clients if they're afraid the experiments may go well. What are the dangers of a well-functioning sex life and an intimate relationship?

Often, clients don't do self-focus exercises either, saying there's no point if the other partner isn't making the effort. Wonder aloud if they're afraid. Ask what has come up that changes things? Sometimes, they've had a row at some recent point and say they don't feel like being intimate as a result. Sometimes, they have the row just before the experiment or pick a fight as they're getting ready. Nothing could say more clearly that PST is scary *or* that one of them doesn't actually want to be doing this at all.

Timing

Some couples genuinely struggle to find time for experiments. This can be antici-pated in the assessment stages and may turn out to be the sole reason why a couple aren't having sex. If they enjoy sex on holidays, away from everyday demands and stresses, it's likely that time rather than willingness or functioning is their problem. It's, consequently, helpful to frame timing as experimental from the beginning. As well as establishing that couples are very busy, it demonstrates the effect of being so busy – feeling stressed, difficulty relaxing, guilt, irritability and just plain exhaustion make it difficult for couples to find time for one another. Often, they'll agree to cancel a Sensate Focus session because they're just too tired or distracted, or some other commitment, such as work or a sick child, gets in the way.

Whatever the reason couples give for missing sessions, restate that timing is experimental and that what happened is good learning. However, in initial con-tracting and when sessions are missed, urge the couple to do *something* if they can, such as the gazing exercise before they go to sleep, and to keep up their own self-focus experiments. They should agree to another time for the experiments as soon as they know they're going to miss one, even if a therapy session inter-venes. If the next time doesn't go into the diary immediately, days and weeks may pass before they get round to scheduling the next date, so failure to do this when advised should be explored thoroughly to ensure the couple do actually want to continue.

When time is genuinely short, work may just be about accepting what's pos-sible at the moment rather than the couple focusing on what they think they ought to be doing or think everyone else is doing. Sometimes one or both partners feel their intimate and sexual connection is an essential stress reliever and/or part of reassuring them that the relationship is okay, so they keep on seeking sex. It may work to continue the work very slowly, trying to keep each partner on board with self-focus and occasional joint experiments.

For couples who take a break from PST, suggest scheduling a regular weekly, or even monthly, intimacy hour when they take a bath together, snuggle up in bed for a chat or a massage, or do some Sensate Focus exercises. Don't create pressure to have any kind of sex on these occasions, but don't impose a sex ban either. They may want to check in occasionally for a session with you, but be clear this is not PST and that sex therapy remains a possibility for the future. If a couple is determined to continue PST despite time difficulties, consider using digital video such as Skype, Facetime or WhatsApp. This is particularly helpful when couples have difficulty with babysitting or getting to their appointments in time after work. However, extremely clear contracting is needed to ensure they can't be overheard and that there's no one else in the room – especially children – whilst a session is taking place (BACP, 2019).

Spontaneity

Some couples don't like the idea of scheduling experiments because, they say, they believe sex should be spontaneous and natural. First of all, point out that the experiments are designed to help establish when is the best time for sex. However, experiments aren't 'sex' inasmuch as they are prescribed activities which are discussed with a therapist – this isn't 'natural'. 'Surprise' sex, which happens when a couple aren't expecting to make love, might be a more accurate description than spontaneity. Usually, interest has been indicated earlier and the couple have been building up to making love. Even when a couple just roll over in bed and start making love, it generally happens at the same time of day or is more likely on a particular day of the week. Couples cite the spontaneity of the early relationship, when they were dating. If they usually had sex during a date, this can't really be described as spontaneous either.

In reality, most people would rather not be too spontaneous where sex is concerned. It's lovely when it happens, but usually the circumstances already have to be right to allow it. For instance, both partners probably want to feel clean, relaxed, unlikely to be interrupted, in an environment where sex is possible and with appropriate contraception, lube and sex toys available if they need them.

If a couple or one partner continues to insist they don't want to schedule experiment sessions, leave them to have them spontaneously. If it works, everyone's happy and if not, you'll all have learned a great deal about what's possible.

Disliking the experiments

Sometimes clients who seemed fully on board when experiments were agreed to grumble about them in the next session, perhaps saying they haven't done them because they're too simple or they've tried this sort of thing before. They won't have unless they've previously tried PST, in which case you'd be very interested in why it didn't work. As with most sabotage, there's likely to be some sort of anxiety which they're not recognising, or they're avoiding it and blaming the therapist or process instead. Often, it's the partner who was more enthusiastic about PST who is dismissive of the process once it gets going. Objections are most common in the early stages of PST before couples properly appreciate the rationale for the experiments and while they remain afraid of failure.

Restating the reasons for the sex ban and taking the experiments slowly is often sufficient to reassure and reengage couples, especially when potential anxiety is directly addressed. If complaints or non-compliance persist, Weiner and Avery-Clark (2017) advise asking couples what they think they should be doing, and creating the next experiments on the basis of their wishes. This can provide useful learning for both therapist and clients, and will almost certainly result in the couple preferring your experiments.

Sometimes couples go even further, just ignoring what's been agreed upon and making up their own experiments. In this case, it's again worth acknowledging their anxiety, even if they don't appear anxious. Complaining and apparent confidence in their own efforts may be very superficial. Take feedback in just as much detail as you would with the agreed-upon experiments, including as much information as possible about how, when and why they switched. Ask them to consider why they think their exercises are more useful than ones you had agreed to and, if they are, why they didn't just employ these rather than coming for therapy. It's important not to appear dismissive, shaming or punishing, but to be accepting and curious.

Check that the couple understands the rationale for the experiments that were set, or consider whether the process is moving too fast. The most apparently confident clients frequently turn out to be the most anxious. It may be too early in the programme for them to be attempting genital exercises, for instance. Or they may have chosen very outcome-focused experiments, still looking for erection and orgasm. You can be curious about why they're doing this when they agreed with your formulation of their situation and the importance of being less outcome-oriented in order to reduce performance and response anxiety.

If they claim to have no anxiety, explore with them why they find such simple experiments so difficult to follow. They'll often say they're too boring, which again suggests their thinking remains outcome-focused and they haven't yet understood that they aren't expected to find experiments exciting or stimulating. Being bored by experiments is useful learning, not a reason to avoid them. Make clear that you're more than happy to explore their ideas but that it's helpful to run them past you before trying them. Reiterate that the PST process has been carefully designed to direct clients' attention towards more positive and affirming thoughts and behaviours, such as building intimacy and feeling in control, freer or more heard.

If, on the other hand, the experiments the couple chose went brilliantly, they feel they've moved on and have given convincing feedback of their learning, you'll have no difficulty in endorsing their choices and congratulating them on their progress. In fact, we actively want clients to take control once their confidence has grown and they're becoming confidently sexual. Letting on that we're looking for them to 'go rogue' would just create pressure, however, and is not usually helpful in the early to middle stages of PST.

Shame

Shame is a huge presence in the lives of many clients, and sex offers even more opportunity for shame to affect our clients' well-being. Couple clients often present with reasons to feel guilty – neglecting one another, affairs, broken promises, unkind words – but shame isn't about behaviours, it's a feeling about the person's very self. Shame is what underlies low self-worth, lack of confidence and self-doubt. It's therefore often an unwelcome partner in the bedroom, the cause of performance anxiety and most of the impossible beliefs people create for themselves.

It takes bravery to have sex or even be just a little bit intimate. Fear of mistakes or being humiliated account for the anxiety associated with sex and for the extraordinary tactics that can be used to avoid sex or PST experiments. Shame is horrible for most people, so it can be helpful to talk instead about 'concern to get things right'. It's so awful for some individuals that they remove themselves entirely from any perception of shame, instead creating a successful persona and belittling others for *their* shame and vulnerability, unable to accept responsibility for their mistakes. PST is hugely challenging for them, as they're required to notice and describe what's happening in their bodies and to entertain the idea of uncertainty and anxiety. A good deal of acting out, avoidance and general blocking is often the result. Yet clients like this often do well in PST, emerging not only with a much improved sex life but with more insight, sense of responsibility, self-control and personal peace. Couples can be transformed from shaming and shamed heart-sink clients to your greatest success stories – couples who can be loving without fear and believe they're loved.

It takes courage to work with such clients, too. They need our calm, confident containment in order to change. We should try not to be frustrated or blame ourselves, but understand clients' fears and frustrations. This helps them see that the world, sex and relationships are not as scary as they've always seemed, even if they've done a good job of hiding this. It's their blocks that give us the opportunity to help, possibly putting right a lifetime of insecurity or bluster.

Breaking the sex ban

Breaking the sex ban often happens early in treatment, when couples begin an experiment, become aroused and then have intercourse. There's often no further compliance problem thereafter. It's as if this is something certain clients need to get out of their system before they can settle down to PST. Just reiterating the rationale for the ban and discussing how it can be managed is often enough therapeutic intervention. It certainly doesn't help to tell clients off.

It's often the partner who seemed least interested in sex, and isn't as enthusiastic about PST, who initiates the violation. Mentioning this when you set the ban may make it less likely. When it happens, the initiator usually says it was something they both wanted at the time and that they don't see why they should be dictated to. The other partner will often admit they remonstrated briefly but felt the opportunity was too good to miss. However, they often disagree with the perception they're being 'dictated to', agreeing that they entered the PST process willingly and want it to work.

It's always helpful to empathise with how scary the process can be even when couples aren't expressing this. This demonstrates your understanding without the couple needing to feel they've shamed themselves by admitting to doubts or fears. In fact, couples often communicate difficult feelings in non-verbal ways, so it's important to be open to meaning in the face of apparent sabotage rather than being irritable about it.

This can be especially difficult with clients who insist their sex drive is too enormous to endure a sex ban. As managing feelings is a major part of differentiation, they should be encouraged to persist and see what they learn as a result. Some therapists cave in and allow masturbation, but this can remove the incentive for couple experiments and the client doesn't learn much about self-management. Shame may underlie their protestations. For instance, someone may feel they shouldn't need sex therapy, so claims to a huge sex drive demonstrate how sexual they really are. If masturbation is the person's only source of stress relief, they'll benefit generally from developing additional affect management resources more suitable to circumstances where masturbation isn't possible. Reassure couples that a complete ban may not last long – depending on their learning – and that their health won't suffer.

Breaking the ban later in the PST process sometimes happens when the couple's therapy is coming to a natural end and they go further with the experiment than planned. Or it may happen when they want to avoid something they think will be challenging ahead. Working out what's worrying them is more important than trying to unpick what happened when the ban was broken – unless, that is, both the couple weren't in agreement about it. This would undo previously accrued trust, making it difficult to continue with PST. Urgent supervision would be needed to help determine how to go forward, as this may be indicative of control in other parts of the relationship.

Consent is discussed further in Chapter 13.

References

BACP (2019) *Working Online in the Counselling Professions*, March, Lutterworth: BACP.

Betchen, S. (2009) Premature ejaculation: An integrative, inter systems approach for couples. *Journal of Family Psychotherapy*, 20;2–3, 1–30.

Bowen, M. (1978) *Family Therapy in Clinical Practice*, New York: Jason Aronson.

Cecchin, G. (1987) Hypothesizing, circularity and neutrality revisited: An invitation to curiosity. *Family Process*, 26;4, 405–413.

Hoyt, M.F. & Bobele, M. (2019) *Creative Therapy in Challenging Situations: Unusual Interventions to Help Clients*, New York: Routledge.

Prochaska, J.O. & Norcross, J.C. (2018) *Systems of Psychotherapy: A Transtheoretical Analysis*, Oxford: Oxford University Press.

Rodríguez-González, M., Skowronb, E.A., de Gregorioc, V.C. & Muñoz San Roque, I. (2016) Differentiation of self, mate selection, and marital adjustment: Validity of postulates of Bowen theory in a Spanish sample. *The American Journal of Family Therapy*, 44;1, 11–23.

Weiner, L. & Avery-Clark, C. (2017) *Sensate Focus in Sex Therapy*, New York: Routledge.

Chapter 13

Sexual consent

A surprising block in PST can relate to the question of sexual consent. Few couples discuss consent (Shumlich & Fisher, 2018), yet it's often a relevant but overlooked issue for PST clients. Consent issues are often presented and mistaken for a different aspect of the relationship. What's described as mismatched libido, for instance, may actually be a consent and coercion complaint, confused by sexual and gender discourses around expectation and desire. As it's unacknowledged, couples often remain in conflict, both resentfully believing their needs are being wilfully denied.

In PST, sexual refusal is often not construed as about consent. Some people have an expectation that sexual refusal is a form of play, a prelude to sexually succumbing. It may be, but this needs to be explicitly agreed rather than assumed. In PST we sometimes sidestep this. We might, for instance, discuss how to avoid hurt feelings when one partner is 'not in the mood'. However, this frames the issue as a conversation about a pursuing partner's hurt feelings, without necessarily recognising or addressing the feelings and wishes of the refusing partner. A conversation about consent, rather than sensitivities, would cover both, as it would produce better understanding of each partner's motivation and feelings.

When we encourage one another to persevere following a relationship rebuff, perhaps what we should instead advise is either respectful retreat or apology and – if appropriate and consensual – a conversation about what happened and how to avoid future 'misunderstanding'. This is crucial, as the pursuit of such a conversation has the potential to turn into pestering or an opportunity for further sexual persuasion. If someone is reluctant to talk, it's usually because the person requesting the conversation isn't listening and/or reacts badly when the discussion doesn't go their way.

Non-consensual behaviour

Though PST is an excellent opportunity to explore a couple's attitude towards sexual consent, therapists often feel out of their depth doing so. This may reflect a tendency to concur with strongly held beliefs. Non-consensual behaviours are often robustly defended as banter or teasing. Even a partner who doesn't enjoy them may also feel ashamed that they're unable to appreciate the fun, aware that their objection would create 'a problem'. Thus, many people find they've assumed responsibility for their own bullying. Once begun, this is a difficult dynamic to end.

Perhaps consent is too rarely discussed because we assume sex between couples in relationships is always consensual. Unfortunately, it isn't. Though persistent sexual persuasion and touching between couples may stop short of intercourse, there may still have been considerable unwanted sexual behaviour before refusal was accepted. Over time, this can result in severe negative effects on the relationship and the coerced partner (Daspe *et al*, 2016). If it's followed by sulking, anger or moodiness, there's clear disregard for the other's feelings and right to refuse. Nonetheless, the behaviour of a partner who continuously pursues and/or gropes despite a negative response may not be treated as unacceptable by either the couple or their therapist. Rather, the refusal may be considered the result of low desire, effectively making the victim the problem (again). To avoid this sort of collusion, it's essential to start discussing consent when it arises. Too many sex therapists appear to have sympathy for the so-called high-libido partner and see the pursued partner as withholding and controlling. It's better to work out what's wrong. First, though, you need to know what's usual, wanted and acceptable for both the couple and not just assume that sex is a regular, loving and happy event.

Changing your mind

There's often more to negotiate and agree to than we ever assume. It's common, for instance, for sexual preferences to change or be rested at certain times in our lives. Many people feel differently about some sexual practices when they've been ill, put on weight or started a family, for example. This is only a problem if their partner doesn't accept their feelings. For instance, once they've had children, many people don't feel comfortable being smacked or patted on the rear as their partner passes by. This may be something they previously enjoyed, tolerated or hated – but now they don't want it to happen in front of their children or at all. They may feel it sends negative messages about the proprietorial treatment of others, they may fear it will be copied by children or that they'll see playful touch as a source of conflict. They may just not like being touched in this way (any longer). Some clients say they feel they've simply grown out of some behaviours. It's not our job to persuade them to change their mind because their partner is disappointed, but to help them both manage the difference.

Sometimes people want sex when they're approached, but feel the circumstances aren't right – they're too tired, don't have contraception, would like a wash first or would like to know the sexual partner better, for example. A big issue is the way desire for sex is communicated. Asking someone to come home for a coffee may mean *come for sex* to the person asking. However, the person they're inviting may simply be excited by the prospect of a nice cup of Java or may change their mind about coffee and/or sex somewhere along the way.

Sometimes people who engage in *some* sexual behaviour but stop short of intercourse or removing their clothes may be as disappointed as the other partner that sex isn't possible at this time. Enthusiastic engagement followed by disengagement is often described as unreasonable teasing rather than a person's right to choose. This is difficult to understand – as well as hugely offensive – since it doesn't acknowledge the sexual engagement that *did* happen as a positive. Such an incident can be reframed for couples as a communication issue to be tackled, rather than a sexual problem to be pitied, whilst remaining clear that unwelcome sexual behaviour is unacceptable.

Expectation of consent

It isn't reasonable to assume that consent to one sexual activity (or a hot beverage) means consent to others. Nor should it be assumed that sex is desired unless someone starts screaming or runs away. Even then, even when someone's unconscious, some people still assume consent. Some men have reacted to the #MeToo movement by not hiring women for jobs, avoiding women and claiming it's dangerous to be with women in case they make a complaint of sexual harassment (Tan & Porzecanski, 2018). In the UK reports of men being terrified of unfair sexual accusations (Dhaliwal, 2018) gave the impression that women were making unreasonable demands of men and marginalising them. Incredibly, it seemed some men were asking what constituted acceptable behaviour, despite #MeToo's clear 'guidelines' that consent needs to be sought rather than assumed. In sexual situations, it's pretty clear whether someone is enthusiastically joining in – surely we aren't hearing from men who are so used to sex with unwilling partners that they've never experienced consent?

It's chilling to hear a large, strong person say about a much smaller, weaker person, 'They said no, but didn't do anything to stop me'. Consent *is* often assumed, and then withdrawal of consent isn't believed, especially if there were other times when it was given or if it was there initially (Darden *et al*, 2019). Often, making someone do something they don't want to isn't considered as bad as letting someone down. This thinking lies behind much sexual coercion, whereby people 'give in' to sex they don't want to please their partner or stop them from being angry

---

Box 13.1   Demonstrating consent

There are several brilliant YouTube videos, such as this one: https://www.youtube.com/watch?v=pZwvrxVavnQ, which explain consent in terms of making someone a cup of tea.

or sulky. Women, in particular, are socialised to put others first, so are more vulnerable to their partner's disappointment. Perhaps this is why women in straight relationships are less likely to recognise or report sexual coercion (Eaton & Matamala, 2014).

The expectation of consent, in the absence of what someone takes as a 'no', places the responsibility for sexual assault on the victim. This reduces consent to a binary nod when it's actually so much more complex and nuanced. For instance, people with low self-esteem or sexual confidence are more likely to comply with sex and be convinced they're unreasonable in withholding it (Darden *et al*, 2019). This ends up being oppressive to both men and women (hooks, 2015), as it's not about sexual pleasure but sexual performance.

Women's responsibility for bolstering the male ego was exacerbated by greater sexual permissiveness from the 1950s–1970s when female sexuality became more legitimised (Frith, 2015). Rather than freeing women from sexual repression, it positioned responsibility for male satisfaction with women. Not just the man's orgasm became required but also affirmation of his sexual abilities, as evidenced by his partner's orgasm. Not wanting sex, thus, became not a minor disappointment but a massive affront to men's sexual identity.

Mansplaining

Talking about abusive behaviour and consent isn't always easy, especially when one partner thinks they understand the other's experience and diminishes it. Men in straight couples sometimes fail to understand women's experience of being groped, cat called and blamed for letting it happen if 'banter' or 'horseplay' go too far (Bates, 2015). Men explaining their experience to them is tiring for many women (Solnit, 2014). Far more than can be counted have used their PST history taking to talk about how this feels patronising and has gradually eroded their desire. Nevertheless, being treated with sexual disrespect is a common experience. If anyone doubts how casually women are verbally attacked and threatened, for instance, it isn't difficult to come across vile abuse on social media.

Straight couples often develop a repertoire of sexual behaviours without necessarily enjoying what they do, but going along with what they think is expected without even considering a discussion of what might be preferable. Gay men, meanwhile, *don't* automatically expect that sex equals intercourse and are more likely to engage in detailed negotiation about what they're going to do sexually (Kornhaber, 2019). Men in gay relationships also seem more likely to acknowledge their needs as competing (Daspe *et al*, 2016). Men are, nonetheless, still subjected to abuse and coercion. Both partners in gay relationships may subscribe to discourses about male sexuality meaning men should always be ready for sex (Braun *et al*, 2009). As a result, anxious men may see sexual refusal as outright rejection and their partners may feel obliged to agree to sex they don't want (Daspe *et al*, 2016).

Fairytales

Kink relationships involving bondage and domination generally include much more consideration of consent, what's going to happen between a couple and how to stop what's happening if someone changes their mind. Interestingly, therapists often consider kink relationships far more dangerous than vanilla relationships in which consent and agreement may never be addressed at all (Richards & Barker, 2013). This may be because we're so socialised about what's acceptable (Rubin, 2011). Fairytale princesses are generally passive, blond and so vulnerable that they aren't even aware of what's happening to them – Cinderella appears to be a victim of trafficking, or slavery at least; Little Mermaid Ariel gives up her voice and, ultimately, her family in pursuit of love; Belle from *Beauty and the Beast* has Stockholm syndrome; Sleeping Beauty and Snow White were actually unconscious when they were kissed and claimed. The original versions of the stories are much darker than the Disney versions too. Sleeping Beauty was originally raped and Geppetto was accused of child abuse when Pinocchio ran away. The story of Rapunzel is based on the legend of St Barbara who was kept prisoner and finally murdered by her own father for refusing to obey him, marry the men he offered and following her own faith. Sanitizing these horror stories shifts the focus to the enviable happy-ever-after outcome and away from the cost this entails. The message that love triumphs over adversity ignores any ongoing sacrifice, usually made by the princess rather than the prince.

While the emerging empowered and non-white princesses in movies and storybooks are to be welcomed, the message generally remains binary – 'kick out the dumb prince' rather than 'negotiate a situation where both prince and princess feel respected'. Princesses' empowerment also portrays them as the holders of responsibility. You don't come across many princes who see the light all by themselves and apologise for their dumb behaviour. Even the portrayal of princes as dumb buys into the discourse that men don't mean it when they hurt women (Rollero & Tartaglia, 2019), thereby negating women's right to outrage.

Pornography

Unfortunately, many children and young people's viewing graduates from Disney to pornography where rough or violent sex is normalised. In advertising its content, a porn site claims, 'No other **sex** tube is more popular and features more Extreme **Brutal Rough Violent** scenes' (their emphasis). The women being abused generally don't look at all happy about what's happening to them. When they do look as though they're welcoming their abuse, this normalises the idea that violence has no consequences. There's also a widespread view that women are the 'gatekeepers' of physical intimacy but 'must compete among themselves by giving men more of what men want if they expect to find male companionship on Saturday night' (Rhoads, 2012: 515). This simplifies and problematises consent for everyone by avoiding negotiation and inherently inviting transgression.

The idea that porn actors' consent is implied by their involvement and that much behind-the-scenes agreement occurs (Lee, 2015) doesn't cut it. Sexual violence is inevitably regularised by its ubiquity, providing the major sex and relationships education for many young people (Wollaston, 2019). Introduction of porn literacy classes to enable young people to critique what they view, facilitated by more contextual sex information, is a popular idea but it's yet to be determined whether it's effective (Albury, 2014). Meanwhile, sexual violence is perpetrated against a background of rape and abuse in pornography. Even if it turns out this doesn't promote violent sex in young people, it serves to disempower those who've been abused. As Chapter 14 explains, disclosing sexual abuse is impossible for some victims. It's unlikely that porn culture, which effectively trivialises sexual suffering, will improve their plight.

References

Albury, K. (2014) Porn and sex education, porn as sex education. *Porn Studies*, 1;1–2, 172–181.

Bates, L. (2015) *Everyday Sexism*, London: Simon & Schuster.

Braun, V., Schmidt, J., Gavey, N. & Fenaughty, J. (2009) *Journal of Homosexuality*, 56, 336–360.

Darden, M.C., Ehman, A.C., Lair, E.C. & Gross, A.M. (2019) Sexual compliance: Examining the relationships among sexual want, sexual consent, and sexual assertiveness. *Sexuality & Culture*, 23, 220–235.

Daspe, M., Sabourin, S., Godbout, N., Lussier, Y. & Hébert, M. (2016) Neuroticism and men's sexual coercion as reported by both partners in a community sample of couples. *Journal of Sex Research*, 53;8, 1036–1046.

Dhaliwal, N. (2018) How a year of #MeToo has made British men more afraid than ever. *The Telegraph*, October 14. www.telegraph.co.uk/men/thinking-man/year-metoo-has-made-british-men-afraid-ever/. Accessed August 5, 2019.

Eaton, A.A. & Matamala, A. (2014) The relationship between heteronormative beliefs and verbal sexual coercion in college students. *Archives of Sexual Behavior*, 43;7, 1443–1457.

Frith, H. (2015) *Orgasmic Bodies*, Basingstoke: Palgrave Macmillan.

hooks, b. (2015) *Feminism is for Everybody: Passionate Politics*, New York: Routledge.

Kornhaber, S. (2019) Cruising in the age of consent. *Atlantic*, July, 96–103.

Lee, J. (2015) Click "I agree": Consent and feminism in commercial pornography. *Global Information Society Watch: Sexual Rights and the Internet*, Melville, South Africa: APC, 40–43.

Rhoads, S.E. (2012) Hookup culture: The high costs of a "low price" for sex. *Society*, 49;6, 515–519.

Richards, C. & Barker, M. (2013) *Sexuality & Gender for Mental Health Professionals*, London: Sage.

Rollero, C. & Tartaglia, S. (2019) The effect of sexism and rape myths on victim blame. *Sexuality & Culture*, 23, 209–219.

Rubin, G. (1984/2011) Thinking sex. Notes for a radical theory of the politics of sexuality. *Deviations: A Gayle Rubin Reader*, Durham, NC: Duke University Press, 152.

Shumlich, E.J. & Fisher, W.A. (2018) Affirmative sexual consent? Direct and unambiguous consent is rarely included in discussions of recent sexual interactions. *Canadian Journal of Human Sexuality*, 27;3, 248–260.

Solnit, R. (2014) *Men Explain Things to Me*, London: Granta.

Tan, G. & Porzecanski, K. (2018) Wall street rule for the #MeToo era: Avoid women at all cost. *Bloomberg News*, December 3. www.bloomberg.com/news/articles/2018-12-03/a-wall-street-rule-for-the-metoo-era-avoid-women-at-all-cost. Accessed August 5, 2019.

Wollaston, S. (2019) *Health and Social Care Committee Report: Sexual Health*, May 21, London: House of Commons.

Chapter 14

Sexual trauma

Many clients have experienced some sort of sexual and/or other trauma, which they may not acknowledge and often minimise. Any form of past trauma can have an effect on relationships, therapy and the therapeutic alliance (McFarlane & Bookless, 2001). Sexual trauma is relatively common, sexual assaults being experienced by at least one in five women in England and Wales (ONS, 2018), and reported assaults against men have recently tripled. In PST the effect of trauma on a client's relationships and sexual expression may be the reason for seeking help or the, as yet unknown, cause of their difficulties.

While some clients tell us about their past traumas, others prefer not to or may not remember them. Someone who has dissociated from their memories may fear they'll have to know detail about what happened if they start talking about it or receive treatment (Steele, 2018). Some people remember what happened but have rationalised the events and don't see them as significant, though this may change during PST. Sensate Focus can trigger abuse memories, whether or not the client remembers them. Some really traumatic memories are not recalled cognitively but are emotional memories, flooding the body with distressing feelings which are then assumed to be a response to whatever is happening at the time (Badenoch, 2018). Flashbacks bring a similar sense of feeling the danger is current, so people often react as though the flashback memory is happening now (Cozolino, 2016).

Some people also remain loyal to the secrecy of their abusive relationship or continue to consider it special in spite of its negative effects. Some believe their silence saved younger siblings from abuse and parents from heartache, and that maintaining silence continues to be protective. It's consequently helpful to assume that all our clients *could have* been sexually abused. This means being respectful towards behaviours which may appear sabotaging to the PST process, but could have protective effects for the clients.

Another reason for failure to reveal abuse is clients' fear that it might have been their fault or that the therapist will think it was. If they weren't believed when they told someone about what happened, they may have additional difficulty in trusting that you'll believe them or won't judge. They may additionally have conflicted feelings if the abuser was someone in a position of trust, that they loved or continue to love, if the abuser made them feel special and if they enjoyed the sex. It can be helpful to mention in general terms – perhaps during some aspect of psychoeducation – that people who experience sexual abuse are often aroused by what's done to them. This is a physiological response, not a choice. This can be illustrated by the tried and trusted example of what happens if someone is poked in the eye. However much they might not want to, they blink. Arousal is the same, and continued arousal leads to orgasm. People also often experience erections or vaginal lubrication when they're frightened.

If trauma is acknowledged, ascertain what help the client had, how much the partner knows and whether the abuser remains a danger. It isn't always helpful for partners to know much detail, especially if a perpetrator is still around. Some partners become angry and vengeful when they find out, rather than offering support. Others feel traumatised themselves. Sometimes abuse is ongoing, posing a major ethical and safeguarding dilemma for the therapist. Sometimes, it even emerges that one of the partners is abusing the other *now*. Risk of violence increases when a less powerful partner mentions leaving or any major changes.

It can be difficult to patiently build trust before mentioning further disclosure where abuse has never been officially reported, and the abuser potentially remains active. Rarely, therapists have enough information about ongoing abuse to make their own disclosure, but ultimately there needs to be a victim who is willing to provide evidence to police. Pushing an unwilling victim could be retraumatising and is likely to cause retreat rather than disclosure.

PST has a better chance of success if trauma is dealt with before starting. Sometimes it's clear this is needed, but some clients want to try PST, especially if they've been dipping in and out of counselling. Clients may feel and act as though they've dealt with what happened but experience difficulties nonetheless. In assessing whether to try PST, you'll need to discuss with both partners how the trauma is affecting the relationship now and how it may affect the PST process. It's important to be sure one partner isn't coercing the other into a route they aren't comfortable with. Sometimes it's the abused client who insists on going ahead, hoping to make their partner happy and to feel normal themselves. Make no promises about outcome if you do decide to try PST, and ensure the couple is aware it may have to stop or stall if trauma intrudes.

Effect of trauma on relationships

Many clients who come to PST because their abuse is interfering with sex and/or intimacy are surprised by this, especially if they thought they'd put what happened behind them. For instance, though some may avoid sex, they may have grown up to be enthusiastic and adventurous lovers, perhaps with a number of sexual partners. Problems often begin when they meet someone special, and suddenly there is much more to lose. Having sex with someone who isn't too close may be fine, but sex with someone they care about may also prompt feelings of being abused or let down by people who should have been caring, safe and reliable. More severe and lasting effects tend to result when the perpetrator was known to the victim (Rellini, 2007), so a partner's love and kindness can be highly triggering.

As 80 percent of women who've been sexually abused report sexual problems (Lundqvist et al, 2004), these are usually assumed to be psychological. However, there's now MRI evidence that the areas of the brain which perceive genital sensation are actually thinner in women who've experienced childhood sexual abuse (Heim et al, 2013), potentially making them more physically vulnerable to genital and sexual pain.

Childhood sexual abuse (CSA)

Some – though by no means all – victims of sexual abuse self-soothe by eroticising and reenacting some aspect of their sexual trauma (Birchard, 2011). Even covert abuse causes many of the same problems as overt sexual abuse, though many victims and therapists don't recognise its significance (Weiss, 2015: 67–70). Be alert for stories which involve emotionally implied, rather than overtly acted out, sexual connection, such as adults commenting on physical development, graphic or sexualised conversation, inappropriate stories or images which can be presented as concern, education or liberalism. The adult may have meant well and been entirely unaware of the damage caused. Nonetheless, the child may have responded in the same way as someone who has experienced physical abuse. Seeing adult sex or nudity at home, homophobia, sex being described as bad or dirty, or never discussed at all, may also be implicated. A single abusive event gives a sense of before and after, so it's much easier for clients to identify what they need to feel better and to respond with trust to therapeutic interventions. When there are several traumatic events, or further trauma surrounds the original incident, clients may have adapted to living with trauma in ways which can be difficult to identify and treat.

Sometimes it isn't the abuse itself which causes long-term effects but the events around them, such as reports to police, going to court or just telling someone. Not being believed, expecting not to be believed or not being supported can be what embeds trauma in the mind and is one of the strongest predictors of post-traumatic stress disorder (PTSD) (Morley & Kohrt, 2013). Indeed, the way abuse is disclosed and handled may be more significant than the nature of the abuse itself. Kristensen and Lau's (2011) study supported earlier research suggesting that having at least one caring and stable parent figure made the development of a sexual pain disorder less likely (Harlow & Stewart, 2005).

Abusers groom other adults too, often making themselves indispensable and trusted family friends. Nonetheless, some people retrospectively blame themselves for letting their abuse happen. Some children feel responsible for any negative consequences of disclosure (Paine & Hansen, 2002), protecting their family's relationship with the abuser or believing their abuse is protecting younger family members. Abusers infect victims with their own shame, telling them they've invited and like their abuse.

Childhood emotional abuse is also associated with thinning of the brain areas concerned with self-evaluation and awareness (Heim *et al*, 2013). All this makes it much harder to shift negative self-appraisal and inappropriate feelings of responsibility. Questions to clients about why they didn't tell someone or fight back, or even trying to develop appreciation that children have little volition, may increase feelings of shame. Be *appropriately* disturbed, but remain containing, avoiding the temptation to self-disclose or to touch or hug the person (Sanderson, 2013). A balance needs to be struck between too much empathy or too little, both of which can be triggering.

Dissociation

Some people dissociate when triggered, a strategy which may have been developed as a way of managing their abuse. Dissociating is more common than we realise and can be valuable at other times when concentration and avoidance of extraneous influence is needed. However, it can become habitual and less helpful when used outside the times it's necessary. For most abuse victims, the danger has passed but they continue to be hypervigilant, ready for trouble. Rarely, someone dissociates so completely that different personalities are used to manage different affects and needs and to have different memories (DeYoung, 2015). There is a continuum of dissociation, however, with occasional vagueness at one end, proceeding through more pronounced splitting to dissociative identity disorder (DID). While DID undoubtedly requires specialist treatment, the affect states or personalities used towards the other end of the spectrum can more easily be seen as ways of managing difficult experiences and feelings. At a basic level, it's possible to work with these simply by asking the client to discuss the characteristics of different parts, especially those which are ambivalent (Fisher, 2017). For instance, clients may not find it too challenging to describe the sexual parts of themselves and the disinterested, disgusted or asexual parts. Given encouragement, clients can be extremely creative, describing the way the parts look, behave and their characteristics. Often, they aren't human and the way they think and feel may be at odds with the client's previously expressed thoughts and feelings. Once externalised in this way, it's possible to look at which parts have been present at different times and what they might think about the next experiment, for instance.

Flashbacks

When vivid flashbacks are experienced during sex or PST experiments, the person may feel as though the partner is the abuser (Kristensen & Lau, 2011). Both the partner and the abused individual may be shocked and upset by such extreme disruption to what should have been an intimate and peaceful experience. When this has happened, sex or Sensate Focus can seem terrifying, so it's often better to take a break and concentrate on recovery from the trauma before recommencing PST. Though sometimes a couple is able to negotiate how to manage such situations, it isn't a long-term solution nor is it really ethical.

Box 14.1   *Sources of support for sexual abuse*

The National Association for People Abused in Childhood (NAPAC):
0808 801 0331; www.napac.org.uk

NSPCC: 0808 800 5000; help@nspcc.org.uk

Positive Outcomes for Dissociative Survivors (PODS): 0800 181
4420; www.pods-online.org.uk

Rape Crisis: www.rapecrisis.org.uk

Safeline: 0800 800 5007 (general); 0800 800 5007 (young people);
www.safeline.org.uk

Supportline: 01708 765200; www.supportline.org.uk

Survivors Scotland: www.survivorsscotland.org.uk

The Survivors Trust: 0808 801 0818; www.thesurvivorstrust.org

Respond (for people with learning difficulties): www.respond.org.uk

---

If PST is paused while the person receives specialist therapy, it may be helpful to use a different therapist and modality, so that the PST is as little contaminated as possible. EMDR is an effective and relatively quick trauma treatment. Accredited practitioners are listed on the EMDR UK & Ireland website (https:// emdrassociation.org.uk/find-a-therapist/).

Male abuse

Though women are five times more likely than men to experience sexual trauma (ONS, 2018), men are abused too, more often by strangers (Stoltenborgh *et al*, 2011). Up to a third of gay men may have experienced physical sexual assault (Braun *et al*, 2009). Straight men are often perpetrators of male rape, demonstrating its use as a tool of power (Vearnals & Campbell, 2001). As with women, it's sometimes used as a form of torture, so we need to be particularly alert when working with asylum seekers. Women abuse men, too, much more often than is reported or recognised (Weiss, 2010). If women find it hard to have their experience believed, how much harder may it be for men in the context of shaming discourses around the performance of masculinity (Javaid, 2016)?

An estimated 25 million US men are thought to be affected, but the actual number could be far higher (Crete & Singh, 2015). Men are less likely to disclose what happened, and less likely to be believed (Elkins *et al*, 2017). Survivors UK think only about four percent of men report their sexual abuse, though disclosure of historic abuse is increasing (ONS, 2018).

It's often assumed men are less affected by sexual trauma (Vearnals & Campbell, 2001), but they may just be better at hiding it. Men are also less likely to identify what happened as abuse (O'Leary & Barber, 2008) and more likely to feel

> **Box 14.2 *Sources of support specifically for abused men and boys***
>
> **Mankind**: 01823 334244; www.mankind.org.uk
> **Safeline**: 0808 800 5005; www.safeline.org.uk
> **Survivors UK**: 0203 332 1860; www.survivorsuk.org

stigmatised (Elkins *et al*, 2017). Nonetheless, Alaggia and Mishna (2014) note that male abuse is a cause of severe depression, suicide, addictions, PTSD, anxiety disorders, personality disorders, sexual identity issues, sexual dysfunctions and difficulty forming close and trusting relationships. Coxell and colleagues (2000) recommend being alert to the possibility of sexual abuse in men and boys with mental health issues, especially self-harm.

As well as stigma and shame, some men fear being thought of as potential abusers themselves (Alaggia, 2005). Many also subscribe to discourses which see self-care and help-seeking as unmanly (Bunton & Cranshaw, 2002). Part of the therapist's task is cognitive restructuring around common masculine discourses and encouragement to accept the vulnerability associated with having been a victim.

Abuse may be revealed 'accidentally', when a different trauma is being dealt with. Treat this seriously as soon as it's mentioned, but do be patient and follow the client's lead (Knight, 2015). Where there is relationship conflict, abuse or anti-social acting out, it may be tempting to judge and attempt to accelerate treatment, but following the client's pace is more likely to be effective. The supportive involvement of partners can enhance both recovery and the relationship (Crete & Singh, 2015).

PST

Where one partner has a trauma history, it's likely the other does, too. When abuse has been disclosed or is suspected, take as long as possible over the history taking and be curious about how intimacy is expressed. Couples may trigger one another, so PST can be slow. Commonly, sex is described as having been great initially, with problems beginning when the couple became close. A history of early consensual sex is associated with CSA, and there may be more risk-taking behaviour.

Secondary sexual dysfunction is relatively common in apparently non-traumatised partners. For example, there may be a genital pain disorder in the abused client and ED in their partner (De Silva, 2001). Partners are often afraid to initiate sex following/learning of sexual trauma, and can become more like carers, leading to lost libido. Sometimes, one partner seeks to overcome the trauma by being very actively sexual, and may feel rejected if the other partner has a more tentative approach or is easily triggered. Some partners also insist on hearing the story of what happened and are hurt when the abused person can't or won't tell them. They need to understand that telling the story can be unnecessarily retraumatising. Even when someone wants to tell their story, they need to be clear about what they hope to gain from this. Their own narratives can contain elements of shame and self-disgust which can be reinforced through the telling (DeYoung, 2015). It can be more useful to first discuss the effects of the event(s) and other relevant stories, such as telling relatives, seeing the abuser or managing feelings, before the story is fully related. This can help the person develop a more mature way of 'remembering' and reinforce their sense of resilience, rather than re-experiencing the events from the viewpoint of their earlier, more vulnerable selves.

Some abused people also find it hard to produce words to tell their story even when they remember it well. Partners need to understand that the logical, mentalising part of the brain, the pre-frontal cortex, goes offline during episodes of trauma or high emotion. Someone's failure to provide adequate feedback may simply be because they can't. The parts of the brain which control speech are also offline during trauma so that events are remembered emotionally rather than cognitively, flooding the body when recalled. Sometimes it's just the body that remembers (van der Kolk, 2015), so a person can feel terrified, angry, frozen or a need to run without knowing why. Being curious about this and trying to understand what's happening is likely to be much more helpful than confrontation (Steele, 2018).

Abuse may be part of a person's story, but not all of it, so avoid making it seem as if the client is defined by trauma. As the couple may be desperate to feel 'normal', it's even more important to emphasise the experimental aspects of PST and that you're looking for helpful information, not right or wrong outcomes. It's important to take things slowly, and not to rush the client(s), seek an outcome or pursue your own agenda to give value. It's tempting, for instance, to rush through the process when clients seem keen to do so or are finding experiments difficult. Remember, though, that many abused clients will have tried to get their abuse over with as quickly as possible, and now need to learn to tolerate their negative feelings in order to access the positive ones. Clients' slow progress isn't a sign of their resistance or the therapist's inadequacy. We just need to accept that pacing is different for different clients and their capacities to be comfortably intimate may still be evolving. The hypervigilance of trauma makes it difficult to be playful (McFarlane & Bookless, 2001) and some clients manage their feelings by flipping between anxious agitation and numbness. If one partner is progressing faster than the other, they may benefit from more self-focus exercises to help them feel they're developing well.

Some experiments need to be adapted to remove potential triggers. For instance, we encourage clients not to talk during Sensate Focus, but silence may be difficult if it feels as though the partner is withdrawing, or allows space for intrusive thoughts or if abuse happened in silence. Clients need to be treated with particular respect and consideration when they've grown used to meeting the needs of others – protecting the abuser, relatives and friends from disclosure, as well as meeting the abuser's physical demands.

It can be helpful to prepare all very anxious and (potentially) traumatised clients with mindfulness and deep-breathing exercises to manage panicky feelings. Suggesting use of a mindfulness app at the initial assessment begins the process early, though some people are panicked by any focus on bodily sensations. Breathing practise may be a helpful exercise to set at the formulation, involving the deepest possible breath in followed by the slowest possible breath out. Clients may be able to feel their heart rate slow as they do this. Keeping a bottle of water handy during Sensate Focus can be useful, as a good glug engages the parasympathetic nervous system. Grounding exercises can be used to reorientate. For instance, tell the client to place their feet firmly on the ground or lie down and be aware of the support beneath them.

Some people want to be hugged and touched when they're panicking; for others, being aware of the space around them can confer a sense of control, which partners need to understand and respect. Some clients benefit from guided imagery which takes them to a calm comfortable place (see page 60). Such interventions are most helpful when used at any early stage, so learning to identify triggers to unwanted feelings can be used to help prepare all clients in case discomfort, anxiety or panic should arise during experiments or subsequently in their lives together.

Self-care

In PST we need to be aware that on any day we may be subjected to profoundly disturbing content that we hadn't bargained for. According to trauma therapist Kathy Steele (2018), working with sexually abused clients requires considerable resilience and awareness, as sometimes their seductive behaviour can create powerful erotic countertransference. This can also make the therapist particularly want to help them but feel inadequate to do so. On the other hand, survivors who identify with the abuser may attempt to control and dominate the therapy. The therapist's sense of self can gradually begin to ebb away.

Self-care is, therefore, particularly important when working with abused clients to avoid vicarious traumatisation and burnout. Becoming over-involved or detached and losing personal satisfaction and confidence in work can indicate burnout (Maslach *et al*, 1996). Some people choose sex therapy as relief from the conflict and hopelessness of some couple work, but unexpectedly find themselves working with different elements of interpersonal trauma. Though you'll need an experienced and qualified PST supervisor, it may be worth finding someone who is also trauma qualified if you find yourself working with a lot of sexual abuse.

Trauma psychologist and lecturer Christiane Sanderson (2013) points out the cumulative impact of working with trauma and recommends developing plans to recognise and manage stress, ensuring that all aspects of self-care are attended to. This includes ensuring enough rest time and holidays, attention to sleep and nutrition, exercise, spiritual needs, partner, family, friendships, pets and hobbies, as well as sufficient supervision and therapy when needed. Many of us settle for the required minimum of supervision and forget therapy once we're qualified. However, both should really be considered professional essentials that we budget for and use as much as we need, not as little as we can get away with.

Working with sexual dependency is another area where therapists often need additional support, as Chapter 15 demonstrates.

References

Alaggia, R. (2005) Disclosing the trauma of child sexual abuse: A gender analysis. *Journal of Loss and Trauma*, 10;5, 453–470.

Alaggia, R. & Mishna, F. (2014) Self psychology and male child sexual abuse: Healing relational betrayal. *Clinical Social Work Journal*, 42, 41–48.

Badenoch, B. (2018) *The Heart of Trauma*, New York: W.W. Norton.

Birchard, T. (2011) Sexual addiction and the paraphilias. *Sexual Addiction and Compulsivity*, 18, 157–187.

Braun, V., Schmidt, J., Gavey, N. & Fenaughty, J. (2009) *Journal of Homosexuality*, 56, 336–360.

Bunton, R. & Cranshaw, P. (2002) Risk, ritual and ambivalence in men's lifestyle magazines. In: Henderson, E.S. & Petersen, A. [eds] *The Commodification of Healthcare*, London: Routledge, 187–203.

Coxell, A.W., King, M.B., Mezey, G.C. & Kell, P. (2000) Sexual molestation of men: Interviews with 242 men attending a genitourinary service. *International Journal of STD and AIDS*, 11, 574–578.

Cozolino, L. (2016) *Why Therapy Works*, New York: W.W. Norton.

Crete, G.K. & Singh, A.A. (2015) Resilience strategies of male survivors of childhood sexual abuse and their female partners: A phenomenological inquiry. *Journal of Mental Health Counseling*, 37;4, 341–354.

De Silva, P. (2001) Impact of trauma on sexual functioning and sexual relationships. *Sexual & Relationship Therapy*, 16;3, 270–278.

DeYoung, P.A. (2015) *Understanding and Treating Chronic Shame*, Hove: Routledge.

Elkins, J., Crawford, K. & Briggs, H.E. (2017) Male survivors of sexual abuse: Becoming gender-responsive and trauma-informed. *Advances in Social Work*, 18;1, 116–130.

Fisher, J. (2017) *Healing the Fragmented Selves of Trauma Survivors*, New York: Routledge.

Harlow, B.L. & Stewart, E.G. (2005) Adult onset vulvodynia in relation to childhood violence victimisation. *American Journal of Epidemiology*, 161, 871–880.

Heim, C.M., Mayberg, H.S., Mletko, T., Nemeroff, C.B. & Pruessner, J.C. (2013) Decreased cortical representation of genital somatosensory field after childhood sexual abuse. *American Journal of Psychiatry*, 170;6, 616–623.

Javaid, A. (2016) Feminism, masculinity and male rape: Bringing male rape 'out of the closet'. *Journal of Gender Studies*, 25;3, 283–293.

Knight, C. (2015) Trauma-informed social work practice: Practice considerations and challenges. *Clinical Social Work Journal*, 43;1, 25–37.

Kristensen, E. & Lau, M. (2011) Sexual function in women with a history of intrafamilial childhood sexual abuse. *Sexual & Relationship Therapy*, 26;3, 229–241.

Lundqvist, G., Svedin, C.G. & Hansson, K. (2004) Childhood sexual abuse: Women's health when starting in group therapy. *Nordic Journal of Psychiatry*, 58, 25–32.

Maslach, C., Jackson, S.E. & Leiter, M.P. (1996) *Maslach Burnout Inventory Manual*, third edition, Palo Alto, CA: Consulting Psychologists Press.

McFarlane, A.C. & Bookless, C. (2001) The effect of PTSD on interpersonal relationships: Issues for emergency service workers. *Sexual & Relationship Therapy*, 16;3, 261–267.

Morley, C.A. & Kohrt, B.A. (2013) Impact of peer support on PTSD, hope and functional impairment: A mixed-methods study of child soldiers in Nepal. *Journal of Aggression, Maltreatment and Trauma*, 22, 714–734.

O'Leary, P. & Barber, J. (2008) Gender differences in silencing following childhood sexual abuse. *Journal of Child Sexual Abuse*, 17, 133–143.

ONS (2018) *Crime Survey for England & Wales*, London: Office for National Statistics.

Paine, M.L. & Hansen, D. (2002) Factors influencing children to self-disclose sexual abuse. *Clinical Psychology Review*, 22, 271–295.

Rellini, A. (2007) Review of the empirical evidence for a theoretical model to understand the sexual problems of women with a history of CSA. *Journal of Sex Medicine*, 5, 31–46.

Sanderson, C. (2010) *Counselling Survivors of Interpersonal Trauma*, London: Jessica Kingsley.

Sanderson, C. (2013) *Counselling Skills for Working with Trauma*, London: Jessica Kingsley.

Steele, K. (2018) From resistance to realization: Integrative psychotherapy approaches with challenging trauma patients. *Personality Development and Psychotherapy*, International Attachment and Trauma Congress, May 6, London: ISC.

Stoltenborgh, M. *et al* (2011) A global perspective on CSA: Meta analysis of prevalence around the world. *Child Maltreatment*, 16;2, 79–101.

Van der Kolk, B. (2015) *The Body Keeps the Score*, London: Penguin Random House.

Vearnals, S. & Campbell, T. (2001) Male victims of male sexual assault: A review of psychological consequences and treatment. *Sexual & Relationship Therapy*, 16;3, 279–286.

Weiss, K.G. (2010) Male sexual victimization: Examining men's experiences of rape and sexual assault. *Men and Masculinities*, 12, 275–298.

Weiss, R. (2015) *Sex Addiction 101*, Deerfield Beach, FL: Health Communications Inc.

Chapter 15

Sexual dependency

Sexual addiction is a growing and controversial area for which help is often sought from sex therapists. It's arguable whether sex therapists are actually better placed to work with this, as it may have less to do with sex than comfort seeking. However, the growth of internet porn has contributed to beliefs that sexual behaviour can become problematic, particularly interfering with relationships and sexual functioning.

A major objection to the sex addiction label is its potential to stigmatise particular sexual behaviours which are considered outside the mainstream (Rubin, 1984/2011). Some research and treatment suggestions have an undeniably judgemental approach (McKeague, 2014), which often seems focused simply on curbing extra-marital relationships, kink and masturbation. However, it's not the behaviours themselves that are the problem, but the way they can become depended on. Sexual dependency is also sometimes known as 'hypersexuality', another term which suggests an excess of sexual behaviour. Again, it's understandable to question how much is too much and it's difficult not to see the term as pejorative. Conversely, there has sometimes been an unfortunately comic approach to sex addiction in the media, associating it with sexual prowess, attractive film stars and others with access to multiple willing partners. In fact, 'sex addicts' are notoriously poor lovers, who often have little interest in partnered sex.

Cohn (2014) argues that labelling encourages blame and robs the client of hope. Hall (2011: 219) agrees that labelling can increase shame and 'restrict power to change', but argues it can also normalise and offer support, relieving partners of blame. Turner (2009) agrees that it can finally bring order to a chaotic life, where it may be one of several mental health and addiction issues. The latest version of the World Health Organization's International Classification of Diseases (ICD), ICD-11, recognises compulsive sexual behaviour as an impulse disorder rather than an addiction.

Patrick Carnes coined the term 'sex addiction' in the 1980s when he noticed an addictive and escalating pattern associated with sexual behaviour, which he elucidated in his seminal work *Out of the Shadows*, now it its third edition (2018). By the time this was published, sex itself had come out of the shadows, with encouragement since the liberated sixties and seventies to use sex as a means of relaxation and soothing. Following orgasm, the body is flooded with feel-good hormones and resets to a state of homeostasis, making sex a highly effective stress reliever.

In Carnes' early days, porn was mainly accessed via 'top shelf' magazines. Anything racier required effort, such as joining an adult film club or seeking out sex workers. Now, people can access sex anywhere just by picking up their phone and logging onto a porn website, chatroom or hook-up app. Though dependency may develop relatively rapidly, there isn't the same need to expand sexual practices now. Nonetheless, it's thought that using sex to manage boredom or stress can cause the brain to become sensitised, so that sexual cues generate a more marked response. Indeed, triggers can start to operate outside conscious awareness, so eventually the tiniest cues can cause cravings (Reynaud *et al*, 2010: 265). This may account for lapses because when people try to stop, the limbic system – associated with hormone control – is activated, rather than prefrontal areas of the brain where urges are managed.

Role of the internet

It could be argued that any behaviour which someone finds soothing has the potential to become addictive. Though activities like gambling, shopping, gaming and viewing porn don't involve substances which act on the body – like alcohol or drugs – they do create a similar surge of dopamine which can be increasingly difficult to attain as dependency develops (Hilton, 2013). Moreover, these behaviours can all involve internet use.

A particular issue with the internet is that absorption in online activity makes it difficult to judge time passing, which can create long stretches looking at different images. Vasopressin is a brain chemical released during sex which increases focus and attention, making it even easier to become absorbed, so that hours pass without awareness. The brain is physically changed by repeating thoughts and behaviours (Hilton, 2013) so that repetition, such as searching the internet to find the perfect image, makes compulsive behaviour more automatic and more necessary. Some people dissociate and describe feeling as though in a bubble or a trance (Weiss, 2015).

Dopamine

Anticipation also produces dopamine, and the more dopamine is produced the more motivated we are to repeat a behaviour – even when it isn't actually pleasant at all. Its release during sex can reduce anxiety and induce a feeling of well-being. However, its presence may prevent the release of other feel-good hormones, such as serotonin (Kafka, 1997). This is the hormone which follows orgasm, signalling that sexual behaviour has ceased, and inducing a feeling of well-being and contentment – the 'afterglow'. It's a sociable hormone, further released when cuddling up after sex. So when its levels are reduced, there's less incentive to have loving partnered sex and no brakes on compulsive sexual activity.

The extreme release of dopamine is also thought to trigger the naturally occurring opioid dynorphin, which neutralises the rewarding effect of dopamine, making the hit harder to achieve (Love *et al*, 2015). As time passes, dopamine release becomes associated with high dynorphin release, fooling the body into thinking it's experiencing dopamine withdrawal. With this come the unpleasant effects of real withdrawal – anxiety, irritability and depression, for instance. Nevertheless, the craving grows so, in common with chemical addictions, the person feels compelled to continue even when they hate what they're doing. In MRI brain scan research, the same areas of the brain that respond in other chemical and behavioural addictions are activated by sexual cues in individuals thought to have a sexual dependency, showing an extreme over-response. Non-affected controls 'like' sexual images to the same extent, but their brains don't respond in the same way (Voon *et al*, 2014).

Supernormal stimuli

When dependency becomes severe, more of the hormonal hit is needed just to feel normal. This is when behaviours can escalate, as it becomes so much harder to achieve the necessary effect just through porn. Exaggerated versions of reality may then become preferable to real life. This applies to sex and bodies in pornography as well as to sex workers and fantasy situations. Once supernormal stimuli become necessary for arousal, partnered sex is often lost (Barrett, 2010). Sometimes people start using sex workers to prove to themselves they can have still sex with someone else – but use of sex workers is thrilling and 'supernormal' in itself (Birchard, 2015).

Many porn users never experience problems, just view porn as a means of obtaining an orgasm, and are done in 10 minutes. However, there are some powerfully seductive elements to porn use. For some people, the idea that they shouldn't be watching is attractive in itself. Snatching time and planning when that can happen makes it all the more interesting. In the end, it isn't an orgasm that's sought, but the excitement associated with clicking on 'just one more' website, and anticipation during the wait for it to load. Once done, this is often followed by shame, which isn't always just about sexual acting out but wasting time, and sometimes money, unnecessarily rather than working, sleeping or spending time with partner or family. As the sexual behaviour is often used to manage shame and anaesthetise negative feelings (Birchard, 2015), shame about the sexual behaviour can trigger further acting out (Potter-Effron, 2002).

Shame

Partners' negative reactions, blame and anger can reinforce a user's sense of worthlessness (Weiss, 2013) which may originally have developed as a result of damaged attachment. It's easy to appreciate how carers' criticism, withdrawal, neglect and abuse can develop into feelings of shame, but simple misattunement can also be shame-inducing (Schore, 2012). Adults are needed to reflect back to children that their understanding of the world is correct. When this fails to happen, the child's resilience and resourcefulness is compromised and their affect-regulating capacity is considerably reduced, so they look outside themselves for comfort. It's the accrual of many misattunements which leaves someone feeling not good enough, as they feel unable to judge what they can expect of the world and what the world expects of them. It needs to be appreciated that shame is about the *self* being flawed, whereas guilt relates to *behaviour*. For some people, whose carers reacted to their needs with rejection, this leaves a feeling that they could contaminate and daren't become too close to others.

People who've grown up to believe their needs won't be met if they have to rely on others, or that they'll be rejected if others become close, sometimes manipulate and lie to keep people at a distance, or they protect themselves from intimacy by finding unavailable partners. When a longing for connection competes with fears of rejection it may feel safer not to become too close and risk discovery of faults and abandonment.

Couples who feel this way often somehow find each other. Carnes (2011) recognised some partners collude with unwanted behaviours, perhaps in order to maintain blame or to avoid sex, choreographing intimacy. Sometimes, Carnes found, aggressive and critical behaviour switches with compliant, enabling roles. Not seeing any options, and often feeling worthless themselves, Carnes says the codependent partner may tolerate abusive, humiliating and degrading behaviour.

Women

Sexual dependency can affect any gender or sexuality, but reliable research about women is more sparse. Sexual acting out seems more common than online porn use, though this is also increasing (Kafka, 2010; Schneider, 2000). However, it does seem that dependency may be more hidden in women than men, with another condition presenting, such as an eating disorder, alcohol or drug abuse, depression or anxiety. Some women present with problems over partner choice or intimacy (Weiss, 2015). Childhood sexual abuse is also a common presenting problem (Finkelhor, 2014). Indeed, women are even more likely to have a history of trauma, particularly severe sexual trauma (McKeague, 2014).

Because of the way they're socialised, for women sex may be seen as a way of overcoming shame and becoming acceptable. Ferree (2010) notes that in women gendered beliefs both contribute to feelings of shame and efforts to overcome it. For instance, they're body-shamed and shamed for being sexual whilst expected to fulfil the sexual needs of partners. Similarly, they learn they need a relationship to be fulfilled themselves but blame their partners when their problems remain unsolved, comparing them unfavourably to the fantasy figures with whom they act out. Nonetheless, women are more likely than men to feel responsible for the health of their primary relationship (Carnes *et al*, 2010).

Love addiction

Feelings of worthlessness, a history of chronic trauma and intimacy difficulties may also underlie 'love addiction'. It's thought to be more common in women, who often present with a 'problem' of regularly ending relationships after a certain time. This may coincide with the loss of hormones associated with early relationship intensity, its euphoria more important to them than intimacy (Weiss, 2013).

Those affected may be registered on multiple dating and hook-up websites, which they check constantly. They may engage in casual relationships but then complain that all partners are only interested in sex. Where they would consider it dangerous to, say, go out to a bar to look for a sexual partner, they'll download apps that allow them to have cybersex or arrange a date with someone they've never even seen, let alone met.

Inappropriate partners are often chosen, making it even less likely the relationship will be successful, and reinforcing the person's belief that they're incapable of loving or being loved. Loneliness appears to make app use more likely and for use to become problematic. This may be because users find it more difficult to self-regulate and so seek external validation through dating apps.

Assessment

Therapists often feel so uncomfortable or lacking in knowledge about sexual dependency that they miss clues (Jones & Hertlein, 2012). As sexual dependency is rarely the presenting problem, it's easy to overlook (Rosenberg, 2014). Ayers and Haddock (2009) report that many therapists pathologise the partner for minding about porn use, and sex-positive therapists may inadvertently dismiss or encourage compulsive behaviour (Weiss, 2013). It's therefore always important to ask about pornography and sexual behaviour in the initial assessment. People often legitimately deny porn use if their behaviour has escalated, so it's also important to include assessment questions about cybersex and use of sex workers.

Sometimes dependency creeps up so that, on presentation, neither the user nor their partner see the behaviour as the problem (Ford *et al*, 2012). However, some people try strenuously to avoid detection, especially if they feel justified in what they're doing. They may, for instance, see their porn use as a necessary stress reliever, to which they're entitled, while their partner may see it as wilful and childish. The longer this continues, the stronger the user's relationship with porn becomes, and the weaker the relationship with the partner. Then the stress of relationship problems causes the user to resort to more porn and sexual problems increase. Suspicions may be aroused when:

- The couple have different bedtimes
- One partner is complaining about the other working constantly
- One or both complain of trust issues
- The couple presents with any form of fidelity issue, such as sexting or texting

- One partner says the other's behaviour makes them feel they're going mad
- One partner says they have 'moved on' sexually or feel the relationship is damaged due to loss of early relationship feelings
- There is trouble completing work or warnings about performance
- Financial difficulties exist
- There is declining physical or emotional health – changes in appetite, sleep, personal neglect (Weiss, 2015).

Tolerance can be assessed by discovering whether the client has begun using the behaviour for longer than they used to (Jones & Hertlein, 2012). Those who regularly go online for distraction, stress relief or to generally feel better may experience withdrawal symptoms such as moodiness, irritability or anxiety if they stop (Griffiths, 2011). It's therefore helpful to explore the length of time spent online, the times of day, the content of online activities (Jones & Hertlein, 2012) and how the behaviour helps with mood management. In addition, assessment needs to address not just trauma and attachment injuries but any enduring unhelpful beliefs, such as avoiding feelings and not asking for help.

History taking should include questions about any wishes or attempts to stop the behaviour and whether the partner knows about them. If not, why is this being kept secret and how would the partner react if they found out? The initial approach for help may have come from the partner who may be unaware of any porn problem or acting out, or who may be driving the therapy. Therefore, treatment-seeking may be a sincere personal choice, accidentally picked up, or someone may have been prompted to seek help after being found out, arrested or acquiring a sexually transmitted infection. Sometimes partners insist someone has a sex addiction because they disapprove of masturbation or porn use, or are trying to rationalise the reasons for an affair or a secret sexual behaviour they've discovered, such as cross-dressing. In such cases, or where the partner has no wish to change, the work may be more about helping the partner to adjust than changing the behaviour.

Treatment

Though there are many groups and approaches claiming to effectively treat 'sex addiction', it's possible that a combination of approaches is most likely to be beneficial. This is perhaps what makes the label of 'sex addiction' so unhelpful. Treating the symptom (addiction) is unlikely to completely and permanently make a difference if the underlying causes remain unaddressed. Matching treatment to the client and their stage of change means therapists must be aware of a variety of approaches or refer the client for specialist intervention. This may be necessary anyway to avoid contaminating PST if the couple are hoping to rebuild their sex life once any unwanted behaviours are dealt with.

Clients generally shift from being unaware or unwilling to change, to considering the possibility of change, then to becoming determined and prepared to make the change, and finally to taking action and sustaining or maintaining change over time. Clients can present at any point in the cycle, so the therapist's challenge is to recognise where they are in this process (DiClemente, 2012).

Goals

It's helpful to be clear about what you're trying to achieve from the outset. It's pointless working towards your goals or the partner's goals if these aren't the client's goals. Clients are often unrealistic about what they think can be achieved, overestimating their ability to give up a behaviour or underestimating the result of merely reducing it. If you treat what they want as experimental, clients usually adjust their expectations and goals with very little prompting.

To engage a possibly unwilling client, a non-judgemental, non-shaming, warm relationship is essential. Gently negotiating with the client what they feel is possible and what they wish to change is much more useful than a heavy-handed summary of what's wrong and insistence on compliance. It's most helpful when the client can discuss what *they* see as the benefits and costs involved in change (Treasure, 2004).

If they're in therapy to please someone else, such as a partner, there's a risk they're hoping to keep you both happy without changing at all. However, you can talk therapeutically with them about their life, and build your relationship to see if they become more engaged. Remaining interested and supportive encourages more realistic appraisal and engagement over time. Where possible, let *them* remind *you* of what brought them to therapy rather than the other way round. It seems ethical for therapists to keep checking in with themselves to ensure they aren't trying to change a client because they disapprove of their behaviour or have sympathy for the partner.

Abstinence

Some clients who say they're comfortable with their behaviour nevertheless want therapy. It can be helpful to ask even these clients whether they'd like to try an experiment with sexual abstinence – either complete or related to the 'problem' behaviour – and what they think might make this easier or more difficult. It's helpful to discuss this in the context of previous attempts to change (anything) and emphasise the experimental nature of the process. When initially discussing abstinence, if this is what the client wants, it's important to work out any immediate changes that can be made, such as reducing opportunity, and to identify times of risk. Some clients are keen to take action to make the behaviour more difficult, such as using a more basic phone, deleting sex contacts, pornographic material and apps, and changing credit cards. Some expect their partner to police their behaviour, but this doesn't help the client take responsibility. Actually, it makes it more likely they'll become sneaky, resentful and increase efforts to get around the prohibitions.

It's essential to plan what the client will do instead of the behaviour, such as going to bed at the same time as their partner, working, socialising or spending time with family. Positives from these alternative activities will help reinforce them. Feedback about their abstinence experiment is extremely helpful in determining the client's approach to self-efficacy and difficulty. For instance, someone who assumes one lapse will result in failure needs help to recognise how often people make attempts that don't succeed immediately. Give examples such as quitting smoking, dieting, learning to ride a bike or pass a driving test. Take the attitude that every 'failure' offers more information to help with the next attempt, and that a failed attempt is better than no attempt at all. Keeping a journal to record daily activities, thoughts, and emotions may help identify triggers and how they were managed.

However, the opposite of addiction is connection, not abstinence (Hari, 2015). Trying to stop any behaviour which offers self and affect regulation will inevitably fail unless there's something to replace it (Heller & LaPierre, 2012). So allow giving up the behaviour to happen in the background while you're foregrounding the therapeutic relationship and the therapy, asking occasionally whether the sexual behaviours have changed. Often clients surprise you by announcing one day that they've been sober for a while. Sometimes abstinence is rejected in the initial assessment, but has been attempted by the end of history taking. Don't overdo the praise if this happens, in case the client then feels unable to report any lapses. However, do be pleased and congratulate them, exploring in detail how they've managed this. After this, or if the person is determined to abstain from the start, seek feedback at every session.

It's often more helpful to get clients away from the computer than from sex, as they'll often swap porn use for online shopping, gambling or other sexual behaviours, such as online sex using a webcam. Because there's a person at the other end, this is sometimes justified as sex with a partner. Other dependencies may coexist, so sometimes a previously unrecognised eating disorder, alcohol or drug problem may become apparent as the sexual behaviour diminishes. Psychoeducation about this risk is therefore essential.

A compromise to complete abstinence can be masturbation to fantasy. Some clients feel their compulsive behaviour is actually less shame-inducing than purely fantasy-assisted masturbation and that the sexual behaviour they've adopted is the lesser of two evils (Jacob & McCarthy-Veach, 2005). Initially, favourite porn images may be used, but this gradually diminishes with therapeutic encouragement to use personal imagination.

It's really useful to discuss in detail how the sexual behaviour helped the client. Often, there's a sense of being 'owed' some sort of treat or recompense for hard work done, or it's the default activity whenever there's any possibility of having enough down time to start connecting with unpleasant feelings or thoughts. The therapeutic relationship, which is trusting and non-judgemental, demonstrates to the client that the feelings they were so scared of are manageable after all, and they gradually develop confidence that they can manage without the (now) unwanted behaviour.

Treatment models

Some people are put off treatment because they expect to be referred to 12-step groups or, indeed, any kind of group. While some clients find these incredibly supportive and shame reducing, others feel they would increase their shame. These clients often benefit more from one-to-one work with someone experienced in dealing with shame and trauma, at least initially.

Most of the addiction models work at ending the behaviour – usually within 60–90 days – and overcoming shame, as well as defining healthy sexuality and sobriety. Motivational interventions are used to encourage clients to recognise the benefits of a more sober sexual life. Support is offered to manage crises and setbacks through individual sessions and groups.

A safe therapeutic relationship is necessary, which privileges the client's needs and pace, fosters self-soothing, self-efficacy and, thus, more balanced attachment security, remembering that the safety they should have expected in their early life is likely to have been compromised in some way (Crittenden *et al*, 2014; Van der Kolk, 2005). The client may also need to make links between trauma in their life and their sexual behaviour, especially if accessing porn related to their own experience of trauma (Jacob & McCarthy-Veach, 2005). Trauma isn't always a single major event, however. Many children and adults live with daily interpersonal trauma caused by, for instance, lack of attunement, parental mental illness, neglect, bullying or domestic violence. Others have come from physically dangerous environments, such as war zones, or lived in poverty. A supportive therapeutic relationship is essential to create a safe enough alliance for such sensitive work. EMDR, mindfulness, grounding exercises, cognitive restructuring and treatment of shame all contribute to recovery.

Psychoeducation involves helping the client understand what's happened within their social context, including recognising social forces such as gender scripts and discourses about 'normal' sexual behaviour (Berry & Berry, 2014). Curiosity is embraced, exploring how behaviours may affect, and be affected by, the thoughts and feelings of the client and others. Triggers and their consequences are deconstructed, encouraging clients to recognise their purpose, such as avoidance of unwanted thoughts and feelings. The client's difficulties are reformulated as an understandable reaction to past difficulties and they're enabled to recognise and understand coping strategies which have outlived their usefulness (Berg *et al*, 2011).

Strengths-Based CBT (Padesky & Mooney, 2012) focuses on seeking and exploring hidden strengths in everyday activities. As with PST experimentation, obstacles are seen as providing helpful information about difficulties and the resilience used when they're encountered. Therapists' approach is positive, enthusiastic and normalising of problems and the unwanted feelings which people may seek to manage sex. Clients' strengths are noted to help create a personal model of resilience using their own words, imagery and metaphor. This helps them plan how to manage challenges, focusing on remaining resilient rather than solution-seeking. Experiments, such as delaying or avoiding the sexual behaviours, are planned in detail, anticipating problems and using feedback to help plan further experiments. Negative events and problems can be greeted as opportunities for practising resilience. Therapists are encouraged to smile more than usual – a fabulous tip which works well to engage clients with all therapies.

Some people believe the most successful outcomes are when group and individual work are combined (Kafka, 2007). The boundaried, cooperative and supportive experience can help to overcome the effects of earlier negative relationships (Birchard, 2015). The idea is that trying to control feelings leads to acting out behaviour. Accepting feelings is the basis of the 12-step model.

Partners

Partners will be understandably shocked, often feeling differently positioned and isolated, as they may feel unable to confide in friends and family. Many describe feeling just the same as if there had been an affair (Whitly, 2003), though Hall (2016) says it can feel worse than an affair. This may be because there's gradual discovery of more and more troubling behaviours. When confronted, the user may deny, justify, minimise or blame others, including their partner who is made to feel as though they're the one with the problem (Weiss, 2015). Partners often blame themselves, however (Weiss, 2013). Many try their hardest to be understanding and helpful but are met with mood swings and withdrawal. Finally knowing why may offer some relief.

Though some partners resent the idea that they may need therapy, it's often helpful for them to join a group or have personal counselling. Initially, they may just want the opportunity to vent (Weiss, 2015), but support will help them be available for aware children as well as help themselves (Carnes, 2011). It's usually better for partners not to see the same therapist, though it can be helpful for the partner to occasionally attend the user's session so they don't feel excluded from their recovery process.

Anger

There's no template for how to behave or recover, and partners may not know how or when to stop being angry. Some think the user will resume the behaviour if they do or that they won't appreciate the pain they've caused if they're forgiven. Some stay angry to remind the user of their debt and to stay connected. Self-righteousness and blaming can also help partners to avoid their own hurt, fear and feelings of responsibility (Carnes, 2011).

Carnes (2011) sees martyrdom as part of some partners' effort to make themselves indispensable. In return, they expect proof of love and care. The more they do for the user, the more they expect from them, which keeps the pair bound together. Hall (2016: 30), however, argues that, for many partners, there is no codependency. She also feels it's important for partners to realise that, though relationship difficulties may contribute to the problem, 'they certainly don't cause it'. Though she says dependency almost always pre-dates the relationship, she warns that knowing changes it. Nonetheless, partners may initially want to know everything about what's been happening, though this rarely makes them feel better. Validating the way they feel, and allowing space to express and explore their conflicting emotions, offers a sense of stability in a situation they could probably never have imagined.

Self-care

The priority is self-care, so keep monitoring how well they're eating and sleeping and give advice about both, as well as offering mindfulness, relaxation and guided imagery. Hall (2016) advises that partners go through several phases of recovery. Despair may be followed by acting out, or numb acceptance may give way to rage or intense hurt when old attachment injuries are triggered.

It can be tempting to change everything – separate from the user, move away, enact revenge – but it's not advisable to react in the early days. Nor should partners be attempting to mend the situation immediately or behave as though nothing has happened. Recovery can't be hurried.

Prematurely encouraging partners to look at their own issues may stall the process if they feel blamed and/or haven't had sufficient time to work through their reactions, which Weiss (2015) says can take up to a year. They may benefit from the sorts of interventions the user is receiving or the work may simply be focused on listening and encouragement. EMDR can be helpful if shock persists or if other disturbing memories have been provoked.

Restoring intimacy

Couples need to give themselves adequate space before attempting relationship repair. It's usual to wait until sobriety is becoming established before attempting therapy together, which is unlikely to be less than three to six months at the very least, and may be considerably longer. Long before this can happen, the couple need to determine and regularly revisit ground rules about both the relationship and sexual behaviours. As they negotiate their future relationship, it's important to emphasise that it will be different and that they need clear boundaries around responsibility and sexual behaviour. When they feel ready to begin joint counselling, this may be with a new but relevantly trained therapist. They need to be clear about the basis for the relationship before moving on to PST.

Cohn's (2014) **Hidden Trauma Model** works with both partners from the start, with a focus on couple dynamics using Imago Therapy developed by Harville Hendrix (1988). Cohn believes many couples affected by sexual dependency both have a history of trauma, so explores the couple's past to see how much of their current relationship experience mirrors earlier disappointments, hurt and frustrations. The couple are then helped to see which of these reflections are accurate and what they would like to change. Collaborative exercises are used to rebuild the relationship from scratch, simultaneously healing old wounds.

Some people are unable to engage with this without some initi
work. Weiss (2015) advises that the chances of the relationship surviv
almost fourfold when both partners receive help. Assessment is n
ensure both are open to new methods of self-soothing and are able to a
ing as a form of comfort. The couple needs to understand that their recc ..y processes have been quite different, one struggling to overcome dependency and the
other striving to accept and adjust (Hall, 2016). Not all are ready to move on at
the same time.

Just as with an affair, partners often want to use joint therapy to discover exactly
what has been happening. It can be especially hard when details have been dripped
out, particularly if the user has insisted there's no more to learn. Some therapists
and organisations insist on full disclosure, which is delivered with the therapist as
mediator. However, both the addict and partner should be clear about what they
hope to achieve. While it's important to feel there will be no more lying, detailed
disclosures don't always help. In fact, learning about some of the behaviours can
be genuinely shocking and make it more difficult to go back. For example, use of
sex workers or sex outside their usual orientation may have happened as supernormal stimuli became more necessary.

PST

It's advisable to take time out from sex in the first three to six months following
disclosure, though some couples find themselves more sexually attracted to one
another (Weiss, 2015). Where problems already exist, resuming partner sex is
likely to be disappointing, so it's usually more helpful to rebuild trust and intimacy first. Nonetheless, some partners want sex to reassure themselves they are
still attractive or to prevent more acting out. Some also think sharing pornography
is a solution, as couple porn tends towards erotica rather than hard porn, but this
risks relapse (Manning, 2006).

PST often helps to rebuild trust as well as the sexual relationship. It's also a
great way to help the couple assume personal responsibility and to differentiate,
which is especially important if the relationship has contained elements of collusion. Because it's an experimental process, and respects each partner's pace, PST
allows remaining pain and vulnerability to be more safely expressed and managed. Pre-existing sexual difficulties are also now able to be addressed. Problems
such as ED can be approached within the context of relationship building, rather
than further pathologising a couple who may already feel very different. Couples
generally exit the process feeling considerably more confident and sexually enabled than they did previously, as well as much more able to be close.

Whether you believe in sexual addiction or not, clients do present with problematic behaviours which began as solutions, and we should be prepared to work
with these. We should also be aware of the chemsex issues discussed in Chapter 16, whereby sex and drug use can evolve from a solution to difficulties into a
life-changing problem.

References

Ayers, M.M. & Haddock, S.A. (2009) Therapists' approaches in working with heterosexual couples struggling with male partners' online sexual behaviour. *Sexual Addiction & Compulsivity*, 16, 55–78.

Barrett, D. (2010) *Supernormal Stimuli*, New York: W.W. Norton & Co.

Berg, R.C., Ross, M.W. & Tikkanen, R. (2011) The effectiveness of MI4MSM: How useful is motivational interviewing as an HIV risk prevention program for men who have sex with men? A systematic review. *AIDS Education and Prevention*, 23;6, 533–549.

Berry, M.D. & Berry, P.D. (2014) Mentalization-based therapy for sexual addiction: Foundations for a clinical model. *Sexual & Relationship Therapy*, 29;2, 245–260.

Birchard, T. (2015) *CBT for Compulsive Sexual Behaviour*, Hove: Routledge.

Carnes, S. (2011) *Mending A Shattered Heart: A Guide for Partners of Sex Addicts*, second edition, Arizona: Gentle Path Press.

Carnes, P.J. (2018) *Out of the Shadows: Understanding Sexual Addiction*, Center City, MN: Hazelden.

Carnes, P.J., Green, B. & Carnes, S. (2010) The same yet different: Refocusing the sexual addiction screening test (SAST) to reflect orientation and gender. *Sexual Addiction & Compulsivity*, 17, 7–30.

Cohn, R. (2014) Calming the tempest, bridging the gorge: Healing in couples ruptured by 'sex addiction'. *Sexual & Relationship Therapy*, 29;1, 76–86.

Crittenden, P., Dallos, R., Landini, A. & Kozlowska, K. (2014) Growing and healing: DMM-FST integrative treatment. In: *Attachment and Family Therapy*, Milton Keynes: Open University Press, 144–166.

DiClemente, C.C. (2012) Motivational interviewing and the stages of change. In: Miller, W.R. & Rollnick, S. [eds] *Motivational Interviewing*, New York: Guilford Press.

Ferree, M.C. (2010) *No Stones: Women Redeemed from Sexual Addiction*, second edition, Downers Grove, IL: Inter-Varsity Press.

Finkelhor, D. (2014) *Childhood Victimization: Violence, Crime, and Abuse in the Lives of Young People*, New York: Oxford University Press.

Ford, J.F., Jared, A.D. & Darrell, L.F. (2012) Structural therapy with a couple battling pornography addiction. *The American Journal of Family Therapy*, 40, 336–348.

Griffiths, M. (2011) Internet sex addiction: A review of the research. *Addiction Research and Theory*, 20;2, 111–124.

Hall, P. (2011) A biopsychosocial view of sex addiction. *Sexual & Relationship Therapy*, 26;3, 217–228.

Hall, P. (2016) *Sex Addiction: The Partner's Perspective*, Hove: Routledge.

Hari, J. (2015) *Chasing the Scream: The First and Last Days of the War on Drugs*, New York: Bloomsbury.

Heller, L. & LaPierre, A. (2012) *Healing Developmental Trauma*, Berkeley, CA: North Atlantic Books.

Hendrix, H. (1988) *Getting the Love You Want*, New York: Henry Holt & Co.

Hilton, D. (2013) pornography addiction – A supranormal stimulus considered in the context of neuroplasticity. *Socioaffective Neuroscience and Psychology*, 3. www.socioaffective neuroscipsychol.net/index.php/snp/article/view/20767. Accessed November 19, 2015.

Jacob, C. & McCarthy-Veach, P. (2005) Intrapersonal and familial effects of child sexual abuse on female partners of male survivors. *Journal of Counselling Psychology*, 52;3, 284–297.

Jones, K.E. & Hertlein, M.E. (2012) Four key dimensions for distinguishing internet infidelity from internet and sex addiction: Concepts and clinical application. *American Journal of Family Therapy*, 40;2, 115–125.

Kafka, M.P. (1997) A monoamine hypothesis for pathophysiology of paraphilic disorders. *Archives of Sexual Behaviour*, 26;4, 348–358.

Kafka, M.P. (2007) Paraphilia-related disorders: The evaluation and treatment of nonparaphilic hypersexuality. In: Leiblim, S.R. [ed] *Principles and Practice of Sex Therapy*, fourth edition, New York: Guilford, 442–476.

Kafka, M.P. (2010) Hypersexual disorder: A proposed diagnosis for DSM-V. *Archives of Sexual Behavior*, 39, 377–400.

Manning, J.C. (2006) The impact of internet pornography on marriage and the family: A review of the research. *Sexual Addiction & Compulsivity*, 13, 131–165.

McKeague, E.L. (2014) Differentiating the female sex addict: A literature review focused on themes of gender difference used to inform recommendations for treating women with sex addiction. *Sexual Addiction & Compulsivity*, 21, 203–224.

Love, T. *et al* (2015) Neuroscience of internet pornography addiction: A review and update. *Behavioural Sciences*, 5, 388–433. http://www.behavsci-05-00388%20(1)pdf. Accessed November 19, 2015.

Padesky, C.A. & Mooney, K.A. (2012) Strengths-based cognitive behavioural therapy: A four-step model to build resilience. *Clinical Psychology & Psychotherapy*, 19, 283–290.

Potter-Effron, R. (2002) *Shame, Guilt and Alcoholism: Treatment in Clinical Practice*, second edition, Binghamton, NY: Haworth Press.

Reynaud, M. *et al* (2010) Is love passion an addictive disorder? *American Journal of Drug and Alcohol Abuse*, 36;5, 261–267.

Rosenberg, H. & Kraus, S. (2014) The relationship of "passionate attachment" for pornography with sexual compulsivity, frequency of use, and craving for pornography. *Addictive Behaviors*, 39, 1012–1017.

Rubin, G. (1984/2011) Thinking sex: Notes for a radical theory of the politics of sexuality. In: *Deviations: A Gayle Rubin Reader*, Durham, NC: Duke University Press.

Schneider, J.P. (2000) Effects of cybersex addiction on the family: Results of a survey. *Sexual Addiction & Compulsivity*, 7, 31–58.

Schore, A. (2012) *The Science of the Art of Psychotherapy*, New York: W.W. Norton.

Treasure, J. (2004) Motivational interviewing. *Advances in Psychiatric Treatment*, 10, 331–337.

Turner, M. (2009) Uncovering and treating sex addiction in couples therapy. *Journal of Family Psychotherapy*, 20, 283–302.

Van der Kolk, B. (2005) Developmental trauma disorder: Towards a rational diagnosis for children with complex trauma histories. *Psychiatric Annals*, 35;5, 401–408.

Voon, V., Mole, T.B., Banca, P., Porter, L., Morris, L. *et al* (2014) Neural correlates of sexual cue reactivity in individuals with and without compulsive sexual behaviours. *PLoS One*, 9;7 e102419. http://journals.plos.org/plosone/article?id=10.1371/journal.pone.0102419. Accessed December 20, 2015.

Weiss, R. (2013) *Cruise Control: Understanding Sex Addiction in Gay Men*, second edition, Carefree, Arizona: Gentle Path Press.

Weiss, R. (2015) *Sex Addiction 101*, Deerfield Beach, FL: Health Communications Inc.

Whitly, M.T. (2003) Pushing the wrong buttons: Men's and women's attitudes toward online infidelity. *Cyberpsychology & Behaviour*, 6, 569–579.

Chapter 16

Chemsex

The term 'chemsex' was coined in the 1990s by sexual well-being advocate and activist David Stuart (2019a) to describe the use of specific drugs to enhance gay sex, sometimes in binges lasting days at a time. Participants hook-up with individuals or join parties via dating apps, frequently identifying with their chemsex group to the extent that other relationships fall away. Crystal meth, mephedrone and GHB have come to be favoured over other recreational drugs as they produce extreme highs, disinhibition and intense feelings of intimacy and bonding (Milhet *et al*, 2019; Stuart, 2019a). This empathic connection is crucial to understanding the motivation for chemsex as a response to feelings of loneliness, chronic shame and trauma (Morris, 2019), feelings of disconnection from society in general and the gay community in particular, especially around the stigma associated with HIV status (Stuart, 2019a).

Stuart (2019b) emphatically sees chemsex as 'a product of the challenges of modern gay sex and hook-up culture in the post AIDS era'. As gay clubs and bars closed around the turn of the century, online dating and hook-up apps took over as the means of sourcing friendship, solidarity and sex. But use of apps required the honing of a perfect profile. For those already feeling the effects of illness or ageing, worries about appearance and internalised homophobia created more isolation and shame (Evans, 2019), exacerbated by the perfect bodies and performance of porn stars and online abuse of their profiles (Stuart, 2019a). The use of drugs not only obliterated such worries but also took the heat out of negotiations over sexual practices and roles, HIV status and safer sex.

The lives of many men are enhanced by the range of practices they're enabled to confidently engage in and the sense of love and community they derive from joining chemsex parties (Milhet *et al*, 2019). The downside, however, is what's concerning health professionals. The drugs used are addictive and potentially unsafe, especially in combination or when used with other recreational drugs and alcohol, accounting for at least one chemsex-related death each month in London (Stuart, 2019a). While disinhibition enables the attainment of new forms of confidence and pleasure, it can also result in injury, unsafe sex and more shame (Morris, 2019). Crystal meth, in particular, actually depletes feel-good endorphins, causing depression and other mental health issues. Preparation of the drug is part of the reinforcing ritual (it can be smoked, snorted or heated and injected, as well as eaten and drunk), adding to its addictive potential (Weiss, 2013). Nonetheless, Stuart (2019b) sees chemsex as very much a social rather than addiction issue.

Despite the sense of community created by chemsex, it ultimately increases feelings of isolation. Some people won't have experienced sober sex or any kind of lasting relationship for many years. Some men describe the development of sexual problems such as erectile dysfunction ('crystal cock') and an inability to climax accompanied by a need to keep climaxing (Milhet *et al*, 2019). Feelings of euphoria, and the ability to continue partying for days without sleep or food, disrupt routines, so that some people spend their weekends partying and the rest of the week recovering alone.

While the drugs and reliance on partying may create dependency and lifestyle problems, seeing chemsex as just an addiction problem risks missing the point. As with other forms of dependency, some form of neglect or abuse, feeling different, oppressed or misunderstood all contribute to the need for connection and comradeship which is here more pertinent than a chemical hit. Labelling and judgement only exacerbate people's sense of isolation (Stuart, 2019a).

Attempting to understand the needs of each individual is likely to be more helpful, and to result in more successful outcomes, than trying to launch chemsex clients onto a neat treatment trajectory. Work with shame and trauma may be far more relevant than early attempts to alter lifestyle. Remembering that chemsex may have offered positive, life-enhancing solutions at some stage is important to encourage clients' sense of self-efficacy. When they want or find new sexual relationships, sex therapy may be extremely helpful in building intimacy, personal validation and functional sex.

References

Evans, K. (2019) The psychological roots of chemsex and how understanding the full picture can help us create meaningful support. *Drugs and Alcohol Today*, 19;1, 36–41.

Milhet, M., Shah, J., Madesclaire, T. & Gaissad, L. (2019) Chemsex experiences: Narratives of pleasure. *Drugs and Alcohol Today*, 19;1, 11–22.

Morris, S. (2019) Too painful to think about: Chemsex and trauma. *Drugs and Alcohol Today*, 19;1, 42–48.

Stuart, D. (2019a) Chemsex: Origins of the word, a history of the phenomenon and a respect to the culture. *Drugs and Alcohol Today*, 19;1, 3–10.

Stuart, D. (2019b) Personal communication.

Weiss, R. (2013) *Cruise Control: Understanding Sex Addiction in Gay Men*, second edition, Carefree, AZ: Gentle Path Press.

Chapter 17

Identity and gender

A chapter considering sexual identity and gender has the potential of 'othering' anyone who isn't cisgender and straight – that is, identifying with the gender assigned at birth and attracted to members of the opposite gender. There's a balance to be struck between recognising difference, and what this may entail, and creating difference by the way it's recognised. Non-judgemental interest in each partner or individual, demonstrating genuine concern for their experience, is what we should be aiming for with all clients.

Experience of gender, sexual and relationship diversity inevitably varies from one therapist to the next and the subject is vast, rapidly changing and exciting. Whilst it's always important to explore clients' individual experience and to avoid stereotyping, we do, however, have a responsibility to know something of the variety of identities we may encounter. This chapter should be seen as a launch pad to further research. However we personally identify, it isn't appropriate to expect clients to educate us about more than themselves, and certainly not to be representative of the group(s) with which they identify (Twist *et al*, 2017).

Identity has been strongly linked with social constructions. For instance, some people argue that gender has intrinsic properties or characteristics, such as male determination and female kindness. A counter-argument is that people express these characteristics because they're expected or socialised to do so. Discourses around sex provide an excellent example of this, demonstrating how they can affect people's well-being when they don't feel they're obeying the rules inherent in the discourses. The rules keep changing anyway, inasmuch as discourses and constructions of sexuality have evolved over history, depending on what's socially expedient. According to Foucault (1976), repression or degradation of elements of sex have been used over history to exert power. Under the Victorians, he said, officially sex simply disappeared. Before the Victorians, in the eighteenth century, sex was openly discussed and enjoyed, the main problem of contraception evidently occasioning some creative practices.

Heterosexuality is a relatively recent construct. Until the 1900s, sexual interest was simply described as 'procreational' or 'non-procreational'. Dictionaries used the word *heterosexuality* to describe an abnormal or perverted interest in the opposite sex, and wasn't used to denote 'normal' sexuality until the mid-1930s

(Ambrosino, 2017). Heteronormativity now is marginalising, as it assumes there's only one way to do sex.

People's rules for themselves, acquired from many socialising influences, exert pressure to conform. Even within the umbrella of straight sex, many activities are marginalised, as Gayle Rubin's (1984/2011) Charmed Circle illustrates. The inner ring of the circle contains 'acceptable' sexual behaviours, such as being married, monogamous, straight, same generation and procreative. The outer circle denotes less-acceptable behaviours, such as casual, gay, cross-generational, paid-for, solo or sadomasochistic sex. It's interesting to consider who decides what's okay and what isn't, how that happens and that this is likely to be different in different places, at different times and in different contexts. Rubin would probably draw her circle differently today and differently again in another 35 years.

We may see the Charmed Circle as encouragement to consider more ways of being sexual as okay, but any definition of what's okay can also be considered limiting. Those inside the circle – while not experiencing the overt discrimination and distaste experienced by those on the outside – are still required to perform those roles to arbitrarily imposed standards. Many PST clients are distressed or experiencing 'dysfunctions' directly related to norms of behaviour they find difficult to achieve.

Gay men

Gay men's relationships are often described as more sexually flexible, communicative, adventurous and creative, attributes which enable them to deal well with sexual problems (Rutter, 2012). Erectile difficulty seems to be the major difficulty affecting gay men (Nichols, 2014), which can be successfully treated with Sensate Focus and self-focus. Some adaptation may be needed, however. When individuals present with ED occurring only in casual encounters, it may not be possible to impose a sex ban on the primary relationship, for instance.

The causes of ED are important to explore. Internalised homophobia, difficulties with coming out, discrimination and HIV status are among the potential pressures experienced by gay couples. Currently, antiretroviral treatment for HIV is effective enough to make the virus undetectable within months of starting treatment, but there may be side-effects, some of which are sexual, including ED. It's also important to take the drugs strictly on time, check their interaction with other drugs and not to skip them to avoid side-effects, like diarrhoea and fatigue, which make people feel unattractive and boring.

Kink/BDSM

Some therapists are often worried when they discover their clients engage in BDSM[1] (Pillai-Friedman et al, 2015), making them reluctant to disclose their interest (Kolmes et al, 2006). However, research suggests participants are well-adjusted and unlikely to have a history or current experience of abuse (Richters et *al*, 2008). Moreover, they're likely to 'be more self-aware, better at communicating needs, desires and boundaries and open to taking more risks' (Pillai-Friedman *et al*, 2015: 198).

There is considerable focus on consent to activity which is 'Safe, Sane and Consensual' or 'Risk-Aware Consensual Kink' and on re-evaluating consent continuously (Richards & Barker, 2013). This may involve safe words, a traffic light system and substantial time spent in planning the 'scene' that's to take place. Though any group may enjoy kink, it has an association with gay men, who may describe the experience as taking them to alternative emotional dimensions and intense feelings of care and intimacy.

Bisexuality

Bisexuality is largely invisible, as sexual identity is often assumed on the basis of a partner's gender (Dyar *et al*, 2014), leading to feelings of isolation (Vencill *et al*, 2018). It's therefore important to ask all couples how they identify at the outset, rather than making assumptions on the basis of the relationship they present with.

Bisexual invisibility may be deliberately or accidentally hidden. It's often treated negatively, as though it's a phase (Vencill *et al*, 2018), which may deter people from coming out as bi (Richards & Barker, 2013). Though both gay and straight partners may question their own sexual identity in response, there's evidence that being in a relationship with another sexual minority can be supportive (Niki, 2018).

Normalising bisexuality can reassure both partners. It makes sense that relationship or sexual difficulties may develop when one has been worrying about what it means, feeling sexually dissatisfied or fearing the other partner wants more. Sometimes this is true; sometimes the partner just wants their sexual identity to be recognised; sometimes there isn't an issue. Unless it's explored, though, there's no way of dealing with concerns that do exist.

Female couples

Three times more women identify as bisexual than lesbian (Gartrell *et al*, 2012), as more women are sexually attracted to a person rather than a gender (Nichols, 2004). Sexual identity shouldn't, therefore, be assumed in female couples. Female couples may present with discrepant desire causing relationship difficulties, loss of desire or lack of sexual behaviour. There is also often irregular but highly satisfying sex.

It has been argued that, without the impetus of male sexuality, lesbian couples slip into sexless relationships. This is by no means always true, however, and a couple's presentation for PST seems to refute this. Indeed, Iasenza (2002) established that lesbian sexual frequency was the same as in straight couples. However, some couples seek help simply because they feel they *ought* to be having more sex, not because they're actively dissatisfied. PST may be an effective way of reconnecting sexually for those who wish to, or of offering alternative ways to be close and sensual. Experimentation can determine what's possible and acceptable when desire differs.

Much of the work may be around validating the couple's intimate and sexual behaviour, including clarifying what constitutes 'sex'. Blocks can occur when one partner sees the other's sexual participation as evidence of love, in which case work is needed on consent and differentiation, with a focus on what does work in the relationship rather than what seems wrong.

Polyamory

Around half of bisexual individuals and gay men have a range of openly non-monogamous relationships (Richards & Barker, 2013). Berry and Barker (2014) recommend a stance of 'informed naivety' when working with polyamorous clients, encouraging an 'open, self-questioning' approach in both clients and therapist. Therapists' awareness of their own relationship with the clients' material, and questioning of their assumptions and judgements, is necessary. It's also important not to assume there's anything pathological about the relationship(s).

Though it may be appropriate to explore relationship rules and practices, as with every relationship, it may not be appropriate to focus on the polyamory itself if this isn't the main issue the client(s) have brought. However, it may be suitable to look at how decisions about having other partners were made if this can be utilised as a way of demonstrating the couple's skill and resilience in negotiating their boundaries.

Trans

Gender identity is not about the way someone relates sexually to others. A person's feeling about their gender may also not relate to their anatomy, so someone can appear 'male' whilst identifying as 'female' (gender dysphoria). Historically, gender dysphoria has been approached from a medical model, which uses hormonal therapy and surgery to establish congruence between gender and gender role. More recently, an identity-based model has recognised that distress is more to do with social stigma (Bockting, 2009). So, whereas there was once an expectation that people would be 'treated' with surgery and hormones, such radical interventions are now not always considered necessary.

Trans identity used to be all about the ability to 'pass' in a different gender, and people went through a struggle to get help. They were required to live in their real gender for a couple of years before treatment and they expected difficulty in being accepted for surgery. This was a highly binary model which is becoming less appropriate as more people see themselves as gender fluid or don't require to 'pass', though this is still important for some.

Cisgender people learn how to 'do' their gender from childhood, but it has to be learned by those who realign (Richards & Barker, 2013). Some people who start out keen to pass may find this isn't a simple matter of 'rebirth'. Though relief to be rid of the past may be expected, that past is often packed with struggle and resilience – a story which may feel as much a part of the person as their gender. For some people, recognition of their identity rather than passing is the important issue.

No treatment is needed to alter gender on a birth certificate, but the person must have lived in their gender for at least two years, must have been diagnosed with gender dysphoria and have a Gender Recognition Certificate obtained from a Gender Recognition Panel (Gender Recognition Act, 2004). This may be experienced as either an exciting or pathologising process, or more often a mixture of both. Gender non-binary individuals are currently unable to change their birth certificates.

Even where recognition is possible, then, it's a complex process which some people may opt not to pursue, especially as increasingly trans identity is simply seen as another way of being (Richards & Barker, 2013). Nonetheless, according to the 2012 Trans Mental Health Study, some 92 percent of trans people report harassment, discrimination or transphobia. While it's important to be able to explore this, it's potentially discriminatory to assume this is what a trans person is bringing to therapy. Sometimes it's never mentioned at all if the problem being brought isn't relevant, such as relationship conflict. Moreover, care is needed when discussing trans identity, say, in a case group or with a supervisor, as trans status is protected (Gender Recognition Act, 2004) and must not be disclosed without the person's consent.

Intersectionality

Exploring the person or couple's experience within all their contexts may confer advantages and disadvantages. It's not for therapists to decide which aspects of someone's experience are the most oppressive or advantageous, or to see them as fixed and immutable. For instance, someone may see poverty, rather than gender, as currently the context which most urgently needs attention. However, if their colour, (dis)ability or trans status makes it more difficult to find work, the intersection of context may increase their difficulty. This could be exacerbated by, say, geography, if living in a remote rural area makes it harder to find work or if there are few trans or black people also living there.

Exploration of intersectionality (Crenshaw, 1989) can open up any form of counselling. Interest in contexts which are enabling can also bring forth stories of oppression, but it's important these are not the only stories we seem to care about. It's also important to realise that all contexts are fluid, and we need to keep up with what's changing or has changed. 'Privilege exchange' refers to discovered differences in positioning that can occur when contexts alter (Mizock & Hopwood, 2016). For instance, trans men may have enjoyed butch lesbian or queer friendships which end when they realign, especially if a group of people have a policy of only admitting cisgendered women (Bockting et al, 2009).

In PST, normalizing sexual problems within the contexts which promote or influence them seems crucial to success, whereas focusing on a single story may close down the work (Berry & Lezos, 2017). Problematizing normative discourses, rather than trying to make the client's situation fit them, is also crucial. This includes avoiding assumptions and stereotypes about trans bodies, such as expecting someone to want to make physical changes. Changes to bodies may be urgently sought, gradually considered or not wanted at all.

Change

Medication to increase oestrogens and suppress androgens is referred to by trans women as Gender-Affirming Hormone Therapy (GAHT). Its feminising effect, including breast development, seems to have positive psychological consequences, as well as improved erogenous sensation all over the body, particularly in the breasts (Rosenberg et al, 2019). Some people have low libido, while it increases for others, sometimes as a response to reduced dysphoria and new sexual sensations. Orgasm changes are common, often becoming more intense. However, testicular atrophy and ED, which occur after about six months of treatment, may be accompanied by difficulty in climaxing (Radix, 2016). Some people adjust their anti-androgen therapy in order to have a libido or to get an erection and orgasm, though ejaculation is often absent. Rosenberg and colleagues (2019) found thighs, back, neck and breasts often become the focus of sex play when erections are absent.

Many trans women report an improvement in sexual functioning after surgery (Udeze et al, 2008), with more than half reporting improved orgasmic intensity (Hess et al, 2018). A vagina, clitoris and vulva can be formed from the penis and scrotal tissue unless the person is circumcised or has had puberty suppressed. An alternative is to use part of the bowel to create a vagina or to opt for just a clitoris and vulva with no vagina. Only about a third of trans women opt for breast implants, as acceptable breasts may develop with hormone therapy.

For trans men, mastectomy and chest recontouring may improve overall wellbeing. Some also have a radical hysterectomy. Treatment with testosterone stops menstruation and produces masculine sexual characteristics, such as a deeper voice and more body hair. It may also increase sexual interest and arousal (Costantino et al, 2013). It's possible to create a penis using tissue from elsewhere in the body, such as the abdomen or back, and the scrotum is formed from the vagina. An alternative is to surgically 'free' the clitoris, already enlarged by hormone treatment, so that it becomes more prominent. Other procedures may be performed for either gender, such as electrolysis hair removal or speech therapy.

Cisgender partners

Changes in their partner's body and identity may result in a period of grief for cis partners when couples stay together through and beyond transition. The initial disclosure often comes as a major shock and not all relationships survive this – but many do. Though it's understandable to be aware of a partner's sense of loss, the person transitioning may be focused on gains, so a balance needs to be struck with couples in therapy. Partners may ultimately be supportive in view of the trans partner's improved sense of self, better mental health and ability to express their sexuality authentically.

Depending on any treatment received, couples may need to experiment with new ways of being sexual together or may need PST to simply reconnect or address pre-existing issues. Some couples continue to perform sex in the same way as before if genitals change little. For some people, however, different sex and new partners is part of expressing their new identity and/or new body. Sexuality may change or become more or less fluid.

Intersex

Not identifying with the gender assigned at birth is not the same as clinical gender ambiguity, which may be chromosomal, hormonal or physical. Fausto-Sterling (2000) sees gender as existing on a continuum, with about 1.7 percent of us intersex. Many people are unaware of this or identify with the gender they appear to be.

Those born with non-specific genital anatomy used to undergo surgery in infancy to conform to the gender chosen by parents. However, sometimes anatomical gender doesn't become apparent until puberty and may not agree with the gender chosen. Consequently, early surgery is now only used as treatment rather than to 'correct' gender; for instance, if there are difficulties with urination.

Non-binary identities

Some people prefer not to adopt binary gender self-descriptions and instead adopt an androgynous identity and may dress deliberately to avoid gender choice. They may use neutral pronouns such as 'they', titles such as 'Mx' and adopt non-binary names. Other ways of being include identifying as somewhere between male and female, neither male nor female, sometimes male and sometimes female, or as a new gender altogether (Beattie & Lenihan, 2018). It's appropriate to ask clients how they like to be addressed and to correct mistakes when they occur.

Other sexualities

At some point in their lives, most people are not sexual, with about one percent actively saying they don't experience sexual attraction (Bogaert, 2004). Some people experience sexual attraction but choose not to act on it (Scherrer, 2008). Some wish to have a romantic relationship which is not sexual (Richards & Barker, 2013). Some people have sexual desire but are not attracted to people, enjoy limited physical intimacy, are sometimes or in some ways asexual, or only feel sexual if there is a particularly strong emotional attraction. Though one might not expect to see asexual people in PST, sometimes couples or individuals seek help to negotiate the boundaries of a relationship or deal with what emerging asexuality or sexuality may mean for them.

Many people have sexual interests associated with a particular object or behaviour. This is often related to clothes such as high heels or underwear, or materials such as silk, leather or rubber. Behaviours may include activities like wearing nappies, being tightly bound or identifying with animals/characters (furries). Some people enjoy cartoon porn, particularly anime, or cosplay dressing as unlikely characters, such as Minnie Mouse and Sherlock Holmes or Mr Darcy and Spider-Man (slash play). As ever, clients are unlikely to discuss this if they sense disapproval.

Now, more than ever, contemporary sex therapists need awareness of not just sexual behaviours and problems but the vast range of influences on clients' lives and our own practice, explored in Chapter 18.

Note

1 Bondage, discipline, dominance, submission, sadism and masochism

References

Ambrosino, B. (2017) *The Invention of Heterosexuality*, London: BBC. www.bbc.com/future/story/20170315-the-invention-of-heterosexuality. Accessed July 22, 2019.

Beattie, M. & Lenihan, P. (2018) *Counselling Skills for Working with Gender Diversity and Identity*, London: Jessica Kingsley.

Berry, M.D. & Barker, M. (2014) Extraordinary interventions for extraordinary clients: Existential sex therapy and open non-monogamy. *Sexual & Relationship Therapy*, 29;1, 21–30.

Berry, M.D. & Lezos, A.N. (2017) Inclusive sex therapy practices: A qualitative study of the techniques sex therapists use when working with diverse sexual populations. *Sexual & Relationship Therapy*, 32;1, 2–21.

Bockting, W., Benner, A. & Coleman, E. (2009) Gay and bisexual identity development among female-to-male transsexuals in North America: Emergence of a transgender sexuality. *Archives of Sexual Behaviour*, 38;5, 688–701.

Bogaert, A.F. (2004) Asexuality: Its prevalence and associated factors in a national probability sample. *Journal of Sex Research*, 41;3, 279–287.

Costantino, A., Cerpolini, S. & Alvisi, S. (2013) A prospective study on sexual function and mood in female-to-male transsexuals during testosterone administration and after sex reassignment surgery. *Journal of Sex & Marital Therapy*, 39;4, 321–335.

Crenshaw, K. (1989) Demarginalising the intersection of race and sex: A black feminist critique of antidiscrimination doctrine, feminist theory and antiracist politics. In: *The Legal Forum*, Chicago, IL: University of Chicago, 139–167.

Dyar, C., Feinstein, B.A. & London, B. (2014) Dimensions of sexual identity and minority stress among bisexual women: The role of partner gender. *Psychology of Sexual Orientation and Gender Diversity*, 1, 441–451.

Fausto-Sterling, A. (2000) *Sexing the Body: Gender Politics and the Construction of Sexuality*, New York: Basic Books.

Foucault, M. (1976) *The History of Sexuality: 1: The Will to Knowledge: The Will to Knowledge v. 1*, London: Penguin.

Gartrell, N.K., Bos, H.M.W. & Goldberg, N.G. (2012) New trends in same sex contact for American adolescents? *Archives of Sexual Behavior*, 41;1, 5–7.

Hess, J., Henkel, A. & Bohr, J. (2018) Sexuality after male-to-female gender affirmation surgery. *Biomed Research International*. www.hindawi.com/journals/bmri/2018/9037979/. Accessed August 18, 2109.

Iasenza, S. (2002) Beyond 'lesbian bed death': The passion and play in lesbian relationships. *Journal of Lesbian Studies*, 6;1, 111–120.

Kolmes, K., Stock, W. & Moser, C. (2006) Investigating bias in psychotherapy with BDSM clients. *Journal of Homosexuality*, 50;2–3, 301–324.

Mizock, L. & Hopwood, R. (2016) Conflation and interdependence in the undersection of gender and sexuality among transgender individuals. *Psychology of Sexual Orientation and Gender Diversity*, 3;1, 93–101.

Nichols, M. (2004) Lesbian sexuality/female sexuality: Rethinking 'lesbian bed death'. *Sexual & Relationship Therapy*, 19;4, 363–371.

Nichols, M. (2014) Therapy with LGBTQ clients. In: Binik, Y.M. & Hall, K.S.K. [eds] *Principles and Practice of Sex Therapy*, fifth edition, New York: Guilford Press, 309–333.

Niki, D. (2018) Now you see me, now you don't: Addressing bisexual invisibility in relationship therapy. *Sexual and Relationship Therapy*, 33;1–2, 45–57.

Pillai-Friedman, S., Pollitt, J.L. & Castaldo, A. (2015) Becoming kink-aware – A necessity for sexuality professionals. *Sexual & Relationship Therapy*, 30;2, 196–210.

Radix, A.E. (2016) Medical transition for transgender individuals. In: *Lesbian, Gay, Bisexual, & Transgender Healthcare*, Berlin: Springer.

Richards, C. & Barker, M. (2013) *Sexuality & Gender*, London: Sage.

Richters, J., deVisser, R.O. & Rissel, C.E. (2008) Demographic and psychosocial features of participants BDSM: Data from a national survey. *Journal of Sexual Medicine*, 5;7, 1660–1668.

Rosenberg, S., Tilley, P.J.M. & Morgan, J. (2019) "I couldn't imagine my life without it": Australian trans women's experiences of sexuality, intimacy, and gender-affirming hormone therapy. *Sexuality & Culture*, 23;3, 962–977.

Rubin, G. (1984/2011) Thinking sex. Notes for a radical theory of the politics of sexuality. *Deviations: A Gayle Rubin Reader*, Durham, NC: Duke University Press, 152.

Rutter, P.A. (2012) Sex therapy with gay male couples using affirmative therapy. *Sexual & Relationship Therapy*, 27;1, 35–45.

Scherrer, K. (2008) Coming to an asexual identity: Negotiating identity, negotiating desire. *Sexualities*, 11, 621–641.

Twist, J., Barker, M-J., Nel, P.W. & Horley, N. (2017) Transitioning together: A narrative analysis of the support accessed by partners of trans people. *Sexual & Relationship Therapy*, 32;2, 227–243.

Udeze, B., Abdelmawla, N., Khoosal, D. & Terry, T. (2008) Psychological functions in male-to-female transsexual people before and after surgery. *Sexual and Relationship Therapy*, 23;2, 141–145.

Vencill, J.A., Carlson, S., Iantaffi, A. & Miner, M. (2018) Mental health, relationships and sex: Exploring patterns among bisexual individuals in mixed orientation relationships. *Sexual and Relationship Therapy*, 33;1–2, 14–33.

Chapter 18

Culture

As Chapter 17 demonstrated, context and culture are crucial to the way we experience and express our sexual selves, and their effect is dynamic. Consequently, sexuality and gender can mean different things, both culturally and individually, at different points in a person's life. The sexual discourses and scripts of our upbringing and environment influence our beliefs, and our personal experience may radically change how we feel able to identify and express ourselves. It's this merging of influences that we can address in PST.

Clients often subscribe to particularly definite discourses about sex, such as the idea that men are always ready for sex or that only intercourse is real sex. Thus, self-critical beliefs may be supported by oppressive discourses which can develop quite casually. Our curiosity and not-knowing opens up options when our clients' 'knowing' closes down their thinking and opportunities. This has never been more important, as now influence is not limited to someone's immediate community but to their online world as well.

The idea that there's some 'natural' way of doing sex, or just of being, contributes to people's feelings of not performing (adequately). Penis-in-vagina (PiV) sex has been promoted by state and religious institutions as the only natural sort of sex. However, PiV sex is only 'better' because it can result in babies, and theoretically having a family organises people to work hard and also provides more workers for the next generation (Burr, 2015).

Liberating conversations

Sexual and gender politics often arise in PST, so being able to discuss dissatisfaction as a more global societal concept can be liberating. It can be a surprise to clients to realise that the messages they receive about sex are not fixed and unchallengeable truths, but culturally and politically constructed ideas which serve a social purpose. Awareness of sexual politics and the ability to facilitate discussion between our clients thus externalises couple conflict and often creates a sense of shared experiencing. Individual clients may also want to bounce ideas around to see how they fit, particularly about their experience of identity.

Some clients who attend sex therapy are eager for an opportunity to discuss the way everyday sexism affects their lives and to point out to their partners how little they understand about what they're experiencing. Indeed, conflict frequently develops following a casual remark made about women's experience which demonstrates how little the occasional observation of, say, cat calling actually contributes to understanding of what this is like (Bates, 2014). Partners' failure to acknowledge the other's experience contributes to much relationship distress and conflict. Seeing is not the same as experiencing, and the sense of being patronised and misunderstood often blatantly contributes to sexual refusal. Many an unaware but well-meaning therapist has bought into patriarchal discourses and behaviours which are unacceptable to their client(s) but which they haven't considered. Indeed, this reflects much casual prejudice, often delivered with pride by those who are keen to announce their 'tolerance' or 'acceptance' and haven't yet appreciated they don't have a right to tolerate, accept or judge. Recognising the privileged positions we occupy as sex and relationship therapists should alert us, in particular, to the importance of stepping back and not knowing about others' experience until they're satisfied we get it – and not just until we're pleased enough with our wokeness.

Some of the discourses around sex are highly gender specific, many appearing to favour men. For instance, women's sexuality has been seen as frightening in its mystery. Women's desire and arousal aren't necessarily obvious, whereas men's erections suggest sexual interest. This has led to a requirement in many places and times for girls and women to develop modesty in their dress and manner. There also remains the belief that women have sexual control in a way that men don't, feeding the belief that men's lack of sexual control is another reason for women to restrain their dress and behaviour (Hollway, 1998). Again, many people – including women – still subscribe to the view that women must be responsible for men's sexual misbehaviour. Nonetheless, women's sexuality has also been seen as out of control and a cause of mental illness. Surgical removal of the clitoris was considered a solution to *problems* such as masturbation, clitoral – rather than 'vaginal' – orgasm, hypersexuality, homosexuality, lesbianism, and sexual frustration in the US and Europe from the nineteenth century onwards (Rodriguez, 2014). Despite now being illegal in many places, it's still used in Africa, Asia the Middle-East, and other countries including the US and UK, as a means of preventing infidelity and signifying female chastity and cleanliness (see Chapter 10).

Though they may initially seem to be a million miles from sex, conversations about such societal influences can sometimes be helpful in PST for partners responding to fixed, oppressive views of their roles. Countless couples refer to sex dwindling because one partner is too busy doing housework, resentment because of a partner's reluctance to participate in domestic chores or nagging to do so. Partners often oppress themselves by trying to live up to unrealistic standards which they think their partner expects, but which partners often don't remotely subscribe to. Complaint about support with chores and lack of time seems to affect sexual frequency and satisfaction (Barrett & Raphael, 2018). Crucially, feeling appreciated may have the most influence on improving sexual behaviour and satisfaction (Træen, 2008). With gender equality still thought to be at least 75 years away, it's one of the most unchangeable aspects of Western society (van der Gaag *et al*, 2019), with other facets of gender and sexuality developing much more rapidly.

Difference

Modern relationships begin and develop very differently from the way they did even 10 or 20 years ago. There is more pseudo-intimacy, thanks to hook-up apps, more casual sexual behaviour and, surprisingly, more rules about the way intimacy develops. As a result, it has become more likely that sexual relationships develop long before the emotional relationship grows, making it more difficult to address sexual problems which occurred before they mattered. Once relationships become more established, it may be harder to admit, say, faking orgasm.

Misunderstanding often causes a world of difficulty that can be overcome with a simple clarifying conversation. Though this shouldn't be taken for granted, older people re-embarking on sexual relationships following separations also often experience sexual difficulties due to misunderstanding, lack of experience or education. Age, stage and background can require profoundly differing approaches to sex therapy and therapists need an ability to explore clients' social, sexual and cultural contexts with sensitive curiosity.

Expectations vary depending on previous and recent experience. Western sexual problems, for instance, are highly performance focused, whereas clients who've been exposed to discourses from other parts of the world may be more concerned with issues like penis size or beliefs associated with behaviour, particularly guilt about masturbation (Hall & Graham, 2014). However, there's a danger of reaching for a cultural explanation when we don't understand, employing cultural stereotyping (Rober & De Haene, 2014). In other words, we expect an individual's culture to explain their behaviour rather than being curious about unfamiliar contexts.

Krause (2014: 21) argues that cultural competence is often thought of as a 'tick box process that simply reproduces the status quo while claiming to make a difference'. This can disguise a patronising attitude and implicit expectation that others want to be like us rather than enjoying their own ways (Brown, 2006). In other words, we may *tolerate*, rather than *explore*, difference (Zizek, 2008), valuing our own way more highly than the ways of others (Rober & De Haene, 2014). We also sometimes expect clients to teach us about their culture, identity or experience as if they are their representatives (hooks, 1994).

It's important to notice our own culture and beliefs, and our relationship with others' difference (Flaskas, 2012) so that difference itself is recognised as applying to everyone, not just those different from ourselves (Totsuka, 2014). A good start is to notice why we're more interested in some contexts than others, and also the risk of not noticing sameness (Burnham & Harris, 2002). For instance, it's easy to miss issues like domestic abuse because a couple appear calm, well-dressed, solvent and educated, or to assume sexual knowledge because a client has, say, a prolific sexual history or a medical background.

A young professional couple, Jacob and Ezzy, presented for PST due to Jacob's early ejaculation and Ezzy's loss of desire. The therapist assumed their sexual knowledge would be adequate, if not good, as they were both well-educated – Jacob was an architect and Ezzy was a midwife. In history taking, Jacob expressed a belief that Ezzy found him unattractive and thought this was why she rejected his advances. He said she even went as far as wearing leggings and a vest, as well as pyjamas, in bed.

Later in history taking, the reason became clearer. Ezzy said she'd grown up in a place where HIV and AIDS was a major problem. In her locality, there were several cases of young girls being raped in their beds by men who believed sex with a virgin could cure AIDS. Consequently, girls were made to wear several layers of clothing at bedtime and to act with extreme modesty around men and boys of all ages, just in case. Though this was many years ago, and far away, Ezzy was still behaving as though the danger was current and it didn't occur to her not to wear so much in bed. She was actually very sexually interested in Jacob, saying he was the most handsome man she'd ever seen.

Nonetheless, Ezzy had never climaxed with Jacob and found intercourse quite painful. Neither of them were aware that stimulation of the clitoris and breasts would arouse her, nor that she needed to be sufficiently lubricated before intercourse would be comfortable. The therapist suspected that Jacob's early ejaculation had developed due to hurried masturbation as a teenager for fear of discovery when he shared a dormitory, and hurrying sex with Ezzy because he believed she disliked it. Instead of recognising her pain, he saw revulsion.

The couple particularly enjoyed psychoeducation, Sensate Focus and exploration of their relative ideas and beliefs, which cleared up many misunderstandings and vastly improved their sexual relationship.

Adaptability

One of the most common culturally related issues encountered in PST is discomfort with masturbation, sometimes for religious reasons. However, it's worth checking this out with the client's religious leader/adviser, as many will agree to masturbation if it's a means to achieving partnered sex. Otherwise, some self-focus exercises may need to be carried out with/by the partner. If there is no actual prohibition but the client is still reluctant to masturbate, exploration of the client's beliefs may help somewhat, discussing their usefulness rather than their legitimacy (Yon et al, 2018). However, deeply held beliefs are obviously important to clients (Friedlander et al, 2006), and it's usually helpful to negotiate what's possible rather than insist on what's unlikely.

Control

It's common for exposure to strict rules or negative stories around sex in child-hood to influence sexual behaviour in adulthood (Wylie *et al*, 2015). In Ezzy's case, for instance, it was seriously shaming for unwed women to indicate any kind of sexual interest. Once married, however, she was astonished to discover she *was* expected to want sex.

Bedroom power struggles are common (Betchen, 2005). Some couples are just used to being in competition or need to prove themselves for fear of criticism. This can have a cultural origin. For instance, in some cultures there's an expec-tation that men will take control of sex with competency they often don't have. Wedding night disasters may result, leading to angry or hurt partners and shamed men. Sometimes relatives even pay for PST if they discover there's a problem, as it's so important for relationships to be consummated and for a couple to have children.

It isn't difficult to normalise such problems when neither partner has any expe-rience and very little knowledge. PST provides a gentle way for the couple to become sexually acquainted and to potentially emerge far more sexually com-petent and confident than many of the peers and family they assume are more sexually skilful.

Stereotyping

Though it's helpful to have broad-brush knowledge about different cultural norms and values, it isn't helpful to make assumptions about particular ethnic or religious groups. We need to be aware that stereotyping can add to the cli-ent's problems or deter them from attending in the first place. For instance, the idea that men are more sexual and women are more romantic can influence their sexual self-schema (Aumer, 2014). If it's felt their therapist expects this, they may feel obliged to play the part. Hence, in eliciting our clients' stories, we should recognise how they prefer to be thought about and referred to, explor-ing their multiple contexts from their experience rather than our clichéd beliefs about their experience.

It's also important to recognise how intersectionality (Crenshaw, 1989) affects us and may be construed by our clients, particularly as therapists are often por-trayed as middle-aged, white, middle-class, educated women or intense, bearded and bespectacled, thin, sandal-wearing men. If we dislike this portrayal, we need to be aware that it's no less ludicrous than some of the ideas expressed about our client groups, especially in terms of their religion and ethnicity (Mulholland, 2007; Ribner & Kleinplatz, 2007). There's a danger of losing our not-knowing position if we see our own privilege or oppression as somehow separate from the experience of our clients, or if we don't consider the intersectionality of our own contexts. It's unusual to think of intersectionality as fluid, but of course it is – context depends on context. What's oppressive in one situation may be a privilege in another (Nash, 2008). Moreover, what we assume is oppressive may not be (Ferguson, 2000), or we may glide over oppressive practices and experiences because we don't recognise them. These issues are among many personal and professional challenges we face that we'll touch on in Chapter 19.

References

Aumer, K. (2014) The influence of culture and gender on sexual self-schemas and satisfaction in romantic relationships. *Sexual & Relationship Therapy*, 29;3, 280–292.

Barrett, A.E. & Raphael, A. (2018) Housework and sex in midlife marriages: An examination of three perspectives on the association. *Social Forces*, 96;3, 1325–1350.

Bates, L. (2014) *Everyday Sexism*, London: Simon & Schuster.

Betchen, S.J. (2005) *Intrusive Partners, Elusive Mates*, Hove: Routledge.

Brown, W. (2006) *Regulating Aversion: Tolerance in the Age of Identity and Empire*, Princeton, NJ: Princeton University Press.

Burnham, J. & Harris, Q. (2002) Cultural issues in supervision. In: Campbell, D. & Mason, B. [eds] *Perspectives in Supervision*, London: Karnac, 21–41.

Burr, V. (2015) *Social Constructionism*, third edition, Hove: Routledge.

Crenshaw, K. (1989) *Demarginalizing the Intersection of Race and Sex: A Black Feminist Critique of Antidiscrimination Doctrine, Feminist Theory, and Antiracist Politics*, Chicago, IL: University of Chicago Legal Forum, 140, 139–167.

Ferguson, A. (2000) Resisting the veil of privilege: Building bridge identities as an ethico-politics of global feminism. In: Narayan, U. & Harding, S. [eds] *Decentering the Centre: Philosophy for a Multicultural, Postcolonial, and Feminist World*, Bloomington, IN: Indiana University Press, 189–207.

Flaskas, C. (2012) The space of reflection: Thirdness and triadic relationships in family therapy. *Journal of Family Therapy*, 34, 138–156.

Friedlander, M.L., Escudero, V. & Heatherington, L. (2006) *Therapeutic Alliances in Couple and Family Therapy: An Empirically Informed Guide to Practice*, Washington, DC: APA.

Hall, K.S.K. & Graham, C.A. (2014) Culturally sensitive sex therapy. In: Binik, Y.M. & Hall, K.S.K. [eds] *Principles and Practice of Sex Therapy*, fifth edition, New York: Guilford Press, 334–358.

Hollway, W. (1998) Gender difference and the production of subjectivity. In: Henriques, J., Hollway, W., Urwin, C., Venn, C. & Walkerdine, V. [eds] *Changing the Subject: Psychology, Social Regulation and Subjectivity*, second edition, London: Methuen, 227–263.

hooks, b. (1994) *Teaching to Transgress: Education as the Practice of Freedom*, London: Routledge.

Krause, I-B. (2014) Cultural differences stand to universalities as practice stands to theory: Comments on Rober and De Haene. *Journal of Family Therapy*, 36, 21–23.

Mulholland, J. (2007) The racialisation and ethnicisation of sexuality and sexual problems in sex therapeutic discourse. *Sexual & Relationship Therapy*, 22;1, 27–44.

Nash, J.C. (2008) Re-thinking intersectionality. *Feminist Review*, 89, 1–15.

Ribner, D.S. & Kleinplatz, P.J. (2007) The hole in the sheet and other myths about sexuality and Judaism. *Sexual & Relationship Therapy*, 22;4, 445–456.

Rober, P. & De Haene, L. (2014) Intercultural therapy and the limitations of a cultural competency framework: About cultural differences, universalities and the unresolvable tensions between them. *Journal of Family Therapy*, 36, 3–20.

Rodriguez, S.B. (2014) *Female Circumcision and Clitoridectomy in the United States: A History of a Medical Treatment*, Rochester, NY: University of Rochester Press.

Totsuka, Y. (2014) 'Which aspects of Social GGRRAAACCEEESSS grab you most?' The Social GGRRAAACCEEESSS exercise for a supervision group to promote therapists' self-reflexivity. *Journal of Family Therapy*, 36, 86–106.

Træen, B. (2008) When sex becomes a duty. *Sexual & Relationship Therapy*, 23, 61–84.

van der Gaag, N., Heilman, B., Taveeshi, G., Nembhard, C. & Barker, G. (2019) *State of the World's Fathers: Unlocking the Power of Men's Care*, third report, Washington, DC: Promundo.

Wylie, K., Markovic, D. & Hallam-Jones, R. (2015) Inhibited arousal in women. In: Hertlein, K., Weeks, G. & Gambescia, N. [eds] *Systemic Sex Therapy*, New York: Routledge, 152–170.

Yon, K., Malik, R., Mandin, P. & Midgley, N. (2018) Challenging core cultural beliefs and maintaining the therapeutic alliance: A qualitative study. *Journal of Family Therapy*, 40;2, 180–200.

Zizek, S. (2008) Tolerance as an ideological category. *Critical Inquiry*, 34, 660–682.

Chapter 19

Contemporary sex therapy

Sex therapists today face a greater range of challenges than ever before. The scope of the work has expanded hugely as we engage with a range of sexualities and identities which are subject to the impact of technology on relationships and sexual expression. The original sex therapy process of Masters and Johnson still provides a backbone for our work, but both the programme and the issues we meet have grown, adapted and been joined by both obvious and nuanced topics, questions and concerns that require us to expand our knowledge and skills. This book has been an introduction to the world of sex therapy – but there's a whole universe of learning to take forward. The book cannot cover anything like the range and complexity of areas now relevant to sex therapy practice. It's been a taste of some of them and will, perhaps, encourage readers to continue their journey.

The range of available training is growing in the UK, with the College of Sexual & Relationship Therapists (www.cosrt.org.uk/) providing a professional community of therapists with which to share skills and knowledge. Established sex therapists are specialising, adapting and enhancing their practice for their particular client groups, and continuing to develop and learn throughout their careers. It feels as though we're at the beginning of a much bigger revolution in the way sex, identity, and volition is performed and appreciated. Those interested in contributing with research will find more masters programmes, and social media offers a new way of reaching and researching cohorts of interest.

The internet is also a medium for sex therapy. Clearly, it has made it easier for everyone to access information (and misinformation) about sex and relationships, with some of that information provided by sex therapists, many having a significant presence on social media. Increasingly, our clients may expect to be able to access online information and resources. It may, indeed, become commonplace to direct our couples to our web pages for psychoeducation or exercises.

In the future, then, more sex therapy may be conducted online. A purely practical issue is that many partners travel for work and find it difficult to attend counselling together. Video messaging makes it easier to sustain long-distance relationships too, but again makes therapy attendance more problematic. Where online sex is part of relationships, sometimes boundaries and consent need examination with a therapist, especially when both partners aren't comfortable with a behaviour or there is jealousy about what else a partner may be engaged in online. This becomes more likely as more partners are choosing not to live together. This is particularly true of older couples, who have established lives and habits they don't want to relinquish, again often making online therapy more viable than face-to-face conjoint counselling.

Though there have been fears about online bullying, the shaming effects of 'perfect' lives portrayed on social media and the risk of losing real life social contact, less-publicised research suggests that the internet enhances relationships. For example, Pew Research (2014) has consistently found people see themselves as benefiting from more social contact and support than less. Significantly, families spend more time interacting with one another both through media like WhatsApp groups and in-person. If they weren't interacting online, many people would be watching television alone or engaged in other solitary activities, so some families interact more. TV viewing has changed too, with people in different households messaging one another as they watch.

The internet makes it possible for people to have sexual relationships without ever physically meeting. We tend to hear about the problems this can create, rather than the many benefits, particularly to people who are housebound or disabled. Such people's right to sexual expression can be affected by fears about their safety, so that even their online access may be restricted by carers (Thompson, 2019). However, the possibilities for people to form rich, loving relationships or just to feel sexual when it wouldn't otherwise be possible, seems positive and may be more proactively researched and addressed in the future.

Nonetheless, couples we see do present with problems related to the internet and social media. Among them are difficulty managing pornography use and the ease of reconnecting with old flames, or igniting new ones. The concept of infidelity has completely changed, with sexting or even just regular texting becoming a major source of relationship distress. Some couples blame mobile devices for the lack of intimacy in their relationships, claiming sex has been interrupted by phone calls, especially ones from work (Hesselberth, 2017).

While many of us feel obliged to respond to work e-mails and calls, there's also often considerable pressure for couples to respond immediately to messages from each other. Delay can cause suspicion and feelings of rejection for the message sender, but also pressure and feelings of claustrophobia for the receiver. Some people have difficulty in composing pithy, meaningful texts, complaining of feeling judged and inadequate when their attempts don't meet their partner's expectations. On the other hand, warm and flirty messages – or even dull, utilitarian ones – are a great way to keep couples feeling connected when their lives are hectic and moments of meaningful intimacy are hard to find.

Support and a sense of community are important for sex therapists, too. Many courses encourage students to use online resources, share drop boxes and create online forums. These are useful for qualified therapists also, with reading groups and peer supervision an economical way to develop learning. In PST, there's usually something to research about every client or couple we work with, so having colleagues to consult is more essential than useful. We should all have excellent supervision too, and a personal development plan to both stay up-to-date and expand our practice. Most importantly, we need space to check in with ourselves, inspect our beliefs, prejudices and opinions, notice our squitches and challenge ourselves. Sex therapy is demanding, surprising, instructive, exciting and incredibly rewarding. Enjoy!

References

Fox, S. & Rainie, L. (2014) *The Web at 25 in the US*, Washington, DC: Pew Research Center. www.pewinternet.org/2014/02/27/the-web-at-25-in-the-u-s/. Accessed August 21, 2019.

Hesselberth, P. (2017) Discourses on disconnectivity and the right to disconnect. *New Media & Society*, 1–17.

Thompson, D. (2019) The internet, social media, relationships and sex. *Tizard Learning Disability Review*, 24;1, 20–22.

Appendix

Case example: Anna and Eric

Anna, 55, and Eric, 57, have two children at university and both work full-time. They haven't made love for 12 years, since Anna became peri-menopausal and moved into the spare room because Eric's snoring and her night sweats were disturbing their sleep. Since that time she has put on some weight and feels uncomfortable about her body. She has also had a low libido for the past few years, having no interest in sex with Eric and only rarely masturbating.

Eric's libido remains undiminished and he still finds Anna very attractive, saying he loves her more each day. He masturbates two or three times a week, using fantasy mostly and porn rarely. He has no problem with erections. In the past, he has worried about early ejaculation, fearing he wasn't satisfying Anna. Though she usually climaxed before penetration, with clitoral stimulation, she enjoyed intercourse and Eric felt he ought to meet this 'need'. However, despite very much wanting to, Eric has been reluctant to approach Anna sexually as he has always been self-conscious about initiating sex.

Both come from families which rarely discussed sex and weren't tactile. They each had a poor sex education, with both learning most about sex by doing it. Anna says she had a 'reasonably enjoyable' sex life from her teens onwards, but Eric had a bad first experience at university, clumsily making love with a virgin who was not sufficiently aroused. Anna stated she could not imagine her parents making love: 'They always seemed past it'.

The couple are both in good health and are finding more time to enjoy leisure together. The decision to seek PST arose during an anniversary weekend away. After a couple of drinks, they both expressed a wish to make love but felt unable to do so. They did, however, cuddle up to sleep.

Anna has more sexual experience than Eric and used to express her interest very clearly earlier in their relationship. However, they now feel awkward discussing sex and communicate poorly, rarely touching at all and fearing a row if they do. They agree their sex life started to wane long before Anna left the bedroom – probably after their children were born – and that they have both lost confidence. Anna is anxious about this, believing she ought to be able to physically show Eric how much she loves him.

Now the children are both at university, and the couple feel they have more time to devote to one another, they very much want to try to resume their sex life together – though they are anxious about what this will involve and admit to feeling very vulnerable.

Anna and Eric's formulation

Problem

No sex
Loss of desire (Anna)
? Early ejaculation (Eric)
Anxiety ++ (Both)

Precipitating Factors – PST

Weekend away
Separate bedrooms

Precipitating Factors – Problem

Busy lives, young children

Predisposing

Poor sex education
Lack of comfort discussing sex

Current Triggers

Thinking about sex or intimacy creates anxiety and potential arguments

Discourses and Beliefs

Eric believes men ought to meet women's sexual needs
Anna thinks sex with Eric is the way she should show her love
? Anna believes sex is for the young
? Eric thinks he needs to make up for his lack of experience

Maintaining Factors

Sleeping apart
Avoiding touch
Poor communication and conflict-resolution skills
They are self-conscious, fearful and vulnerable

Positives

Sparkling moment – they *did* talk about sex on their anniversary and booked PST
They're highly motivated
The way they feel is very similar
They're still nuts about each other
Their sexual abstinence, which makes it easier to resume intimacy from scratch

Therapist Goals*

Improved communication
More comfort with touch
Improved sexual confidence

**These are not yet SMART goals, but will be once they have been broken down
into smaller aims which contribute to the formulation aims.*

Client goals

In the formulation discussion the couple made clear that they shared the wish
to resume a regular sex life, which would include intercourse. They said
'regular' sex would mean it should happen a couple of times a month. The
therapist thought her goals would contribute to their overall goal. The couple thought they would know communication had improved when they were
talking regularly, including discussing sex. Similarly, Anna felt they would
know touch was more comfortable when they didn't find themselves automatically avoiding it. Eric thought he would know he felt more comfortable with
touch when he started initiating touch without any fear of rejection. They both
thought that being able to talk about and initiate sex would be a sign of their
sexual confidence and that looking forward to the PST experiments might also
be a sign of this.

As therapy progressed, making time for the PST experiments showed them
they had more time for intimacy than they'd imagined. They decided that, after
therapy, they would continue to put aside a couple of hours twice a week for intimacy. They no longer felt this had to include intercourse, but might if they felt like
it. They thought they would be able to talk about how they each wanted to spend
their special time and weren't concerned that they'd feel rejected if one of them
wanted to make love and the other just wanted cuddles. They both felt this demonstrated comfort with touch and improved communication. By this point, the couple were enjoying sexual touch together and had reached the stage where this felt
more like lovemaking than an exercise, though they had not yet had intercourse.
This 'just happened' one day, even though it hadn't been planned, and the couple
left therapy soon afterwards feeling their goals had been exceeded. At follow-up,
their progress had been more than maintained, as they felt their relationship and
lovemaking were getting better every day.

SPECIMEN TREATMENT PLAN

	Partner 1	Couple	Partner 2
1	Mindfulness 1 Kegels Self-discovery	Gazing Routine creation Readiness for therapy questionnaire Sex ban Psychoeducation: Menopause	Mindfulness 1 Kegels Self-discovery
2	Mindfulness Kegels Self-discovery	Hugging Gazing Tracing Sex ban Psychoeducation: Desire	Mindfulness Kegels Self-discovery
3	Mindfulness Kegels Self-discovery	Gazing Sensate Focus 1 Talking point – consent Sex ban Psychoeducation: Body image	Mindfulness Kegels Self-discovery
4	Mindfulness Kegels Self-discovery	Hands on Hearts Sensate Focus 1 with additions	Mindfulness Kegels Stop:start
5	Mindful awareness Kegels Self-discovery Fantasy	Hands on Hearts Sensate Focus 1 with additions Tracing	Relaxation Kegels Stop:start
6	Mindful awareness Kegels Self-discovery Fantasy	Gazing Sensate Focus 1 – bag of wonders Psychoeducation: Anxiety	Relaxation Kegels Stop:start
7	Mindfulness Kegels Grounding Self-discovery	Gazing Sensate Focus 1 – small kisses, licking, bag of wonders	Relaxation Kegels Stop:start
8	Mindfulness Kegels Fantasy Self-discovery	Gazing Sensate Focus II – interim Psychoeducation: Sexual identity	Relaxation Kegels Mindful awareness Stop:start
9	Mindfulness Kegels Guided imagery Self-discovery	Sensate Focus II Plus Talking point – embarrassment	Relaxation Kegels Mindful awareness Stop:start
10	Mindfulness Kegels Self-discovery	Sensate Focus II Plus	Relaxation Kegels Stop:start
11	Mindfulness Kegels Self-discovery	Sensate Focus II – mutual Talking point – Hurt feelings Stop:start	Relaxation Kegels
12	Mindfulness Kegels	Sensate Focus II – mutual Stop:start	Relaxation Kegels

	SPECIMEN TREATMENT PLAN	
Partner 1	Couple	Partner 2
13 Mindfulness	Sensate Focus II – mutual	Relaxation
Kegels	Penile-vulval stimulation	Kegels
	Stop:start	
14 Mindfulness	Containment 1	Relaxation
Kegels	Talking Point: Romance	Kegels
15 Mindfulness	Containment 2	Relaxation
Kegels	Stop:start	Kegels
16 Mindfulness	Experimental Phase	Relaxation
Kegels	Discussion: Future sex	Kegels
17 Mindfulness	Follow-up	Relaxation
Kegels		Kegels

This specimen treatment plan demonstrates that couples may not be given the same self-focus experiments. The numbered phases don't represent the number of sessions – clients might repeat, say, block 7 several times, progress rapidly through 8, 9, 10 and then stay in 11 for several sessions. New exercises are introduced on the basis of feedback, with self-focus exercises being varied more than mutual ones.

Exercises

The following case examples can be used as exercises to practise creating a formulation and treatment plan. Remember, though, that any treatment plan you create will only be a guide. Experiments will change depending on the feedback received from clients.

- What are your hypotheses about each of the couples?
- What formulation and treatment skeleton would you devise?
- What are the major issues you would want to address?
- What could you offer each partner if they sought PST individually?

Baz and Mica

Baz, 51, and Mica, 47, have been married for 21 years and have two daughters, aged 14 and 17. During the past couple of years Mica has been experiencing very heavy and irregular periods plus some night sweats and hot flushes, especially in months where a period is missed. Her GP says she is peri-menopausal.

Mica says the couple were having sex with intercourse twice a week until about three years ago when their younger daughter started secondary school and Mica resumed full-time work. She's exhausted and feels resentful that she remains responsible for most of the household chores. She thinks tiredness and lack of time have affected their sex life, explaining they make love more when they're on holiday.

Baz believes Mica lost interest in sex before she went back to work. He says that, for years, she would push him away even if he just wanted a cuddle until, in the end, he gave up trying, so they now have little physical contact at all. He has noticed his erections are not as reliable as they once were, though he can achieve penetration. They last made love on his birthday.

Both the couple masturbate – Mica only once or twice a month and Baz three or four times a week for about 10 minutes, using porn.

Mica observes that they've both built up resentment. She feels Baz should do more to recognise how tired she is. In history taking she said she would feel more like making love to him if he was more helpful. She thinks he doesn't listen when she tells him how unsexy and unattractive she feels, especially when she sweats. Baz thinks this is just an excuse and fears she may have gone off him. He's very sad about the affection – and even passion – he feels they have lost, but this is expressed as anger.

'Why would I want to have sex with someone who's angry with me?' Mica asks.

'Have sex with me and I won't be angry,' Baz responds.

Despite their relationship issues, they'd like to be able to enjoy sex together again and even just to feel sexual. At the moment, they both feel inadequate, are highly anxious about the treatment and fear it won't work.

Niamh and Patrick

This professional couple, in their mid-thirties, met last summer and have recently bought a house together. They say they have a great deal in common and both feel this relationship will last. Their families and friends approve and they're thinking about having a baby. However, Patrick is rarely able to climax during intercourse.

Patrick has had delayed ejaculation with other partners, but thought he was over it. It worries him because he says intercourse is the *only* way Niamh will climax. Neither of them enjoy oral sex and Patrick says Niamh doesn't stimulate him 'properly', so there is little foreplay. In history taking, both admit they have faked orgasm to end intercourse.

Niamh says she's had a number of partners, none of whom have complained about her technique. She feels under pressure to orgasm, but she often doesn't do so now – indeed, she is much less interested in sex these days. Recently, the couple stopped having sex because Niamh becomes so sore and bruised. There is now little physical contact between them.

Patrick has cut back on masturbating to porn which he used to do most days, but this hasn't helped. He is vague about the masturbatory technique he uses and seems unable to communicate his preferences to Niamh.

Both say their relationship is practically perfect apart from this, but are very worried this will force them apart.

Cynthia and Colin

This couple in their sixties have been together for 38 years and have two sons who are married with children of their own. Colin retired from his retail job three years ago, but Cynthia has continued working in an office. They've always had an active and fulfilled sex life and enjoy each other's company very much. Recently, Colin had treatment for an enlarged prostate which had been interrupting his sleep, as he had to keep getting up at night to wee. He had also found himself 'dribbling' sometimes after weeing, which affected his confidence and self-esteem. He had consequently been looking forward to having surgery, but since then he has only had a 'pathetic' erection and he's worried this means the end of his sex life. Cynthia says it doesn't matter as they can still be sexual, but Colin is unconvinced and has been refusing even to kiss her. It was Cynthia who booked an initial assessment for PST.

Clare and Diana

Clare, 61, and Diana, 49, are primary school teachers who've been together for nearly eight years. Diana was previously married and has two sons, aged 14 and 11, who mostly live with her but spend every other weekend with their dad.

Clare had a 21-year relationship with another teacher, which ended when she was 51. Since this, she's had difficulty with orgasms and rarely climaxes when she and Diana make love. This doesn't happen often, as Diana says she's had a low libido for a few years, mostly due to work stress.

In history taking Clare reveals that, though the couple are very much in love, she's frightened that Diana will change her mind about the relationship. Her ex-husband argues that their sons should not be exposed to 'this sick relationship', and Clare worries that the pressure this creates will prove too much for Diana.

Hafeez and Hans

Hafeez, 28, and Hans, 25, have been dating for two years after meeting at work. They're planning to go travelling together next year and are keen to sort out their sexual problems before this. They both say sex was great for the first six months, but then Hans started to develop problems with his erection, finding it would 'just disappear'. Hafeez has a theory that this followed Hans' first attempt at insertive penetration, because Hafeez found it uncomfortable. Though Hans disagrees with this, the couple haven't repeated the experiment.

In history taking, Hafeez said this was because he doesn't want to put Hans under pressure, but also admitted he was worried the experience had put Hans off him a bit, something he didn't want Hans to know. Meanwhile, in his history taking, Hans said he feared Hafeez thought he was 'abnormal'.

When you explained to the couple that there would be a sex ban, and that the PST process would begin with sensual rather than sexual exercises, both seemed surprised and disappointed. Hans wonders whether he should attend by himself.

Liana and Winston

Liana, 68, and Winston, 73, are both widowed and met through church, which provided considerable comfort to them both when their partners died. Their relationship grew gradually and they were both thrilled when they realised they were falling in love. They're keen to be sexual together, but attempts at intercourse have been painful for Liana who hasn't had partnered sex for 20 years and is worried she won't satisfy Winston.

In history taking, Winston tells you he's been using sex workers for a number of years but has stopped in the past couple of months. He has never used condoms. He is concerned about hurting Liana and eager to get started with PST.

Zain and Saleem

This couple, in their late thirties, have been married for 10 months and tell you they're deeply in love. Both come from large families and never had their own bedroom or personal space. Saleem's father suffered from depression and Zain's mother died when he was 13, having been ill for several years. Zain's family doesn't know about their relationship.

Saleem had only had two previous sexual experiences before they met, both of which were casual, and on both occasions he ejaculated almost immediately. On the couple's first attempt at lovemaking, Saleem ejaculated when they were only kissing. He has had other casual sexual relationships since then, which Zain is aware of. Zain says he only has sex with Saleem, but this happens rarely. In the past few months, Zain has sometimes been unable to get or maintain an erection. Saleem says this is because he masturbates in the toilet at work and watches a lot of porn. Zain denies this is excessive.

Saleem is extremely anxious and has recently seen his GP who prescribed a low dose of the antidepressant fluoxetine. Zain has little faith in the PST programme; it was Saleem who insisted they seek help, and he is paying.

Maisie and Jap

Maisie, 24, and Jap, 27, have been in a relationship for two years and living together for just over a year. In all that time, they've never had intercourse, though they are sexually active and orgasmic. They're planning to get married next year and would like to have their sexual problems sorted by then. They've tried to have intercourse but Jap often climaxes before the penetration attempt, as soon as his penis touches Maisie's vulva. Recently, he's been losing his erection during sex anyway.

Maisie's first attempt at penetration, aged 16, was painful and she bled a lot. She hadn't expected this, as she had enjoyed other forms of sex with her boyfriend and had been orgasmic. In retrospect, she thinks they were both so keen to get on with intercourse that she hadn't been sufficiently aroused. Subsequent attempts didn't go well, however. To begin with, intercourse was possible but soon became too painful, so they gave up trying.

When this three-year relationship ended, Maisie remained single for a couple of years, scared anyone new would expect penetrative sex. She wants to have intercourse with Jap and finds it ironic that she doesn't know whether she now can. Jap has always climaxed quickly with partners, though the problem has never been as bad as it is now, and he has not had ED before.

Both have been to their GP and Maisie has been referred to a gynaecologist. Jap's hormone levels appear normal but the GP has prescribed Cialis to help with his erections, which the couple have not yet tried. They both masturbate successfully and say they had a 'normal' sex education. They each say their families were comfortable talking about sex and answering questions, and both sets of parents are still married.

Maisie is a sports journalist and Jap is a European account executive with an international company, which means they both travel a lot. They're concerned about making time for the exercises, but are nonetheless hopeful and enthusiastic.

Index